Privatizing Prisons

Privatizing Prisons

Rhetoric and Reality

Adrian L. James, A. Keith Bottomley,
Alison Liebling and Emma Clare

SAGE Publications
London • Thousand Oaks • New Delhi

SAGE Publications Ltd
6 Bonhill Street
London EC2A 4PU

SAGE Publications Inc.
2455 Teller Road
Thousand Oaks, California 91320

SAGE Publications India Pvt Ltd
32, M-Block Market
Greater Kailash – I
New Delhi 110 048

British Library Cataloguing in Publication data

A catalogue record for this book is available from
the British Library

ISBN 0 8039 7548 1
ISBN 0 8039 7549 X (pbk)

Library of Congress catalog card number 97–066423

Typeset by Photoprint, Torquay, Devon
Printed in Great Britain by Biddles Ltd, Guildford, Surrey

Contents

Acknowledgement

Crown copyright is reproduced with the permission of the Controller of Her Majesty's Stationary Office.

Preface

In the summer of 1991, faced with the irresistible prospect of having the first contracted-out prison in the country opening no more than 15 miles away from the university where two of us worked, we had already discussed the possibility of undertaking some research at Wolds when we were approached by one of the companies which was tendering for the contract. This company which was, in the event, unsuccessful, had had the foresight to recognize that there may be some merit in including an element of external evaluation in their bid (the only one to do so as far as we know). Given our interest, we agreed to be associated with their bid, but recognizing that their tender might not be successful, we decided also to register our interest independently with the Home Office. When we contacted them, it transpired that it had not apparently occurred to the Prison Department to either undertake or commission any evaluation of what many regarded as the penal experiment of the century!

Unknown to us, Steve Twinn, who was to be the first Director (Governor) of Wolds, had also had exploratory discussions with Professor Tony Bottoms at the University of Cambridge's Institute of Criminology about the possibility of some evaluation of Wolds. Thus, when Group 4 eventually won the contract in the autumn of 1991, these elements were brought together in a bid to the Home Office Research and Planning Unit from the Centre of Criminology and Criminal Justice at the University of Hull, in association with the Cambridge Institute of Criminology.

It is perhaps worthwhile commenting that, in view of the political significance of developments at Wolds, we initially sought joint funding from a charitable source and the Home Office. This was partly because it had emerged from our early discussions that the Home Office thought that any evaluation undertaken or funded solely by them was likely to be viewed with some scepticism by potential critics of the experiment, apart from there being internal administrative problems arising from the question of providing government funding for research into a privately run institution. In the event, however, we were unsuccessful because the organization we approached thought the research should be *wholly* independent of the Home Office! As a result of our abortive early attempts to secure joint funding and subsequent delays in negotiations with the Research and Planning Unit and the Remands Contracts Unit (as it then was), we submitted the final proposal in March 1992, confirmation of the final agreement being received at the end of June, some three months after the opening of the prison.

It may also be worthwhile recording here that, as we describe more fully in Chapter 5, our original proposal had been for the study to include a comparison with an appropriate public-sector prison. This would have enabled us to have compared developments at Wolds with those in an establishment run by the Prison Service but whether for financial or other reasons, the Home Office decided against this. When we embarked on the research, therefore, we were conducting what was in essence a case study, a fact which undoubtedly influenced our approach to the project, to which the comparative element was only subsequently added.

Another methodological limitation, which is directly related to this, is that what some will regard as a major dimension of the 'privatization' of prisons – the impact on public-sector employees, their trade unions, and employer/staff relationships – does not receive the attention which it might otherwise have done. Thus, although we devoted a considerable amount of our efforts to exploring the experiences and attitudes of staff, we recognize that this important element has not been given the attention which it would otherwise have been given and which it undoubtedly merits, both as a legitimate area of prison research and as an important element in the politics and economics of contracting-out the management of prisons. It is also clear that because the research agenda was large and our resources were limited, there are many other questions to which we still have no answers and some crucial issues about which, for reasons we explain, we are able to say comparatively little.

It is equally important to acknowledge the enormous political sensitivity of such research and it is hardly surprising, perhaps, that a feature of most research on the privatization of prisons is that it is very rare to find evaluations by researchers who appear or even claim to be 'independent' or 'unbiased'. This is something of which we were conscious throughout, in a myriad of ways, and it permeated many of our discussions within the research team. In this context, and in terms of the more general struggle for objectivity and balance which is intrinsic to any research but which is so much more difficult in a situation such as this, we would emphasize what we regard as the considerable advantages of a team approach, not least of which is the mutual support which it provides. Each member of the team brought with him or her different backgrounds, experience, predispositions and approaches and we had to manage some lively discussions arising from both the context of the research and from these differences! We believe that in the final analysis, however, we have achieved a good balance and that this would have been much more difficult to achieve without the medium of the research team. However, having read this book, others may reach a different conclusion about this, and we anticipate that both the proponents of contracting-out and those who are against it will readily find fault with our work as a consequence of the politically and ideologically laden issues involved, if for no other reason!

Apart from our debt to each other as members of a hard-working research team, we should like to take this opportunity to express our sincere gratitude to all of those staff, at all levels, in both public- and private-sector prisons who gave so much of their time and took so much trouble in facilitating the research on which this book is based. We should also like to express our gratitude to those prisoners who talked to us, both formally and informally, during the course of the research. The views and experiences of all of those who have participated have been invaluable in helping us in our efforts to try to understand the complexities of prison life in times of change such as these and we hope that those who read our account will recognize the issues we have addressed and feel that we have done these justice. One of the few things we can say without fear of contradiction is that without the willing co-operation of all concerned, this research would not have been possible!

We should also like to place on record our thanks to Professor Tony Bottoms in his role as consultant for providing much-valued injections of reflective comment and objective criticism; and to staff in the Research and Planning Unit at the Home Office (now the Research and Statistics Directorate), particularly John Ditchfield and Diane Caddle, for all of their support during the course of the research and its publication. However, the end product and responsibility for this is, of course, ours and ours alone.

Adrian L. James
A. Keith Bottomley
Alison Liebling
Emma Clare

January 1996

1

Private Prisons Rediscovered: International Developments in the Twentieth Century

The sudden revival of interest and major drive towards private-sector involvement in prisons in the 1970s and 1980s – with the ostensible aims of improving conditions, controlling costs, facilitating innovation and improving the quality of regimes – should be seen in the broader context of a political, social and economic climate of declining faith in the state to manage traditionally 'public-sector' services. During this period, the USA, Canada, several Australian states and the UK had conservative governments in power whose political ideology gave increasing emphasis to reducing the role of the state in the delivery of public services. These countries also had the highest proportionate and fastest-growing prison populations (Lilly and Knepper, 1992; Shichor, 1995; Zimring and Hawkins, 1994). The private sector was thought to be capable of delivering higher quality services in a more efficient and accountable fashion. Privatization was seen as an additional resource, as a stimulus to change, and as a way of responding quickly and flexibly to the urgent need for an expanded prison capacity. The 'Great Confinement' (Christie, 1994; Weiss, 1989) stimulated the enthusiastic pursuit of private-sector financing and management of prisons. As Sparks has argued: 'Both the "need" for prison places and the "viability" of alternatives are matters of political decision and ideological preference, and in any case the free market preferences of governments sympathetic to privatization and their high demand for prison places are more than accidentally related' (Sparks, 1994: 25).

The Early History of Private Involvement in Prisons in the USA

> Plagued by facilities that are crowded, costly, dirty, dangerous, inhumane, inefficient, and subject to riots and law suits, many officials are looking to the private sector as an alternative source of supply. (Logan, 1990)

By June 1994, the prison population in the USA had exceeded one million. State prisons (for those convicted of felony crimes, normally serving sentences of one year or more) held 919,143 prisoners;

federal prisons (for those convicted in federal courts) held 93,708 prisoners (Proband, 1994: 4). These figures do not include the US jail population (local municipal jails and county jails; for misdemeanants (convicted of petty crimes) or those awaiting trial or serving less than one year), which has been estimated at more than 400,000 (Shichor, 1995). The imprisonment rate for prisoners sentenced to more than one year had reached a record 373 prisoners per 100,000 population – double what it had been a decade earlier (Proband, 1994: 4). 'Truth in sentencing', a 'War on drugs', and a 'crackdown' on violent crime culminating in the infamous 'three strikes' mandatory life sentence legislation which originated in Washington in 1992, together resulted in sharply increasing demands on prison spaces, spiralling costs and deteriorating prison conditions.

Slogans like 'hard time for armed crime' characterized the public and political sentiments behind the fastest growth in the size of a prison population in history. California increased the size of its prison population more than fourfold in a decade – a 'singular event in American correctional history' (Zimring and Hawkins, 1994: 83), and yet representative of a pattern of unprecedented expansion across more than 90 per cent of American states. This very marked increase in pressure on prisons, the vast prison construction plans which accompanied it, and the gap between public support for 'more prison' and taxpayers' willingness to cover the costs, made private financing of prison construction and management almost inevitable (see Borna, 1986; Ryan and Ward, 1989). The costs of each prison place were rapidly increasing. The total state expenditure on prisons in 1984 had been about $6 billion. By 1990, it had more than trebled, to around $20 billion (Shichor, 1995: 11). It was during the very early stages of this (now rapidly escalating) prison population 'explosion', that private sector involvement in prisons re-emerged in the USA.

Private-sector involvement in prisons in America can be traced as far back as the nineteenth- and twentieth-century practice of prison labour leasing, an arrangement whereby prisoners were housed, clothed and fed by private contractors in return for their labour. For this exchange, the contractors received a fee from the state and a 'contract' lasting a number of years. Ryan and Ward describe the emergence of this labour lease system, which was especially common in southern states at the end of the Civil War, and its cruelly ironic 'replacement' of slavery, for those who transgressed the law (Ryan and Ward, 1989: 18; see also Shichor, 1995: 34–43). They describe the neglect and brutality shown to such 'leased prisoners', whose morbidity rate was alarmingly high and who were overwhelmingly black (see also Sellin, 1976). Contractors were responsible for the maintenance and discipline of prisoners, and concerns were voiced that such leasing arrangements exposed prisoners to the dangers of injustice: contractors would have a vested interest in lengthening the sentences of good workers and in neglecting their welfare (Shichor, 1995). However, even reluctant states pursued the practice. Leasing practices contributed to a need for fast, economic and labour-intensive industrial development, such as railroad, mining and plantation work. States were paying off heavy war debts, reconstructing their economies, and adapting to the abolition of slavery, whilst also maintaining growing prison populations, so that using otherwise expensive-to-maintain prisoner populations for hard work made good economic sense. Growing concerns over the supervision and control of private companies and their treatment (and containment) of prisoners led to the resumption of some degree of control over the operation of leased prisons by the state and the restriction of lease arrangements to labour only.

This variation on the lease arrangement ('the contract system') was more common in northern and eastern states, whereby the prison was managed by the state, but workshops ('prison factories') were run by outside contractors for profit under the combined ethos of reformation through hard work and discipline, repentance through public labour, and covering costs (see Melossi and Pavarini, 1981; also Shichor, 1995: 26–43). Other examples of the role of private industry in prisons included the 'piece price' system whereby prisoners were observed and managed by public prison staff, but were paid according to their productivity by private contractors. Objections to such exploitation were made most powerfully by labour organizations in the community, who feared competition, but despite opposition the contract system persisted, albeit under increasing constraint, throughout the first half of the twentieth century. It made prison cheap for the state and profitable for manufacturers, who exerted considerable power over prisoners and prison life.

Prison industries gradually began to produce goods for state-run services, most famously on public works such as roads and bridges, or penal farms, the former sometimes using 'chain gangs' (Ryan and Ward, 1989: 17–20; see also Durham, 1989). According to Shichor, the gradual phasing out of privately contracted industry and its replacement with state-run production was a reassertion of control over prisons by the state (Shichor, 1995: 32–3). Prison industry contributed to the costs of imprisonment, instilled the 'work ethic' into prisoners, and sometimes returned a profit, whether it was privately managed or not. Through hard (and cheap) work, financial and reformist goals could be simultaneously met (Shichor, 1995), although accounts of corruption by manufacturers, neglect of prisoners' health, foul conditions and brutality suggest that reformist goals were often subsumed by the drive for profit and cost–reduction. Shichor gives a graphic account of the establishment of a 'private prison' in California in 1851, when the state leased out its own prison for 10 years (from a position of bankruptcy) and then built San Quentin prison to replace the contract a decade later. Both were subject to scandal and corruption. The prison was eventually returned to the state in 1860 after a settlement of $275,000 in favour of the leasee, after a long process of litigation and public concern over many aspects of the prison's management (see Shichor, 1995: 39–41).

It was the combination of humanitarian protest, economic depression curtailing the willingness of private companies to offer contracts, a declining need for the sorts of goods unskilled labour produced and outside labour opposition to unfair competition which led to the eventual decline of leasing out during the early part of the twentieth century (see DiIulio, 1990; Shichor, 1995). The return of private industry to prison (and in some notorious states a little later, the return of the 'chain gang' during the latter part of this decade) came in the 1970s, during a renewed search for efficiency and profit and in the early stages of the prison population explosion outlined above.

The Renaissance of Private Prisons

As in other countries, the resurgence of private-sector involvement in American corrections began with services (education, medical treatment, catering, work and training) but extended to the management and operation first of juvenile and then of adult establishments during the 1980s. This renaissance of the contracting-out of selected prisons in the USA occurred in the mid-1980s for similar practical reasons to those which led to its re-emergence in the UK more than a decade later (see Chapter 3) – including financial, political and managerial reasons, with the prison population crisis acting as perhaps the single most significant factor. However, there were distinct features of the development of the privately contracted management of prisons in the USA. Entrepreneurs canvassed for business in a climate which was receptive to their campaign. Increasing legal requirements, alongside deteriorating conditions in overcrowded facilities and stringent budgetary control, led to what the private sector came to see as a market opportunity.

States were facing expensive law suits by federal courts, who were finding states to be in violation of the Constitution's prohibition of 'cruel and unusual punishment' and demanding limits to be set on prison populations unless more places could be found (McDonald, 1994; Shichor, 1995). The US Supreme Court had ruled in 1968 that prisoners could sue state governments if conditions were found to be unsatisfactory (House of Commons, 1987b). States faced serious and persistent overcrowding, and the problem of having no money to build new prisons. Court orders had been passed in 39 states by 1988 demanding the alleviation of overcrowding, for example, by early release (Shichor, 1995). By 1991, 40 states had been found by the courts to be 'unconstitutional' because of the poor and overcrowded conditions in their prisons. A 'tax revolt' meant that the public demand for more imprisonment was accompanied by votes against the bonding proposals which were needed to fund such enterprises (McDonald, 1994). Private companies lobbied for contracts, arguing that procurement procedures could be avoided and the financing of privately owned facilities speeded up – the only alternative seemed to be a 'cap' on the number of prisoners in numerous states, in order to comply with the requirements of the increasingly interventionist courts. Enhanced early release practices and other solutions to the penal crisis, such as community alternatives to custody, sentencing restrictions and fines, were not likely to be politically acceptable.

There were other significant factors behind the move to and acceptance of privatization as a viable policy option: changing penal trends away from rehabilitation and training towards containment, incapacitation and deterrence represented a significant if somewhat negative shift in penological and public thinking (Durham, 1989; Shichor, 1995). Rising crime rates fuelled public demand for prisons *as* and *for* punishment. The incapacitation or 'protection of the public' function was an easier administrative task to 'hand over' to private companies and their employees than the 'treatment and training' of offenders. Longer sentences, mandatory minimum sentences, reduced parole eligibility, and a declining faith in rehabilitation were all part of a reconceptualization of the imprisonment task.

Community treatment centres and half-way houses had been contracted-out to private firms since the late 1960s. The contracting-out of non-secure correctional facilities had been readily accepted, with the voluntary sector already playing a major role in the provision of 'less visible' criminal justice services. As Krisberg et al. argued, 'the growth of the private sector was actively advocated by juvenile justice reformers of the early 1970s' (Krisberg et al., 1986: 28). The first secure facility to be contracted-out was the Weaversville Intensive Treatment Unit for juveniles in Pennsylvania, in 1975 (Borna, 1986; Sellers, 1993). It housed 20 juveniles in high-security accommodation. Typically, for such a small facility for juveniles, it had a more philanthropic than profit-centred approach. The second was the Okeechobee School for Boys, in Florida, which was substantially larger, housing 400 juveniles, and which opened in 1982. Private-sector involvement in the management of prisons remained confined to such (largely non-profit making) juvenile facilities throughout the early 1980s. This development was accompanied by the contracting-out of immigration detention centres by the Immigration and Nationalization Service (INS) in the early 1980s on the grounds of speed and finance. This provided the 'seedbed' out of which the relevant experience and opportunity to expand grew (McDonald, 1994).

The 'early players' in the above developments – Corrections Corporation of America (CCA) and Wackenhut – went on to secure the first contracts for managing adult prisons in the USA (see McDonald, 1994). Thomas and Logan refer to the founders of CCA as the 'fathers' of the correctional privatization movement in the USA. Formed in 1983, CCA had the advantages of opportune timing, access to substantial working capital, the movement of experienced administrators from the public to the private sector and 'charismatic leadership' (Thomas and Logan, 1993). A healthcare model already existed, as privately managed hospitals emerged under the direction of companies such as Hospital Corporation of America. Within a few years, CCA had been awarded contracts in Florida, Tennessee, New Mexico, Texas and California:

> . . . these initial contracting experiences were of vital importance to those who saw potential in the private sector option. Those proponents of privatisation were not disappointed. The initial contracting efforts demonstrated that private corrections firms bring construction projects to fruition substantially faster and at a significantly lower cost than could government agencies, that the transition from public to private management of 'takeover' facilities could be accomplished smoothly, that the *per diem* costs of private management of correctional facilities yielded important cost savings, and that the quality of services private firms provided were equal to and often better than those of government. (Thomas and Logan, 1993: 220)

These claims were hotly disputed by the increasing anti-privatization movement, who identified problems of expansion, corruption, exploitation and secrecy (see, for example, Ryan and Ward, 1989). The fear of job losses was inevitably a matter of considerable concern to public-sector employees in such a labour-intensive occupation, but an additional major grievance expressed by corrections managers, staff and unions in America was that improvements to prison management and conditions were actively desired by the public sector; staff wanted to work professionally in decent conditions. The National Sheriffs' Association argued, with some justification, that local politicians had under-financed local jails for years, allowing them to deteriorate and to become overcrowded, and they were now looking to the private sector for a cheap and fast solution to problems caused by inadequate finance. Lower staffing levels, poor conditions of service and poor quality recruits were bound to result from any such search for both improvement *and* profit (see Ryan and Ward, 1989: 32–3).

Early ventures into prisons were restricted to minimum security facilities. It was during the mid-1980s that rapid expansion of private-sector involvement in the management of prisons took place, and received public, academic and political attention. By 1986, there were more than 30 institutions – immigration detention centres, juvenile facilities, work-release or half-way houses – either owned or operated by private companies in the USA.

It was also in 1986 that CCA offered to take over the whole of Tennessee's prison system, at a cost to them of $250 million, on a 99-year lease following a court ruling that the state had violated the US Constitution on the grounds of inadequate conditions (McDonald, 1994; see also Cody and Bennett, 1987). Although this offer was eventually turned down, as an event it signalled the potential power and scope of the privatization movement. Opposition continued to rally, from local townspeople and prison reform groups, from the National Sheriffs' Association, the American Bar Association, the American Federation of State, County and Municipal Workers, and from criminal justice organizations (see McDonald, 1994; Ryan and Ward, 1989). As McDonald shows, by 1987 'the debate had died down' (McDonald, 1994: 31). Expansion by the private sector had been slower than early indications had suggested, but new privately managed prisons continued to open, in parts of the prison estate (such as maximum security) that were originally expected to eschew the introduction of private-sector management. By 1988, there were a number of privately managed county jails which were referred to as 'maximum security' – but these establishments did not require anything like the same level of security provision as state facilities.

Recent Developments and Issues in the USA

The recent development of privatization in the USA thus began with the 'shallow end', namely low security, juvenile and adult womens' establishments, with the extent of public objections to private-sector involvement in criminal justice appearing from the outset to depend on how visible the power exercised seemed to be. Private companies anticipated the needs of government and were able to meet them. Unlike the public sector, private companies were far more responsive, future-oriented and flexible. According to Logan (1990), private prisons would secure a criminal justice system that was 'safe, humane, efficient and just' in a way that the public sector was failing to achieve.

By 1991, private corrections firms operated 60 secure adult facilities in 12 out of 50 states (including four maximum security facilities in Texas) and housed 20,000 local, state and federal prisoners (McDonald, 1994). This constituted less than 3 per cent of the US prisoner population (Lilly and Knepper, 1992). By 1994 the number of adult prisoners held in private prisons in the USA was estimated to be around 30,000 out of a total prison population of more than one million (Ryan, 1994).

The most decisive practical consideration influencing the appeal of private-sector management of prisons was cost. There were three areas where it was believed that costs could be reduced significantly by competition: the financing, the construction and the operation of prisons. Delays in the securing of finance for new prisons were increasing costs; by by-passing voters, the public could have more imprisonment at a lower price. Operational costs could be reduced by 'more effective management' (for example, more reliance on electronic surveillance), and crucially, by more power to hire and fire. There would be less waste in the private sector – as the workforce would be more controlled, less unionized and less secure. The government could push down the costs of corrections, whilst hopefully maintaining (or even improving) standards, through the introduction of minutely detailed contracts. At the same time, it would cause the public sector to become more internally reflective, accountable and responsive to the demands of a cost-constrained government. Privately managed prisons would thus provide an alternative standard against which to measure the performance of public prisons, thereby bringing about improvements in the public sector by defining higher standards, raising expectations and facilitating innovation.

Public-sector unions, reform groups and other opponents of the privatization movement declared that privatization might be inherently expansionist and that vested interests would stimulate demand (see Lilly and Knepper, 1992). But despite at times organized and vociferous opposition, expressing the view that contracting-out 'passes some of the risks of innovation from the public to the private sector' (Logan, 1990: 167) and that improved management and greater accountability would be secured through the contract and increased monitoring, private-sector involvement in corrections steadily gained ground. The main issue was not whether prisons were publicly or privately managed, but rather there was a perceived need to make 'low visibility power' more visible.

Other major reasons favouring private-sector financing, construction and management of prisons in the USA at this time were that it would make the true costs of imprisonment visible, facilitating comparison and control, and would lead to greater efficiency. It would add new expertise and specialized skills, encourage experimentation and innovation, and introduce an additional layer of accountability (the market). By requiring the development and use of objective performance measures, it would raise standards in both private and public prisons. It was the opinion of senior British Home Office officials in the late 1980s that the early evidence from experience in the USA suggested that many of these improvements had been effectively secured by private-sector prison management and ways found to monitor the standards required (Home Office, 1988b: 4). Their report recognized that the constitutional, legal and operational background of the US prison system was quite different from that in Britain and that any judgement about the success of the initiatives taken in the USA must be made with those differences in mind (Home Office, 1988b: 4). However, cost-effectiveness had been achieved and the evidence of apparently improved efficiency and accountability provided sufficient justification to a UK government eager to replicate the development on home ground.

On a broader front, the ideological climate in the USA during the 1970s and 1980s had been ripe for an alternative penal venture, with social, political and economic forces all favouring increased privatization. The government had failed to deliver efficient, humane prisons and had in fact demonstrated the need, in the contemporary context, for a private-sector remedy. The quality of regimes was low, the costs were exceedingly high and demand exceeded supply (Logan, 1990), so that under such circumstances privatization seemed the obvious solution and was in tune with the broader socio-economic ideology. It was in the USA that public ambivalence about government first gained momentum; the public were rethinking the role of the state, capitalism was manifestly in crisis and right-wing economists emerged during the late 1970s and early 1980s with an ideology that would limit the power of government yet allow it to pursue specific interests. This declining trust in government – a belief that it should no longer be the main actor in maintaining social order – took hold. It seemed that the state could no longer manage the economy – perhaps the market would do better. The 1980s' candidates were elected to 'get the government off our backs'. Prisons were a significant 'core' government function. Thus, it is an important dimension of the re-emergence of private management of prisons both in America and Britain, that this development was part of a much broader ideological debate about the proper scope and size of government. As Logan argues, the 'invisible hand' was usurping the 'iron fist' of government, despite the imperfections of the market.

The Reagan administration (like the Thatcher government in the UK which followed, see Chapter 3) were elected to dismantle the state, in which prison privatization was a significant 'test case'.

The Early History of the Private Sector in Australia

Although Australia does not have quite the same early history of private/commercial involvement in the prison system as America, with its tradition of prison labour leasing, nor any direct parallel to the private management of local gaols in England from early times to the last quarter of the nineteenth century, it does have a unique history of its own in this respect dating from the time of its colonial foundation.

Virtually every transport fleet that set sail from England after 1788 with its cargo of convicts bound for Australia operated under contract from the British government, which was quick to see the economic and administrative advantages of the privatization of penal transportation. In so far as convict transport ships were floating prisons, the detailed specifications laid down for contractors on every aspect of the voyage now read amazingly like the contracts for the privately managed prison in England and Australia 200 years later:

> By the end of the eighteenth century . . . the private contractor faced an imposing list of government demands. From the number of lifeboats to the size of the rations, all was laid down, along with the exact responsibilities to convicts borne by captain, surgeon and officers. (Hughes, 1987: 144)

Perhaps even more prophetically, directly foreshadowing the present-day contract monitors and Controllers, naval agents and surgeons (employed by the government) were put on board each transport to keep a close eye on conditions and the treatment of convicts. They had to keep official diaries, relating to sickness, fumigation and cleaning of the ship, and supervise all aspects of the contract requirements (Hughes, 1987: 140; Shaw, 1966: 110). The 'surgeon-superintendents' were later given more powers including the daily inspection of convicts and responsibility for their punishment (Shaw, 1966: 120–21).

Once the convicts had been safely delivered (or not, as the case often was!) to the penal settlements, a further major government economy was discovered whereby, after 1800, the majority of convicts became 'assigned' to work for free settlers, who became responsible for feeding, clothing and sheltering them – at far less expense to the government than keeping them employed on public works. Thus, Shaw records that in 1828–9 whereas it cost the government over £15 a year for convicts kept for punishment or employment ('on the stores') in New South Wales (cf. £14 in Van Diemen's Land), assigned convicts cost only £4 (Shaw, 1966: 254). Despite the system of convict assignment being roundly condemned (along with most other aspects of transportation) by the Molesworth Committee on Transportation in 1838, it was not abolished until 1849. So, for fifty years, 'assignment' could be said to have been the first (unacknowledged and 'experimental') privatized 'open prison' system for convicts (Hughes, 1987: 283; Shaw, 1966: 587), creating a precedent that has not yet been repeated in quite such an ambitious or arguably successful fashion since.

The main challenge facing successive Governors of the penal colony in the first 30 years of the nineteenth century was to reduce the cost incurred by the Exchequer at home for a rapidly expanding system of penal transportation. Between 1810 and 1821, Governor Macquarie succeeded in reducing the overall cost of transportation of a convict from over £100 a year to less than £30 – which was less than it cost to keep a prisoner for a year in a hulk on the Thames (£40) or in the new Millbank Prison (£50) (Shaw, 1966: 98–9). However, all his efforts at economy were overtaken by the flood of convicts sent to Australia following the end of the Napoleonic Wars (Hughes, 1987: 300), and the overall scale and cost of transportation eventually became unacceptable to the British government, thereby hastening the end of an unparalleled system of convict management as a joint venture involving government and private enterprise.

Private Prison Developments in Australia

By the late twentieth century, Australia became the second major country to 'rediscover' privately managed prisons, and currently has the highest proportion (28 per cent) of its prisoners accommodated in privately managed prisons, with an average overall imprisonment rate of 81 per 100,000 population (Harding, 1994). Perhaps as a result of the speed and scale with which private prisons have been introduced and spread in Australia, a substantial body of research and critical academic literature has emerged from there (see, for example, Biles and Vernon, 1994; Chan, 1992; Harding, 1992a, 1992b; Moyle, 1993, 1994).

In several states in Australia, similar (but later) political, economic and social developments occurred as in the USA: problems of finance ('Australia's deteriorating economic circumstances', Moyle, 1993), increasing prisoner populations (largely as a result of 'Truth in sentencing' legislation), the management of politically recalcitrant prison staff, the search for more effective prisoner programmes and the anxieties caused to governments by increasing court intervention, combined together to produce a receptiveness to the idea of exploring the possibilities and potential of privatization. Significantly, also, the extent of direct American involvement in developments in Australia has been considerable, including not only the formation of American-linked consortia, but also the appointment of Americans to key management posts in several of the new private prisons (Beyens and Snacken, 1994).

Australia has eight separate jurisdictions – namely seven states (New South Wales, South Australia, Queensland, Northern Territory, Victoria, Tasmania and Western Australia), and the Australian Capital Territory, each of which has a separate criminal justice system and corrections service. Two states – Queensland and New South Wales – have privately managed prisons in operation (Queensland has two); a third State – Victoria – plans to contract-out three of its largest prisons, so that by 1997 it aims to have over half its prison population in privately managed establishments. In addition, at the time of writing, Victoria has invited tenders to finance, design and construct three further prisons, including one for women prisoners. Finally, South Australia has contracted-out the management of Mt Gambier prison for women to Group 4 Securitas, which opened in 1996.

Queensland

Queensland was the first Australian state to contract-out the management of a prison. To date, two of Queensland's 11 correctional centres are managed by private companies. Borallon prison was opened under private management in January 1990. It holds 244 male medium-security prisoners. It cost $22 million to build (about £12 million) and its contract fee was $9.7 million for the financial year 1991–2 (Moyle, 1994). The contract was awarded initially on a three-year plus two-year option to Corrections Corporation of Australia (CCA), which is a consortium of Wormald Security Australia and John Holland Holdings, and Corrections Corporation of America (Chan, 1994). CCA manages the prison, providing managers, administrators, instructors and healthcare staff, whilst Wormald supply the correctional staff (Moyle, 1993). Queensland Corrections Service had been operating the cheapest prison service in Australia, at a cost of $39,000 per prisoner per annum, but its initial motivation for the introduction of competition was primarily to undermine the power and influence of the Prison Officers' Union in Queensland, which had been resisting new working practices. A review of correctional facilities in Queensland (Commission of Review into Corrective Services in Queensland) carried out by Mr J. Kennedy (1988) led to the establishment of the Queensland Corrective Services Commission

(QCSC) in 1988. According to Stan Macionis, the Deputy Director General of QCSC:

> In his report, Kennedy recommended that one prison under the jurisdiction of the QCSC should be operated and managed by the private sector under contract to the Commission. His rationale for this recommendation was to create a market for corrective institutions in Australia and Queensland and, for the first time, to introduce competition which would provide a real measure against which to test the performance and costs of the QCSC. (Macionis, 1994: 1)

Arthur Gorrie Remand Centre, Queensland's second private prison, opened in 1992. It is a remand and reception prison, and holds 380 prisoners, of which 20 are immigration detainees. The successful tenderer (from a shortlist of seven companies invited to tender for the contract) was Australasian Correctional Management (ACM), who were awarded a five-year contract, renewable for two further years. Its operating budget was $11.5 million for the year 1992. A controversial aspect of the Arthur Gorrie Centre's role has been seen as its involvement in the classification of prisoners upon reception into custody, a process which leads to the development of a sentence management plan, which in turn may influence the type of establishment, activities, work and release opportunities open to the prisoner (Harding, 1994).

According to Macionis, the four reasons for introducing private management into prisons in Queensland were: 1   the benefits of competition, and the stimulus for improved performance by the public sector; 2   perceived cost savings and improved efficiency; 3   the need for 'cultural and attitudinal change in the management and operation' of prisons, including a greater emphasis on rehabilitation and offender programmes; and 4   the need for comparative information with which to make future decisions (Macionis, 1994; see also McDonald, 1994; Moyle, 1993).

In view of the fact that Queensland has subsequently achieved a substantial reduction in the rate of imprisonment, this has been cited as a counter-argument to the corrections-commercial complex thesis of Lilly and Knepper (1990) whereby 'prisons for profit' leads to an inevitable rise in the size of prison populations (see Harding, 1994).

New South Wales

The New South Wales Corrections Service has had a troubled recent history, receiving sustained and hostile media attention in the wake of several disturbances and deaths in its state-run prisons. Its 'near collapse' in the late 1970s (Harding, 1994) has been documented by Nagle (1978). The motivation for introducing a privately managed facility, according to some commentators, was therefore to create a distance between the state and some of its worst problems – although media criticism has continued to focus on the State as the responsible party. The main problems identified by observers of the public-sector system were 'inadequate facilities, staff shortages, lack of staff training, and inappropriate management practices' (Chan, 1994: 44).

Private involvement in the management of prisons in New South Wales was first considered by the coalition government in 1988, following a successful promotional meeting with Corrections Corporation of America (CCA), chaired by the then Minister for Corrective Services, Mr Michael Yabsley (Baldry, 1994). According to Baldry, at the time of its Australian promotional tour CCA was making a loss (Baldry, 1994: 126). A dramatic increase in the size of the prison population following the election provided additional support for the building of new prisons. The imprisonment rate in New South Wales increased from 101 per 100,000 to 129 per 100,000 between 1988 and 1991 (Baldry, 1994: 129). Public finance was available, however, to build three new establishments. Unlike the situation in the USA, it was not overcrowding, litigation or lack of public funds which precipitated the decision to 'go private', but rather, according to Baldry, the 'client state nature of Australia's relationship with the US' (Baldry, 1994: 129–30). As the US market seemed to slow down, in the wake of particular investigations into poor management, and as individual contracts were failing to be renewed or in some cases, were abandoned, private corrections corporations began to look to Australia for business.

A consultant's report (Kleinwort Benson Australia Ltd, 1989) recommended privatization on the basis of overseas experiences, at a time of large and persistent increases in the size of the prison population, on the grounds that it could build and operate a prison more easily, efficiently and effectively than the public sector (Baldry, 1994; Chan, 1994). The Report argued that:

> The private prison could be used as a precedent for introducing an alternative style of management or *accelerating change within public prisons* . . . benefits will accrue to the Government by *releasing funds from the Government's capital budget* for alternative use in the short to medium term . . . [and] . . . a private prison would also provide a benchmark to *assess the efficiency* of the present New South Wales system. (Kleinwort Benson Report, 1989: 17, cited in Moyle, 1993; original emphasis)

As a result of these developments, and following the Prisons (Contract Management) Act 1990, New South Wales Corrections Service opened its first privately managed prison in 1992. Junee Correctional Centre was (somewhat 'naively', according to Baldry, 1994) contracted-out to Australian Correctional Services Pty (ACS), which was a consortium of Thiess Contractors, ADT Security, and Wackenhut Corrections Corporation – a US company with some limited experience of private prison management in that country. The prison accommodates 600 medium and maximum-security prisoners. The contract was secured in the hope that a private company would be able to solve the problems of escalating costs, overcrowding and 'recalcitrant unions' (Baldry, 1994). Three of Junee's first senior managers were 'imported' from the USA. In addition to the normal mechanisms for complaint and scrutiny (the Ombudsman, and official visitors), there is a liaison officer (the equivalent of the Controller in the UK) employed by the Corrections Service in Junee.

Victoria

Victoria too had a history of difficulties with the public sector and its prison system. In 1992, its 'anti-privatization' government was replaced by one 'strongly committed to contract management of a significant part of its prisons and corrections system'. The new conservative Liberal government passed the Contract Management Act 1993 (Vic) in September 1993. This was soon followed by the kind of confrontation between the government and the Prison Officers' Union in Victoria, which privatization was intended to tackle. In December 1994 there was industrial action by prison officers (including a strike on Christmas Day which interfered with prisoners' visits from families) as plans were announced to embark on a large-scale privatization programme involving up to half of the state's prison population. A contract was signed in October 1995 with Australasian Correctional Services Pty, to finance, design, construct and manage a 600-bed medium-security prison in Fulham, which is due to open in 1997. In addition, two further prisons are expected to be contracted-out in the near future. The government has indicated that it expects substantially lower costs, together with improved services to prisoners (Nathan, 1995d).

Western Australia

Western Australia's prison system was the most expensive of all the Australian states at a cost of $55,000 per prisoner per annum. This relatively high cost was due to the absence of economies of scale, with a total prison population of 2,100, held in 16 establishments (most of which were concentrated around the Metropolitan area), and the delivery of programmes in relatively small establishments (average population around 150). During the 1980s the Western Australian prison system went through a period of enormous change and modernization. New prisons were opened (for example, the very modern Casuarina Prison) and Freemantle Gaol, the Victorian 'rep-lica' of Victorian prisons in the UK, and the site of serious riots in 1988, was closed and turned into a museum. The Corrections Service of Western Australia was incorporated into the Ministry of Justice in 1993. The Prisons Department amalgamated with the Parole Board, to become the Department of Corrective Services.

An interesting aspect of Western Australia's response to the developments in private prisons that were taking place in several other states was an operational review that was carried out and which effectively 'bought out' prison officers' overtime. The policy of the Australian Prison Officers' Association (POAA) was to advocate 'genuine consultative labour relations' as an alternative to further privatization. The following resolution came from the 1992 Annual Conference of the POAA, based on experience in Western Australia:

> Correctional administrators and policy makers are urged to turn their attention to the world's enduring successful economies, particularly those that don't enjoy vast natural mineral or primary resource wealth. These Northern European and more recently Japanese economies have as an ongoing feature genuine participation and consultation with the workforce and their unions. They have not privatised their corrective functions. (Belton, 1992: 10)

In the summer of 1994 the Western Australian Corrections Service introduced a deal with its staff which became known as 'the package'. Its basic conditions were the abolition of overtime and the removal of some of the privileges associated with state employment as Corrections staff. The restructuring plan was intended to save \$8 million per year and included cut backs in holiday entitlements and sick leave, and working an extra 80 hours per year for a higher basic salary (see Brown, 1994; Pollard, 1994). The package was introduced as a way of 'staving off' the threat of market-testing for an initial period of three years, at which time a renegotiation of pay and conditions might occur.

One hundred and thirty staff were shed as a result of the deal – or were not replaced when 'natural wastage' occurred – staff were deployed more economically, and a 'best practice' model of management was introduced. This was based on the following principles: consultation with employees; vision and strategic planning; the skilling and training of staff; the devolution of more power and responsibility to staff; flexible and flatter organizational structures; and continual performance measurement. 'It is also a system which encourages continuous improvement through an ongoing examination and evaluation of operational systems to ensure that it is functioning in a responsive, accountable and efficient manner' (Stacey, 1992: 5).

As the report also argues, the application of these principles to the management of particular establishments was considered appropriate because 'there is clearly a need to develop more cost efficient and effectively run prisons within Western Australia utilising the operation of "private" prisons as an industry benchmark' (Stacey, 1992: 5).

It is clear from the Western Australia experience that the introduction of prison privatization in some of the states has been welcomed and unashamedly used by governments in other states as a 'tool' with which to break the monopoly of the Prison Officers' Association.

Commentators on developments in Australia are divided in their views about the success or otherwise of 'contract management' of their corrections services. Harding argued:

> Its impact has so far been positive, in terms of costs, conditions and prisoner programs. The prison system is becoming less introverted, not only as the stranglehold of uniformed officers over prison regimes starts to be confronted but also as middle managers and senior administrators respond to competition. (Harding, 1992a: 7)

The managerialism which has appeared in the US and UK criminal justice systems is equally evident in Australian penal thinking (see, for example, Hall, 1995). An interesting difference between Australia and the UK is Australia's Freedom of Information Act. However, this Act does not include information covered by 'commercial-in-confidence' considerations and it is proving inadequate as a method of monitoring performance (see Moyle, 1993). For example, the contracts are exempt on the grounds of commercial secrecy (Baldry, 1994). Australia has no formal Inspectorate, but has an Ombudsman who investigates complaints and publishes annual reports. A crucial feature of the Australian context is the ongoing interest in custodial matters generated by the Royal Commission into the deaths of Aborigines in custody (see Biles and MacDonald, 1992).

A particularly striking feature of the Australian experience to date has been the speed with which privately managed prisons have been introduced in so many states – despite a climate of at times quite hostile criticism – resulting in the highest proportion in any country of prisoners held in establishments managed by the private sector. It seems that chronic difficulties in the resolution of staffing problems, and long-standing criticisms of the public sector, have rendered the introduction of competition particularly attractive to state legislatures in Australia: 'The public prison system has not exactly delivered the goods in Australia – in terms of recidivism rates, programs, humane standards and public safety' (Harding, 1994: 2). However, the way in which prison privatization was introduced was highly unpopular in some circles, with commentators arguing that insufficient time was allowed for public debate or proper scrutiny of the US firms seeking expansion into the Australian market (see Zdenkowski, 1994). This unwelcome (to some) expansion/invitation of private-prison entrepreneurs into Australia has been described as another example of 'colonialism' – after nuclear power, healthcare and other industries – with 'economic imperatives' taking precedence over arguments concerning 'social cohesion, well-being and citizen's rights' (Baldry, 1994: 126).

Privatization in Europe and Elsewhere

There has been similar development elsewhere in Europe. France, for example, faced with similar problems as those faced by prisons in the UK, 'has, if anything, a stronger and more recent history of private sector involvement in corrections' (Vagg, 1994: 305). There was already extensive involvement of private companies in the prison industries and workshops whilst the major form of custody for juveniles was also provided largely by non-governmental organizations or associations. However, although concerns similar to those expressed in other jurisdictions about the constitutionality of private prisons were raised, it was decided in France, as elsewhere, that whilst new laws might be needed, there was no constitutional reason why the administration of prisons could not be separated from the administration of justice.

Also faced with the problem of chronic overcrowding (Gallo, 1995), French initiatives in the privatization of prisons in 1987 (following a visit to the USA by the French Minister of Justice at about the same time as the visit by the Home Affairs Committee) reflect a completely different approach from that of the UK, aimed at minimizing capital costs by shifting these to recurrent expenditure. Initially, radical and extensive proposals for the provision of additional prison places by the private sector, which would have constituted over 40 per cent of a greatly expanded prison system, were progressively watered down, partly because of the cost of the proposed scale of provision. Four consortia were therefore asked to design and build prisons providing an additional 13,000 places and to provide a range of services – for example, food, plant maintenance, transport for prisoners, medical and drug rehabilitation services – at a fixed cost per inmate for a ten-year period.

These opened two years later and are now owned by the French government. By 1994, however, the number of private institutions had risen to 17, accommodating over 10,000 prisoners (Gallo, 1995). Although the original intention had been for total privatization, in the event, as a result of pressure from prison administrators, the French

Parliament and of a change of government in 1988, prison management and security and control remained the task of the prison service (Beyens and Snacken, 1994; Gallo, 1995). As Vagg comments, '[t]he only new factor was, therefore, the scale of contracting out of ancillary services' (Vagg, 1994: 307).

As Beyens and Snacken somewhat cynically observe, 'what happens in Paris today, happens in Brussels tomorrow' (1994: 8). Following visits to the new French semi-private prisons, and faced with problems of prison overcrowding (mainly due to a rise in remand and long-term prisoners together with a reduction of prison capacity caused by the need to refurbish prisons built last century), deteriorating prison conditions and escalating costs, the Belgian government decided in November 1993 to follow the French lead and to involve the private sector in the building of two new prisons. Whilst such circumstances prevail in Belgium, therefore, and faced with 'serious overcrowding, budget problems, the example of French semi-private prisons and the lobbying of international private companies' (Beyens and Snacken, 1994: 9), further co-operation with the private sector must remain a strong possibility.

In The Netherlands, long known for its moderate and humane penal policy, there has also been almost a fourfold increase in the prison population in less than 20 years and there is now a large prison building programme underway. In what has been described as 'a form of back door privatization' (van Swaaningen and de Jonge, 1995: 26), there has also been a process of decentralization and budgetary devolution since the early 1990s and it has now become official policy to transform the penal system into a government agency. This has given much greater autonomy to prison Governors, as a result of which 'every service except the actual control functions can be carried out by private enterprise' (van Swaaningen and de Jonge, 1995: 26).

In Germany, the first privately financed contract has been awarded to private contractors by the federal state of Berlin for the construction of a new prison and a number of other regional authorities 'have been approached by prison companies and have received presentations on the merits of private prisons' (Nathan, 1995c: 17), whilst other European governments have received such presentations. Some admit to monitoring privatization developments elsewhere and are reported by Wackenhut Corrections Corporation to be in various stages of considering the privatization option, although at the time of writing, there do not appear to have been any firm decisions to privatize reported (Nathan, 1995c). However, throughout Europe the same pressures are evident as prison populations increase – in Russia, Poland and neighbouring Baltic countries, Spain, Denmark, Norway,

Sweden and The Netherlands (Christie, 1994). It is in this context that Christie speculates that the huge growth in the prison population in the USA might reinforce what happens in Russia, concluding his analysis with a vision of an impending penal apocalypse.

Under circumstances such as these, few could deny the potential for a major expansion in the privatization of prisons in Europe and beyond. In France, for example, SIGES (a subsidiary of Sodexho SA) is one of the largest companies providing services in French prisons. Following a recently formed international strategic alliance between the Corrections Corporation of America (CCA) and Sodexho to market private prison services, the President and Chief Executive of CCA indicated that the company intend 'to make a significant impact on the global corrections market at a time when every criminal justice system is seeking fiscally sound, technically innovative ways to solve their corrections problems' (Nathan, 1994a: 17; see also Gallo, 1995: 88).

Similarly, in addition to the growing markets in the USA, Canada and Australia, New Zealand is now entering the field of prison privatization, after some initial hesitation and political delays. Two major reports (the Report of the Ministerial Committee of Inquiry into the Prisons System (Roper, 1989) and the Department of Justice Resource Management Review submitted to the New Zealand Department of Justice (Strategos Consulting Limited, 1989)) recommended the introduction of private-sector involvement in specified (and limited) areas of prison management during the 1980s, including escort and court duties, remand centres and canteen services. A decision was taken to await the outcome of developments in America and Australia before any firm commitment was made to private-sector involvement, with the notion of 'full privatization' being rejected in 1988. However, in November 1994, the new government passed the Penal Institutions Amendment Bill (No. 3), which provided enabling legislation for the introduction of privately managed prisons. There are plans for two prisons to be privately financed, designed, built and managed by the private sector, in Auckland: one a 250-bed remand prison, and the other a 350-bed medium-security facility. Six firms submitted bids for the contracts, and the government hoped that the first contracted-out facility would be operational before the end of 1996 (Nathan, 1995a: 20).

Meanwhile, CCA is reported to have identified markets in Brazil, Mexico and China 'which in the long term could represent the majority of earnings' (Nathan, 1995b: 20), and Wackenhut's 1994 Annual Report also refers to developments in the South American market (Nathan, 1995c: 17). Apart from the USA and Australia, however, both CCA and Wackenhut claim that their prime target is the UK (Nathan, 1995a). It is therefore to the privatization of prisons in the UK that we shall turn our attention in Chapter 3. Before doing so, however, we shall explore briefly in Chapter 2 some of the issues and difficulties raised by attempts to evaluate such initiatives.

2

Evaluating Private Prisons

Our review in Chapter 1 of the 'renaissance' of private prisons in the final quarter of the twentieth century has illustrated the many different factors that have contributed to their introduction and development, particularly in the USA and Australia. The major influences have ranged from the highly political and ideological to the more mundanely pragmatic and instrumental, typically in a context of serious penal–fiscal crisis, which is becoming increasingly common world-wide (see Christie, 1994). Similarly, the accompanying and often heated debate about the merits (or otherwise) of privatized prisons has been conducted across a wide spectrum of argument, from considerations of the ethical, moral and constitutional principles that are raised to the practical consequences and future implications/potential of the contracting-out of the management of prisons.

Before proceeding to a more detailed examination of how the private-sector management of prisons emerged on to the professional and political scene in the UK in the late 1980s, thereby providing the context and *raison d'être* for the comparative research project reported in this book, it will be instructive to consider the attempts that have been made in other jurisdictions to evaluate the early achievements of the private-sector management of prisons. The primary focus here will be upon empirical evaluation studies that have tended to adopt an essentially pragmatic approach to the task, rather than the arguably more significant ethical and moral critiques, to which attention will be paid in later chapters. In view of the focus and scope of our own research, we shall concentrate primarily upon those studies that have evaluated adult prisons and correctional facilities rather than institutions for juvenile offenders or other forms of custodial detention.

Cost Comparisons

Whatever other political and penological influences may contribute to the introduction and development of private prisons, it is clear that one of the primary considerations affecting the decision to contract-out the management of prisons to the private sector is the belief that the state will thereby save a significant amount of taxpayers' money. It should come as no surprise therefore that the main emphasis in most of the early and many of the subsequent attempts to evaluate private prisons was upon cost comparisons between the private and public sectors. In order for such comparisons to be valid, a number of methodological problems have to be addressed. In particular, the private and public penal establishments or correctional facilities being compared should be as directly 'comparable' as possible, on all factors other than that of their privately/publicly managed status, controlling for such factors as size of inmate population, types of prisoner, security level, physical design, etc. Furthermore, it is essential to take account of all the otherwise 'hidden costs' involved in the running of penal establishments, whether in the private or public sector (see McDonald, 1994), and to calculate costs on the same basis across the two sectors, for example, expressed as a *per diem* rate for prisoners or as a fixed sum assuming 100 per cent occupancy. Otherwise, misleading conclusions may be drawn, as Charles Logan was fully aware in his comprehensive review of the 'cons and pros' of private prisons:

> Simple comparisons like those presented above can be used to support opposite conclusions: that proprietary prisons are less expensive – or more expensive – than their governmental counterparts. The key word here, and a source of confusion, is 'counterpart'. Researchers who compare institutions must face the fact that facilities vary widely on a great many factors that affect costs; so much so that most simple comparisons of *per diem* rates are not very meaningful. (Logan, 1990: 96)

In fact, in one of the first studies to be carried out into the estimated savings in the running of the Hamilton County Penal Farm (Silverdale) in Tennessee, which had been contracted-out to the newly formed Corrections Corporation of America (CCA) in October 1984, Logan himself and Bill McGriff (the county auditor) did not select any establishment from the public sector for comparative purposes but simply estimated the likely costs of Silverdale if the county had continued to run it (see Logan and McGriff, 1989).

On the other hand, Levinson's well-known evaluation of the Okeechobee School for Boys (Florida) – a secure facility for juvenile delinquents, which had been transferred to the private, not-for-profit Jack and Ruth Eckerd Foundation in 1982 – was seriously flawed by the fact that the population of Okeechobee included far more ethnic minority juveniles and serious offenders than did the Arthur G. Dozier School in Marianna, which was used for comparative purposes, even though for certain matched comparisons Quay's typology of offenders was used to standardize the two populations (see Levinson, 1985).

In view of the technical difficulty of selecting two closely matched penal establishments and other problems such as that of not having full details of the various hidden costs, any cost comparisons of the private and public sectors should be treated with great caution and interpreted with care. Nevertheless, the majority of studies to date of the relative costs of broadly comparable private- and public-sector prisons suggest that certainly in their early years the cost of private-sector prisons represents a saving on what might have been expected from the public sector. Thus, when CCA took over Silverdale Work Farm, they charged the county 12.5 per cent less per prisoner per day than it had cost to run under county management. A conservative estimate of savings to the county in the first three years under private-sector management indicated that there had been savings of between 5 and 15 per cent (Logan and McGriff, 1989: 6).

Sellers' detailed comparison of three matched pairs of correctional facilities for adults in Pennsylvania, New Jersey and Tennessee (Silverdale again) concluded that 'all three privately-operated facilities operate at less cost than the three publicly-operated facilities' (Sellers, 1993: 84), despite the fact that all the salary structures in the privately managed prisons were the same or higher than comparative government salaries, including benefits. The average inmate *per diem* costs was $46 (privately operated) and $74 (publicly operated), with the greatest difference between a matched pair of facilities being $50 per day (Weaversville vs North Central) and the smallest being just $4 per day (Butler County Prison vs Salem County Jail) (Sellers, 1993: 84 and see Table 4.11).

In contrast, a similar study of three matched (private/public) pairs of adult and juvenile establishments in Kentucky and Massachusetts, carried out by the Urban Institute in 1987–8, revealed that the costs were quite similar for all three pairs, with the difference between no more than plus or minus 10 per cent per inmate per day (Hatry et al., 1993). In Kentucky, the cost of the privately run minimum-security Marian Adjustment Centre was 10 per cent *higher* than the publicly managed Blackburn Correctional Complex; similarly, in the survey of juvenile facilities in Massachusetts, the cost of the private facilities was around 1 per cent higher than the public (Hatry et al., 1993: 197). The authors commented that one of the reasons for these findings was that 'competition for these contracts, at least thus far, has not been sufficiently large to drive the cost significantly lower, if indeed lower costs are feasible' (Hatry et al., 1993: 197). Indeed, in Kentucky the initial private-sector bids were all much higher than the unit costs budgeted by the state.

Early evidence from Australia, where Queensland was the first state to contract-out the management of an adult prison, Borallon

Correctional Centre (opened under private management in Ja 1990), showed cost savings in 1992/3 of approximately 10 pei per prisoner, when compared with Lotus Glen Correctional Ci (Macionis, 1994). The main problems in interpreting the finding of this comparison relate first to the different security mix of prisoners at the two establishments – with Borallon accommodating mainly medium-security prisoners (80 per cent, with the rest low or open category), whereas Lotus Glen had 40 per cent medium security, 40 per cent low or open, but a significant 20 per cent high-security prisoners – and secondly to the apportionment of central office overheads costs to the two facilities.

Another interesting feature of the comparison of costs over the first two years' operation of Borallon and Lotus Glen is that between 1991/2 and 1992/3 the costs of privately managed Borallon increased significantly, whereas those for Lotus Glen decreased, leading one economic commentator to speculate that this trend towards differential costs might continue so that for these and other reasons 'the comparison of costs between Borallon and Lotus Glen is an imperfect exercise' (Brown, 1994: 211).

To summarize the findings to date on cost comparisons between the private and public sector, it would seem appropriate to quote from the conclusions of an avowed advocate of the privatization of prisons:

> Private prisons will not necessarily be less expensive than those owned and run directly by the government. A very safe generalization from the broader literature on contracting for public services is that often it saves money, but sometimes it does not. (Logan, 1990: 117)

Evaluating 'Quality'

An equally important consensus to emerge from studies of the economics and cost-effectiveness of private prisons is that:

> . . . any study of costs should be complemented by an examination of the 'quality' dimension of prison operations. Appropriate decisions in relation to the contracting out of prison management can only be made when both cost and quality aspects are taken into account. (Brown, 1994: 211)

In 1990, Logan concluded that 'there has been almost no systematic empirical research comparing private and government-run prisons *in terms of quality*' (Logan, 1990: 147; emphasis added). Although, some five or six years later, the situation has not been exactly transformed in this respect, there have been several interesting qualitative evaluations that have added a crucial dimension to the debate, even though the complexities of qualitative methodology are no less than those associated with cost comparisons.

In order to evaluate 'quality', consideration must be given to what constitutes a 'good prison' and from whose perspective this judgement should be made – prison managers, discipline/treatment staff, prisoners, politicians, members of the public? In practice, most evaluation studies have focused on prison conditions and internal 'regime' aspects, rather than attempting more ambitious external evaluations in terms of rehabilitation or re-offending rates. It is perhaps not entirely without significance that the era of the development of private prisons has coincided with the decline of the 'rehabilitative ideal' within prisons. In such a penal climate, private firms can hardly be expected to achieve overall rehabilitative objectives that have been largely discarded by the public sector. Moreover, the perceived need to measure performance (which, as Chapter 3 argues, is also rooted in more widespread political changes) has resulted in the creation of 'key performance indicators' (KPIs) and evaluation criteria for both the private and public sectors, that are likely to accelerate the present trends towards simple 'warehousing' or 'humane containment' (Keating, 1990: 134) – although there is some evidence of a renewed interest by the Prison Service Agency in developing KPIs for measuring re-offending and encouraging prisons to address offending behaviour.

Not only are the objectives of the evaluation of quality quite complex, linked as they must be to the overall correctional policies and priorities of prison services, but the methodologies required are more demanding of time and resources than typical economic cost-benefit analyses. Opinion surveys and interviews of staff and prisoners are an essential prerequisite, combined with observational data to supplement institutional records of regime activities, disciplinary offences, etc. Few studies to date have met all these methodological criteria, but nevertheless several have produced interesting findings to complement the quantitative data reviewed above.

As part of the Urban Institute's matched study of private and public facilities in Kentucky and Massachusetts, Hatry, Brownstein and Levison (1993) examined 'service quality and effectiveness', covering a wide range of aspects grouped into: 1 conditions of confinement; 2 internal security and control; 3 social adjustment and rehabilitation; and 4 management and staffing:

> For a substantial majority of these performance indicators, the privately operated facilities had at least a small advantage. By and large, both staff and inmates gave better ratings to the services and programs at the privately operated facilities; escape rates were lower; there were fewer disturbances by inmates; and in general, staff and offenders felt more comfortable at the privately operated facilities. (Hatry et al., 1993: 198)

The researchers attributed much of the 'success' of the privately run establishments to the enthusiasm of staff, who tended to be younger (albeit less experienced) than the longer-serving staff in the public facilities:

> By and large, staff in the privately operated [facilities] appeared to be more enthusiastic about their work, more involved in their work, and more interested in working with the inmates than their public counterparts. Management-wise [*sic*], the privately operated facilities appeared to be more flexible and less regimented, with staff subject to less stringent controls. These elements seem to have made life in the privately operated correctional facilities more pleasant for both inmates and staff. (Hatry et al., 1993: 199)

In contrast, in the evaluation of the Okeechobee School for Boys (run by the Eckerd Foundation) it was judged that a programme of equal quality to that at the Dozier School was being delivered, but that Dozier was a happier place to work than Okeechobee. An independent corrections expert who visited both institutions, to give a subjective assessment of qualitative dimensions, reported much more favourable impressions of the publicly operated Dozier School (Levinson, 1985: 81–2).

In one of the first qualitative studies of Silverdale, Brakel surveyed the opinions of a sample of 20 inmates, who rated the institution very highly on many of the key 'quality' factors:

> . . . the inmates could not care less about who runs the prison, by what political mandate or on what contractual terms. Their paramount interest is much simpler: decent conditions and decent treatment. (Brakel, 1988: 240)

These findings are perhaps to be treated with some caution, given the small size of the sample on which they are based, and the fact that the questionnaires were distributed by the chaplain, to prisoners known to be 'reasonably articulate' (Brakel, 1988: 181). Shichor makes the further points that in its first year Silverdale had a $200,000 cost overrun, and in 1986 there was a riot in which prisoners demanded better food, more adequate recreation and generally better treatment (Shichor, 1995: 214)!

In what is probably the most detailed qualitative study of private and public prisons to date, Logan compared the 'quality of confinement' in three women's prisons in New Mexico: private, state and federal. He recognized the problems of establishing a methodology for comparing prison 'quality' – 'the major obstacle to such research is the difficulty of defining the ''quality'' of a prison' (Logan, 1992: 578):

The criteria proposed here for comparative evaluation of prisons are normative, rather than consequentialist or utilitarian. They are based on a belief that individual prisons ought to be judged primarily according to the propriety and quality of what goes on inside their walls – factors over which prison officials may have considerable control. (Logan, 1992: 579)

The subsequent analysis was based on a 'doing justice' model of punishment and a 'confinement model' of imprisonment. Eight dimensions of the quality of confinement were selected: Security, Safety, Order, Care, Activity, Justice, Conditions and Management. These were converted into 333 empirical indicators, as the basis for pairwise comparisons among the three prisons. Data were extracted from institutional records, and interviews of staff and prisoners were carried out at each prison, except at the federal prison where inmates were not interviewed. The response rate was quite high, ranging from 40 per cent of staff at the federal prison to 95 per cent and 82 per cent of prisoners, at the state and private prisons, respectively. The private prison out-performed the state and federal prisons across nearly all dimensions (often by quite substantial margins) except for Care and Justice, where it was equal with the federal prison (Logan, 1992: 589).

It was interesting to find that on the results of the inmate surveys only, the state prison out-scored the private on every dimension except Activity; when looking at staff surveys, the private prison easily and consistently out-scored the state prison. There was a cluster of dimensions (designated a 'Welfare Model') on which the state prison out-scored the private and federal prisons, namely Activity, Conditions and Care. On a second cluster ('Governance Model') the federal and private prisons out-scored the state, namely Justice, Order, Security, Safety and Management (Logan, 1992: 599). Thus, no clear-cut conclusion about the consistent superiority of the private over the public sector emerged from this qualitative analysis: 'Regardless of the data source examined, there were many similarities among the 3 prisons, and for each one there were large numbers of both positive and negative indicators. Moreover, in absolute terms, quality was high at all three prisons' (Logan, 1992: 601). Nevertheless, Logan felt able to conclude that 'by privately contracting for the operation of its women's prison, the State of New Mexico improved the overall quality of that prison while lowering its costs' (Logan, 1992: 602) – suggesting that where data are unexpected or inconclusive, conclusions are sometimes still drawn in the light of the researcher's predisposition in favour of either the private or public management of prisons (see below for further discussion).

Private vs Public Prisons: Weighed in the Balance

Any summary of the findings of the evaluation of private vs public prisons must be tentative and provisional. Perhaps the most eloquent attempt was that of John DiIulio:

> ... at this stage it is impossible to answer most of the important empirical questions raised by the privatization movement. Despite a variety of claims to the contrary, there is absolutely nothing in either the scholarly or non-scholarly literature on the subject – no journal article, no government report, no newspaper story, no conference proceedings, no book – that would enable one to speak confidently about how private corrections firms compare with public corrections agencies in terms of costs, protection of inmates' civil rights, reliance on particular management technologies, or any other significant dimension. The necessary comparative research simply has not been done, and reliable empirical data are still scarce. (DiIulio, 1990: 156)

However, apart from a general reluctance to make dogmatic claims about the unqualified merits of either the private or public sector in the management of prisons – at least not on the basis of empirical evaluation studies – an interesting consensus that seems to have emerged is that *significant variation of performance and quality* is to be found within both private and public sectors alike. Thus, conclusions of a very similar kind can be quoted from those on both sides of the debate. For example:

> My own conclusion so far is simply that private prisons will fall variously within the same range of quality as do those run by government employees. Some private prisons will be better than some public prisons, and *vice versa*. (Logan, 1990: 148)

> As the Okeechobee Project has shown, in corrections neither the public nor the private sector is all good or all bad; there are pluses and minuses on both sides. . . . What most certainly needs to be avoided is either side denigrating the other. Under that scenario, all the players lose. (Levinson, 1985: 92)

> The crucial point, however, is that the administrative performance of public prison and jails has not been uniformly bad, and there is no reason to suppose that the performance of private facilities would be uniformly good. To believe otherwise one would have to believe that there is something magical about the private sector. (DiIulio, 1990: 171)

> ... there is no sure way to know whether private prisons will end up more or less humane, on average, than public ones. Every tale of bad conditions or brutality at a private facility can be matched by a story about the horrors of public prisons and the superiority of private prison conditions. The anecdotes cut both ways, and settle nothing. (Donahue, 1989: 169)

By their very nature and timing, most of the 'evaluations' that have been carried out so far have focused primarily on internal comparisons of 'processes' and 'means' rather than on 'outcomes' or 'ends'.

Ideally, of course, evaluations should attempt to address issues related to both outcomes and process (Roberts and Powers, 1985: 99). Typically, however, the goals of most studies are more modest:

> Process studies have as their goal an understanding of what is happening in a particular program, why it is happening, and whether it is happening the way it was intended to happen. As such, these studies focus on means rather than ends. ... Thus, the basic question is not one of whether privately run correctional programs are more or less effective and/or efficient than their public counterparts in some monolithic or global sense but rather, in what specific ways and in relation to what particular types of problems or client populations might one approach be superior to another. (Roberts and Powers, 1985: 100)

However, even if significant differences were to be found between privately and publicly managed prisons, the extent and confidence with which any such differences could be attributed to distinctive and unique features of private-sector or public-sector management *per se* would be very problematic. Thus, at the conclusion of his detailed comparative study of women's prisons in New Mexico, Logan identified a number of features that might explain the relatively high performance of the private prison, including greater operational and administrative flexibility, higher morale, enthusiasm and sense of ownership among line staff, and stricter 'governance' of the inmates. Nevertheless, although he believed that the private operation of the prison contributed at least in part to these features, he admitted that 'we cannot say precisely to what extent the differences observed among the prisons were due to privatization, nor can we isolate the aspects of privatization that might account for the differences' (Logan, 1992: 602). He called for further research, not only to see whether the apparent advantages associated with private management could be replicated, but also 'to go beyond merely measuring differences and to begin accounting for them as well' (Logan, 1992: 602).

When claims are made, in further justification for the privatization of prisons, on grounds of its impact on the generation or acceleration of change in prisons in the public sector, the nature of the argument and the case to be made becomes yet more problematic. Among the fundamental assumptions underlying the wider movement towards the privatization of public services is that the private sector can do most things more cheaply and efficiently – spurred on by the competitive market situation in which they are forced to operate (Donahue, 1989). Furthermore, where the public sector operates alongside the private sector in delivering the same service (such as correctional facilities), it is often firmly believed that this competition will in turn bring about significant economies and improved quality of service in the public sector: 'Perhaps the major contribution of private prisons is that they will provide an alternative standard against which to measure public prisons. . . . Privatization may force improvements in government operations by defining higher standards and raising expectations.' (Logan, 1990: 145).

Whatever the mechanism whereby this improved performance in the public sector is assumed to be generated, for example whether by simple threat of 'market-testing' or privatization, or by responding to the professional challenge that has been set down to them, the fact is that it is virtually impossible to *prove* that any such effect is due to privatization rather than to other factors in the ever-changing economic and political environments. There is evidence from economists that 'the performance of publicly owned providers of goods and services can be substantially improved over a relatively short space of time' (Brown, 1994: 200). More specifically, in Australia, there is evidence showing that government enterprises have increased their productivity at a much greater rate than firms in the private sector, so that 'there seems to be no inherent factor preventing publicly operated prisons from similarly improving their economic productivity' (Brown, 1994: 215).

Evaluation – By Whom? For Whom?

A final unfortunate, and perhaps unavoidable, feature of most of even the research-based literature in the privatization of prisons debate is that it is very rare to find evaluations by researchers who appear or even claim to be 'independent' or 'unbiased'. It quite quickly becomes apparent, when reading accounts of the findings of research studies, where the authors' sympathies lie (Shichor, 1995: 231). In one of the most recent reviews of empirical evaluations in this area, David Shichor makes a strong plea for the need for truly independent research: 'It is important that the evaluation be designed by independent researchers who do not have a vested interest either *pro* or *con* in the privatization debate and who are not paid by private companies.' (Shichor, 1995: 228). However, he recognizes the special problems and sensitivities surrounding evaluative research into the performance of private correctional facilities. On the one hand, evaluators need the co-operation of those whose programmes are being evaluated but who are often not interested in or even hostile to the evaluation exercise. Many managers and programme administrators in the public as well as in the private sector feel that 'independent evaluators' are actually there to look for trouble in their institutions, whereas any possible benefits for them accruing from a positive evaluation are perceived as being minimal, as Levinson recognized in the course of his pioneering evaluation of Okeechobee:

> What are the purposes to be served by an objective evaluation? Is it to find and disseminate the truth? Is it to justify political decisions by providing an acceptable PR (public relations) atmosphere at the initial stages of a project? Will anything change because of the Okeechobee evaluation? (Levinson, 1985: 87)

As a team of 'independent researchers', with the task of evaluating the first UK initiative in contracting-out the management of a remand prison, the four of us started out with varied preconceptions and sympathies which we felt would not unduly influence the way we conducted our research or the conclusions we would eventually reach. As the research progressed, we became aware of the many tensions and dilemmas in attempting to maintain an independent role on which the ultimate value of our work would, in our view, so crucially depend. Indeed, we each emerged with slightly different positions on some of the key empirical questions and normative judgements. The extent to which we were able to retain our professional (and political) independence both in the carrying out and the reporting of the findings of our research will be for the reader to judge! In the final analysis, whatever empirical data are generated and might appear to portray, the interpretation and response to such data will, for most readers, be significantly affected by their basic beliefs and ideological orientations, and therefore located and understood within a predetermined value framework:

> The central moral issues surrounding private prisons and jail management have little to do with the profit motive of the privatizers and much to do with the propriety, in a constitutional democracy, of delegating the authority to administer criminal justice to nonpublic individuals and groups. (DiIulio, 1990: 177)

3

Contemporary Developments in British Penal Politics

The political, social and economic factors which produced the circumstances in which private-sector involvement in the management of prisons began to appear in other countries also helped to create the climate in which the contracting-out of the first prison in Britain became possible. Before considering developments in Britain, however, it is important to acknowledge that, in spite of the strong opposition which crystallized around the idea of 'privatized prisons' and 'prisons for profit', which presented this as a radical departure and a major compromise to the state's proper responsibility for law and order, the not-for-profit sector had long since breached any monopolistic state responsibility for the penal system.

Indeed, the supposed monopoly of the state had never been complete and many opponents of these developments have overlooked the long tradition of private-sector involvement in the provisions for young offenders. When reformatory schools were introduced in 1854, followed by industrial schools in 1857, they were inspired and created by the private sector and run under private management. Although much of the responsibility for such residential provisions for children and young people in trouble was progressively taken over by the state, and the role of the voluntary sector in this respect has decreased (Rutherford, 1990), there have been numerous and rapid developments during the last 15 years reinforcing private-sector involvement which have been at least partly in response to their declining role in residential provision.

Of particular importance was the significance attached to voluntary-sector involvement in boosting the impact of what had become known as 'intermediate treatment' (IT) for juveniles, first introduced by the Children and Young Persons Act, 1969. The voluntary sector had, in fact, been extensively involved with the provision of a wide range of IT schemes from the outset, but during the 1970s there was a progressive and substantial loss of confidence in these which reflected the more general disillusionment with welfare-oriented preventative services which were part of the discredited rehabilitative ideal and the welfare model of justice which had dominated the 1960s.

However, in 1983 a Local Authority Circular (LAC 83/3) was issued, announcing the availability of £15 million over a period of three years to aid the development of intensive IT. This initiative had three main aims, which reflected these and other issues: to shift IT from prevention to providing alternatives to care or custody; to provide bridging finance to enable IT projects to be established prior to closure of institutions as part of the shift from residential to community care; and to facilitate local inter-agency liaison between those organizations concerned with juvenile offending, in order to improve the efficiency and effectiveness of the juvenile justice system. LAC 83/3 gave a prominent place to the development of alternatives to care and custody by voluntary organizations such as Barnardos and National Children's Homes, which had traditionally provided a range of residential care, in order to augment provisions made by local authority social services departments. It is clear, therefore, that major provisions in an important sphere of the penal system – that which revolves around juvenile and young offenders – have long been delegated by the state to others.

In addition to developments such as these, there had been private- and voluntary-sector involvement in a number of other areas of the penal system for some time prior to the opening of the first con-tracted-out prison. For example, the first contract for the private operation of immigrant detention centres was let by the Home Office in 1970, when Securicor Ltd became responsible for the Harmonds-worth detention centre near Heathrow (Rutherford, 1990). In addi-tion, private-sector construction companies have long been involved in the building of prisons and the provision of various services; a range of voluntary-sector organizations has been involved in the provision of bail hostels and accommodation for offenders and ex-offenders; and yet other voluntary organizations have provided vari-ous services for offenders being dealt with in the community.

Thus, although the contracting-out of the first prison to private-sector management was clearly a momentous development in terms of British penal policy, the image of a penal system as one which, until then, had been the sole preserve of the state, is an illusion. As Vagg has observed:

> Any brief inspection of the degree to which criminal justice was in state hands would . . . conclude that a large number of facilities, from juvenile homes and probation hostels to immigration detention facilities, were actually operated by private companies or voluntary organizations. What was being proposed was a change in scale, with contracting-out becoming

a core rather than a peripheral feature of criminal justice. (Vagg, 1994: 294)

The Political Context of Privatization

The Changing Tide of Politics

Such issues notwithstanding, it is clear that for many on both sides of the debate, the privatization of Britain's prisons was seen as a political landmark, not only within the relatively narrow confines of penal policy but in the much larger context of Thatcherite political philosophy. Before considering the way in which this came about in Britain in detail, therefore, it is important to delineate some of the key dimensions of the political context which facilitated such changes.

As we have already argued, during the 1970s the face of world politics began to change and

> a new politics became established in the West. There were different national variants but many common themes. . . . The trigger for this was the collapse of fixed exchange rates in 1971–2 followed by the quad-rupling of the oil price in 1973 and the ensuing generalised world recession. (Gamble, 1994: 12–15)

In Britain, this weakened government authority and led both directly and indirectly to the adoption of a range of deflationary measures, rapidly increasing large-scale unemployment, wage restraint, economic instability and industrial unrest.

It was this context which was so powerful in setting the scene for the Conservative victory in the 1979 general election and in shaping the political philosophy which was to become the hallmark of Margaret Thatcher's administration. Central to this, according to Brake and Hale (1992), was the economic philosophy of Friederich von Hayek (Chair of the academic board of the Adam Smith Institute in the early 1980s), whose ideas were so influential in shaping those expounded by Mrs Thatcher and her government.

It is, perhaps, ironic therefore that according to Gamble, 'Hayek has always had reservations about conservatism as a sound ideological basis for politics . . . [because] Conservatives could not be trusted to protect freedom' (Gamble, 1994: 142) because both 'doctrinal' conservatism (which arises in periods of social and political upheaval, such as that seen in Britain in the 1970s, and is the 'politics of social breakdown') and 'positional' conservatism (which is concerned with the administration of an existing order) involve, *inter alia*, according to Hayek, 'the use of arbitrary power' (Gamble, 1994: 143).

This reservation is reflected in the work of Butler, Pirie and Young of the Adam Smith Institute who wrote with what, in retrospect, seems ironic prescience:

> Unfortunately, once legislators come to believe that they are the standard and measure of justice, there is little that can be done to restrain them, no limit to the scope of the new rules that they impose in their attempts to fashion a new society closer to their own beliefs. Those beliefs are often temporary and changing, which is not a recipe for preserving a stable system of justice. And, however prolonged one particular viewpoint might be, the confusion [between administrative power and the preservation of justice] tempts legislators to suppose that they can run an entire country as one might run a factory, by administrative command – another source of discontent and disruption, because it necessarily comes into conflict with deeply held ideas of justice. (Butler et al., 1985: 232)

It is interesting to note in this context, in passing, that the authors also outlined proposals for limiting the exercise, proliferation and abuse of administrative power which have a strong libertarian ring and which would, in key respects, have limited the extraordinarily high levels of government intervention in criminal justice which has been one of the hallmarks of Conservatism since 1979. As Butler and his colleagues went on to argue:

> Most people, particularly legislators, have a vision of an ideal world. That is not to say that they have any right to impose that vision on others. But the confusion of administrative law and justice leads legislators, through idealism as much as anything, to attempt to impose their administrative ideals on the general public as well as on the government sector. Lacking clear concepts and devoid of constraints on their power . . . it is then possible for a country to drift very far from the ideal of a liberal society. (Butler et al., 1985: 235)

Many commentators would have little difficulty in recognizing this as an acute and highly accurate description of what has subsequently happened to criminal justice in Britain in the years since these words were written.

From the influence of Hayek (such reservations apart), and the work of others such as Milton Friedman, emerged the view that democracy and, indeed, freedom could only be based upon free-market choices. As Gamble argues:

> One of the most important areas where this approach was applied by New-Right economists lay in the field of public expenditure and taxation. The existence of a substantial sector in which services were provided by public bodies meant a large area where administrative rather than market criteria held sway . . . The argument was that good intentions and high ideals were not enough. Any service would be more efficiently provided if it was subject to competitive tender and free from administrative controls and political interference. (Gamble, 1994: 56)

Once elected, therefore, Brake and Hale argue that in order to pursue their economic policies, 'the Conservatives had to construct an ideological climate which justified its unpicking of the Welfare State' (Brake and Hale, 1992: 171). Therefore, building upon these ideas and Conservative philosophy more generally, Mrs Thatcher's government developed:

> . . . [a] determined campaign to replace socialism with a market economy, a distinct project: to reduce State involvement in the field of welfare provision and to break the power of the trade unions. To succeed with either aim it felt it had to develop a strong State in the arena of law and order. (Brake and Hale, 1992: 2)

In similar vein, Gamble argues that in order to ensure that its economic policies were successful, the government had to demonstrate that it could not be coerced and that it would confront any direct challenge to its authority. The unifying theme of the 'New Right' was 'the combination of a traditional liberal defence of the free economy with a traditional conservative defence of state authority . . . [this] involves a paradox. The state is to be simultaneously rolled back and rolled forward' (Gamble, 1994: 35–6). Thus one of the main planks of Mrs Thatcher's policies was, in Kavanagh's words: 'the restoration of the authority of government. This involved both strengthening the . . . forces of law and order, and resisting damaging claims of interest groups' (Kavanagh, 1990: 13). Consequently, the logic of these dicta was that the state:

> . . . should be interventionist only in the area of law and order. Indeed, the maintenance of public order and the policing of crime is a prerequisite for the proper functioning of the market. . . . [This] led to a revival of the classical theory of criminal responsibility which echoed the individualism of the marketplace. (Brake and Hale, 1992: 17)

The Emergence of the Conservative Criminology – Party Politics and Penal Policy

To such an emerging political philosophy the rehabilitative ideal and the welfare model of justice, which had dominated penal policy in the 1960s and 1970s, were anathema. Apart from growing concerns about the excesses of intervention in the name of treatment, the emphasis of such deterministic perspectives on the needs of the offender, on treatment rather than punishment, and on the social and economic determinants of crime were antithetical to a philosophy based on individual responsibility and the social contract (for a fuller discussion, see, for example, Hudson, 1987). It was therefore important that they should be rejected outright. This disjunction was also clearly a major factor in bringing law and order to the fore in the campaign leading up to the 1979 general election and in making it, more than at any other time in post-war Britain, a matter of party politics. As King has argued:

> The construction of crime as a major social problem demanding an immediate and effective government response has for at least the past hundred years allowed politicians in general, but the political party in power in particular to define the problem, distil the issues and offer solutions which promote and sustain its particular collective vision of the ideal society and the ways of achieving that ideal. (King, 1989: 291)

It also seemed clear that public opinion was in favour of change in that 'there was ample survey evidence that the electorate was well to the right of the major parties on issues like . . . law and order' (Kavanagh, 1990: 73) and that between 1964 and 1979, public opinion had shifted decisively to the ideological right. These issues were clearly reflected in the Conservative Party manifesto which outlined their commitment to:

1   See the problem of crime primarily from the viewpoint of its victims rather than its perpetrators.
2   Support a deterrent strategy, i.e. stiffer penalties.
3   Believe individuals have free will and should be accountable for their actions. Everyone, rich and poor, has the choice of obeying or breaking the law but if they take the latter course they should be in no doubt as to the penalties they must face. (Jones, 1994: 356)

When the Conservative Party came to power in 1979, therefore, many expected the increase in crime to be dealt with by traditional Conservative remedies such as strengthening the police force and seeking stiffer penalties for serious crimes. However, Aughey and Norton identify a dilemma faced by the Conservatives:

> The Radical Conservative response posited that the return of a Conservative Government by itself was insufficient to preserve the delicate balances within the constitution. . . . The aim was not to create some new visionary constitutional structure and relationship, but rather to restore those that were presumed previously to have existed. In an important sense, it was not just radical, it was also reactionary. (Aughey and Norton, 1984: 143)

To Conservatives, the concept of punishment is related to liberty within an established order. Its purpose is not to reform the guilty but to preserve order through force. Hence, the emphasis is upon punishment, upon the rights of the victim, and upon the guilt of the lawbreaker, not of society. Thus:

> Conservatives have difficulty in going beyond the individual in discerning the root of criminal behaviour. . . . If there is public disorder, if there is a spiralling crime rate, the prescription is largely more of the same. . . . But if such reforms fail to have the desired effect, Conservatives have

difficulty in knowing where to turn next. Even a policy of more of the same generates demands on resources which can no longer fully be met. . . . For the Conservative Party, the party of 'law and order', it is a perplexing conundrum. (Aughey and Norton, 1984: 146–7)

In spite of this potential dilemma, law and order featured prominently in the campaign leading up to the 1979 general election and the issue became increasingly a subject of heated party political debate. As Brake and Hale argue:

In the ideological battle waged by the Conservatives before and after 1979 the Conservative Party successfully projected itself as the party of law and order. Conversely, the Labour Party has been pilloried as the bastion of permissiveness which uncritically supports the poor, the deviant, the feckless and the idle regardless of individual worthiness. (Brake and Hale, 1992: 17)

In consequence, the relationship between the parties has become increasingly adversarial. As parties have sought to make political capital from the law and order issue, popular perceptions of the differences between the parties have become the targets of party political rhetoric and the Conservative stance, seen as the tougher of the two, has been an electoral plus for the party. This assessment is shared by other commentators who argue that by the mid-1980s the Conservatives had 'succeeded in making themselves the party of "law and order"' (Jones, 1994: 357) and that 'Assuming the mantle of the party of "law and order" has proved a congenial, and electorally rewarding, task for the Conservative Party' (Aughey and Norton, 1984: 141).

However, these same factors also led to the emergence of a 'Conservative criminology'. The overall shape of penal policy was necessarily determined by the over-arching and far-reaching political and economic philosophy. Consequently, 'the government, as in its economic policy, has chosen to accept and support only those policies which enhance its own narrow political ideology' (King, 1989: 293). Thus anti-statism, libertarianism, free-market economics and penal policy became inextricably intertwined and shaped the emerging Conservative criminology.

Under these circumstances, therefore, there were powerful political and ideological imperatives continually to generate new thinking about penal policy and it is this which holds the key to understanding the rapid growth in private-sector involvement in the penal system by the end of the decade and why '[o]ne of the curiosities of the Thatcher government was that it became more radical as time went on' (Gamble, 1994: 130). As a consequence of these imperatives for continued innovation within the rubric of the prevailing Conservative ideology and political philosophy, when the manifesto for the 1987 election was published, it contained a controversial set of ideas designed to reconstruct the state and to:

> renew the radical momentum of the Thatcher project in the third term. Having got the economy right, as they believed, and having won a third successive popular endorsement, the Thatcherites saw the reconstruction of the public services as a key task in refashioning the British state and British civil society . . . a set of ideas for managing all institutions in the public sector and involving devices such as internal markets, contracting out, tendering and financial incentives. . . . One of the features of all the different reforms aimed at reforming the public services was that the government was determined to by-pass public-sector professionals and establish new modes of service delivery. (Gamble, 1994: 135–6)

Public Policy, Private Interests – Lobbying for Change

It is clear, therefore, that the thinking of certain economic and political philosophers of the so-called 'New Right' was an important influence in shaping Thatcherite policies and although 'the New Right did not represent a single coherent perspective . . . [f]or all sections of the New Right a crucial ideological task was to establish the legitimacy of their ideas within the British conservative tradition' (Gamble, 1994: 146). There were several right-wing 'think-tanks' which became increasingly prominent under the Conservative government, but we want briefly to consider the particular role of the Adam Smith Institute (ASI), because this was undoubtedly one of '[t]he key think-tanks on the liberal and libertarian wing of the New Right' (Gamble, 1994: 146) and, as we have already argued, it provided a platform for the ideas of Friederich von Hayek, who had such a profound influence on the development of Thatcherism. It has also, at the very least, made a very specific and influential contribution to the debate about private-sector involvement in the penal system.

As Ryan and Ward rightly point out, 'Just how much influence the ASI has is difficult to gauge as it works largely behind the scenes; but it boasts that many of its policies have been implemented by the Conservative government' (Ryan and Ward, 1989: 45), a claim which even a quick reading of *The Omega File* (Butler et al., 1985) rapidly confirms. Just within their consideration of criminal justice, which is but a part of their overview of a wide range of policy areas, there are many ideas which have subsequently been seen in practice: unit fines; electronic tagging; the reform of parole to ensure greater openness, including the introduction of automatic release on licence for shorter sentences and increased judicial control; the development of punishment in the community and the replacement of probation with alternatives; and the creation of a unified family jurisdiction based on a presumption in favour of parental autonomy which, *inter alia*, would separate the civil and criminal justice functions of existing juvenile courts.

More significant for our purposes is their diagnosis of the ailments of the prison system as one which 'suffers from three faults inherent in all government: high cost; inadequate supply; and a shortage of capital investment' (Butler et al., 1985: 259). As they went on to argue, the solution to these problems was that:

> Ultimately, new managerial ideas have to be introduced. This is unlikely to occur with the context of the present, politically-managed system, and some more radical solution is therefore attractive. . . . [I]n the United States . . . the new solution has involved two main proposals: the use of independent firms to build, own and operate prisons and detention centres; and competitive bidding amongst outside firms to provide real work for inmates. (Butler et al., 1985: 259)

They go on to observe that, apart from Securicor's responsibility for the detention of suspected illegal immigrants:

> . . . it is surprising that the idea of independently built and managed prisons has not gained a wider acceptance. . . . We suggest that the innovative methods of the private sector have a very important role to play in the provision of prisons in Britain, and that the government should take urgent steps to initiate private sector involvement. (Butler et al., 1985: 260)

From this, they argue that the case for contracting-out management and using manpower more effectively applies to all prisons, including those used to punish young offenders, regardless of security level. The main differences – for example, levels of security, the amount of association permitted, types of discipline – could, they argue, easily be allowed for by the government issuing standards to the contracting prisons in the same way that local authorities set out standards in contracts with private refuse firms – a somewhat insensitive and inappropriate analogy, some might think! – and although this would require government (or independent) monitoring to ensure that agreed standards would be met, they believed that this would not really pose any great problem.

The work of Butler and his colleagues was followed shortly after by an enthusiastic review of the achievements of private prisons in the USA by Young, who depicted the British prison system as a typical case of 'a state service being run to benefit the producers of the service, the employees, rather than the inmates and the taxpaying public' (Young, 1987: 4), and who claimed that in the USA private prisons had achieved dramatic improvements in the conditions for prisoners, no adverse consequences for public-sector prison employees, and significant cost savings. Young's review (or eulogy, as Ryan and Ward describe it) is perhaps stronger on rhetoric than fact and his ' "hard conclusions" are, to put it politely, a shade premature' (Ryan and Ward, 1989: 46). Nonetheless, in an increasingly rhetorical debate, the absence of substantial evidence easily passed unnoticed and the general approach of the Institute was undoubtedly such that it was assured a sympathetic hearing for its views in government circles.

Thus, although it is, indeed, difficult to determine just how influential the work of the Institute was, few observers will fail to notice the close similarity between its proposals and what was to transpire. By way of elaboration, an interesting insight into the activities of the ASI is offered by Jenkins (1993) which, in addition to illustrating the ideological commitment of its staff and their determination to establish 'the legitimacy of their ideas', seems to suggest that its role was of considerable influence:

> In 1985, two of its senior members, Eamonn Butler and Peter Young, put the idea to the government. For Peter Young, the idea of private prisons had a symbolic political importance for the institute – if you could persuade government to privatize prisons, you could get them to privatize anything. 'At the time it was regarded as a bit beyond the pale. . . . David Mellor and some of the senior civil servants . . . thought the idea was a bit of a joke'. Nonetheless, the institute kept lobbying the Number Ten policy unit, which was more receptive to this kind of idea. Looking back, he feels pleased that the once zany idea is now part of government policy. 'It's a good victory, that one, prison privatization. Quite an amusing one.' (Jenkins, 1993: 19)

In addition, Michael Forsyth, who was later to become a junior minister at the Home Office with responsibility for prisons and who played an active part in promoting the idea of private prisons within the Conservative Party, had close links with the ASI (Ryan and Ward, 1989: 47).

It is evident, however, that a much wider range of interests was involved in the political process than just the ASI. Indeed, it can be argued that the privatization of prisons was a classic example of how to lobby a government, with pressure being brought to bear by business interests, Conservative politicians, and free-market theorists, although as Ryan has argued, 'the full story of how vested and commercial interests operated and overlapped with political interests is even now not entirely clear' (Ryan, 1994: 10). To turn again to Jenkins' account, 'it wasn't just ideological interests that were making the noise. Quite independently, business was trying to influence the government' (Jenkins, 1993:19). Christopher Hutton Penman, managing director of Racal Chubb Security Systems (who had been building high-tech prisons abroad) and a director of one of the first private prisons consortia, Contract Prisons, is quoted by Jenkins as saying:

We very quickly came to the conclusion that our task was far more to persuade the government to go down this route and pass the necessary legislation. We spent a lot of time talking to MPs, and the Number Ten policy unit, and we just kept pushing away at the door until it started opening. (Jenkins, 1993: 19)

Similarly, Beyens and Snacken observe that the lobby from industry was strong and persistent, reporting that at a privatization seminar in the Netherlands in 1993, the Director of Corporate Communications of UK Detention Services (UKDS) (who subsequently won the contract for Blakenhurst), R.D.N. Hopkins, said:

It took us two or three years to finally convince the government that this was indeed the right course of action. . . . Prisons were not working and there was a viable alternative. . . . UKDS was very much involved in bringing forward the arguments in favour of the case. It was a time when privatization was the watchword of the Conservative government. (Quoted in Beyens and Snacken, 1994: 6)

At the same time, Carter Gobell, a US private consultancy specializing in criminal justice who are associated with Group 4, the private security company which eventually won the contract for the management of Wolds Remand Prison, was undertaking extensive research to identify possible sites in Europe where the best opportunities might lie for expanding the private correctional market (Lilly, 1993).

Other connections between politicians, industry and the development of private prisons can be identified without difficulty. There has been active lobbying by Racal Chubb Security Systems since the late 1970s, in the light of their experience of building high-tech prisons abroad, whilst British construction companies are also closely involved. For example, John Mowlem (who are substantial donors to the Conservative Party) and Sir Robert McAlpine & Sons (one of whose Directors is Lord McAlpine of West Green, a former Conservative Party Treasurer) were the main contractors responsible for the building of Wolds Remand Prison and were both part of UK Detention Services, a company specifically formed with the Corrections Corporation of America (CCA) for the purpose of competing in the corrections market.

In addition, in the early 1990s, Sir Norman Fowler, ex-Conservative Party Chairman, was a member of the Management Board of Group 4; Premier Prisons, who won the contract for the management of Doncaster prison, was formed by a UK supply and management services company, SERCO, and the American private corrections company, Wackenhut; more recently, Premier Custodial Developments Ltd. was formed by Wackenhut and Trafalgar House, the UK construction firm which rebuilt Strangeways, to bid for contracts to finance, design, build and manage new prisons; and

members of the Home Affairs Committee, which was so influential in
the policy-making process which paved the way for much greater
private-sector involvement in the penal system in Britain (see below),
included Sir Edward Gardner, who chaired the Committee and
subsequently retired from parliament to become Chairman of Contract Prisons PLC (partly owned by US company, PRICOR, and
Chubb), and John Wheeler, Conservative MP and member of the
Parliamentary All Party Penal Affairs Group, who was also former
Director General of the British Security Industry Association.

It has also been argued that there is evidence of the emergence of
monopolies within the lucrative corrections market – for example,
Commercial Metals Co. is reported to be the only producer of the
ribbed steel window bars preferred by prison builders – and it is
salutary to consider the fact that crime control in the USA alone cost
in excess of $24 billion in 1990 (Lilly, 1993). Thus, although Vagg
has argued that 'It is probably not accurate to describe England as
having even a nascent "corrections-commercial complex"'(Vagg,
1994: 308), others such as Lilly and Knepper (1992) and Christie
(1994), who provides a detailed and graphic account of the world-
wide growth of the crime-control industry, are more sceptical. As
Lilly argues:

> Punishing people is big business. . . . It is a multinational industry, which
> involves not only obvious players like security firms, but also less obvious
> ones like catering companies, suppliers of prison furniture and clothing,
> and anyone who sells goods or services used in jails. The danger for
> public policy is obvious: there are global interests, with a direct interest in
> world-wide incarceration. (Lilly, 1993: 20)

Penal Pressures Towards Privatization

Much has been made by some commentators of the influence of
developments in the USA on those in Britain – for example, Beyens
and Snacken have claimed that 'What happens in the United States
today, happens in the United Kingdom tomorrow' (Beyens and
Snacken, 1994: 5). Alternatively, however, as Vagg has suggested,
there is a strong case for arguing that 'The impetus towards private
prisons in England had only one thing in common with America: the
increasing prison population. . . . The primary pressure for privatization was not practical but political' (Vagg, 1994: 298).

This view is largely shared by Rutherford (1990: 56) who
observes, however, that the proponents of prison privatization have
downplayed ideological considerations in the debate, stressing
instead pragmatic considerations such as the need to modernize the
ageing prison estate and to improve overcrowding and insanitary
conditions. Having considered the political and ideological pressures

Table 3.1   *Average prison population, 1973–88*

Year	Remand	Sentenced	Total
1973	5,109	31,665	36,774
1974	5,471	31,396	36,867
1975	6,087	33,733	39,820
1976	5,605	35,838	41,443
1977	5,911	35,659	41,570
1978	6,235	35,561	41,796
1979	6,629	35,591	42,220
1980	6,283	35,981	42,264
1981	7,289	36,022	43,311
1982	7,779	35,928	43,707
1983	8,287	35,486	43,773
1984	9,028	34,321	43,349
1985	9,973	36,305	46,278
1986	10,318	36,571	46,889
1987	11,432	37,531	48,963
1988	11,667	38,282	49,949

Source: *Prison Statistics, England and Wales, 1983* (Cmnd. 9363) and *Prison Statistics, England and Wales, 1988* (Cm. 825). London: HMSO.

which created the climate in which prison privatization became a practical possibility, therefore, it is also important to consider, if only briefly, the practical pressures, and in particular the increase of the prison population since 1979, which helped to shape the debate (for a more detailed discussion of which see, for example, Morgan, 1994; Rutherford, 1990; Stern, 1993; Windlesham, 1993).

During the 1970s, the prison population grew steadily and when the Conservatives came to power in 1979, the average prison population stood at 42,220, consisting of 35,591 sentenced prisoners and 6,629 on remand – some 17.5 per cent of the total (see Table 3.1 and Figure 3.1 for graph format). Between 1979 and 1988, the year in which the crucial Green Paper *Private Sector Involvement in the Remand System* was published (Home Office, 1988b), publicly exploring the scope for private-sector involvement in the prison system for the first time, the average population increased by 18 per cent to 49,949, by which time the remand population constituted over 23 per cent of the total. The remand population had therefore increased by no less than 76 per cent during the same period.

The main cause of this increase was twofold. First, although there had been a fall in the number of untried and unsentenced prisoners received into custody immediately following the implementation of the Bail Act, 1976, the number began to increase again in 1979 and continued to do so until 1987, when it began to fall again. Secondly,

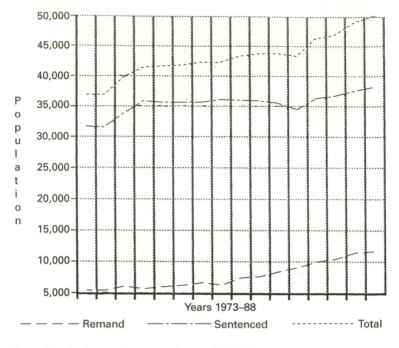

Figure 3.1 *Average prison population, 1973–88*

there was a continued increase in the length of time spent in custody – for unconvicted males, there was an increase in the average time spent on remand from 36 days in 1978 to 54 days by 1990 (NACRO, 1992). Thus in 1988, of the 9,000 untried prisoners held in custody awaiting trial, 6,150 had been held for up to three months, 1,950 for over three and up to six months, and 1,000 for over six and in some cases more than twelve months (NACRO, 1990). The combined effect of these twin pressures was the burgeoning of the remand population.

This trend had not gone unnoticed and the May Committee (Home Office, 1979), in its inquiry into the Prison Service, had observed that 'remand periods in England and Wales are frequently excessively long and have generally been increasing' (para. 3.66) and that everything possible should be done 'to bring defendants in custody to trial as soon as possible' (para. 3.67), a concern echoed two years later in the report of the Royal Commission on Criminal Procedure.

Throughout the period during which this increase occurred, there were expressions of concern from many quarters, not only about the number of people being held in custody on remand, but also about the conditions in which they were confined. As the Home Affairs Committee argued:[1]

> Cell-sharing, long periods locked up and, for the majority, all the considerable disadvantages of the old Victorian prisons . . . would be intolerable enough when inflicted on persons found guilty of an offence, but for the many prisoners awaiting trial, and innocent before the law, these experiences are completely insupportable. (House of Commons, 1981: para. 54)

Three years later, the same committee returned to the same issue, pointing out that:

> Overcrowding is at its worst, and conditions are at their most squalid, in the local prisons and remand centres in which remand prisoners are housed. . . . It is commonplace for remand prisoners to be accommodated two or three to a cell built in Victorian times for a single occupier; to be locked in for most of the day; and to be subjected to sanitary arrangements which are an affront to human dignity. (House of Commons, 1984: para. 1)

And again, only two years later, the Chief Inspector of Prisons, in his annual report for 1986 wrote:

> The physical conditions in which many prisoners had to live continued, therefore, in many cases, to border on the intolerable. For remand prisoners in particular, whose numbers increased sharply during the year, conditions were particularly poor. Overcrowding, coupled with the lack of in-cell sanitation and the sharing of limited and inadequate facilities on the landings, represented much human misery. Many inmates in local prisons spent almost all day locked up, two or three men in a cell intended for one, with no integral sanitation and little to do. (HM Chief Inspector of Prisons, 1988: para. 4.02)

Indeed, as Morgan comments, 'In report after report successive Chief Inspectors [of Prisons] chronicled the "degrading" and "insanitary" accommodation, the "enforced idleness", the prolonged daily cellular confinement, and the general lack of access to facilities, to which the untried are routinely subject' (Morgan, 1994: 144).

Confronted by the problems caused by the increasing prison population and the steadily deteriorating conditions in which they were confined, the government was also faced with a powerful Prison Officers' Association (POA), whose members exercised a substantial amount of control over the nature and delivery of prison regimes and whose practices led to increasing staffing levels and high levels of overtime (see King and McDermott, 1989). Such pressures led to the *Fresh Start* initiative in 1986, which sought to rationalize the use of personnel by fundamentally reorganizing prison officers' working arrangements and the management of prisons, in order to re-establish a degree of control over spiralling staffing costs.

Despite such responses, it has been argued that the government was still presented with major difficulties in addressing the pressures in the prison system because of the resistance of the POA to change (Rutherford, 1990; Ryan, 1994; Ryan and Ward, 1989; Stern, 1993) and that privatization was part of a strategy to overcome this opposition. Beyens and Snacken have also argued that:

> In Australia, England and Wales and the United States, limiting the power of the trade unions has been an important consideration for privatization. . . . Attempts to introduce new (regime) programmes were hindered by . . . prison officers, who resist change. (Beyens and Snacken, 1994: 2)

although Rutherford's more qualified assessment is that whilst 'It might be cynically suggested that prison privatization has arisen as a means of bypassing the POA or at least reducing its power. . . . It must, however, be concluded that no evidence is available that gives weight to this connection' (Rutherford, 1990: 61).

Throughout this period, the principal response of the government was to increase massively the resources made available to the prison system. Expenditure increased in real terms by 72 per cent in the fiscal years between 1980 and 1987 (Rutherford, 1990), with the government embarking on a major programme of prison building, an apparent anomaly in view of the prevailing ethos of the government's policies. From 1982 onwards, however:

> . . . the government began vigorously to pursue its 'Financial Management Initiative' (FMI), designed to encourage efficiency and cost savings by applying private sector management methods to the public sector, and imposing market disciplines on them. . . . Privatisation and the FMI were of course linked, for increasing restrictions on staff levels and resources in the public sector increase the opportunities for competitors from the private sector. (Newburn, 1995: 38; see also Humphrey, 1991)

Thus, as Ryan (1994) has argued, when the debate about privatization got under way in Britain, the issue of whether the private sector could manage prisons more cheaply, and therefore by implication more efficiently, than they were currently being run by the public sector was of central importance.

Penal Policy and Change

It was in this ideologically vibrant and politically volatile context that the policy to introduce private-sector involvement into the prison system gradually took shape. As outlined above, the first proposal for the privatization of prisons, which came from the ASI in 1984, received little attention in government circles and three years later, there was still no apparent support. The situation was to change rapidly, however, as Ryan emphasizes:

> Speaking to the House of Commons in July 1987 the then British Home Secretary, Douglas Hurd, made it plain that he was not in favour of extending the government's privatisation plans to include the private sector. . . . In under two years . . . [he] had changed his mind, and in March 1989 announced to the Commons that the private sector would in future be authorised to both build and/or manage remand prisons. . . . By 1992 legislation was in place giving the Home Secretary powers to introduce private prisons into the rest of the prison system . . . if the experiment in the remand sector proved a success. (Ryan, 1994: 9)

How, then, was such a *volte face* possible in such a short space of time? A number of diverse influences can be identified.

Failure of Existing Policies

First, it became evident that the government's policies of attempting to ease the pressures on the prison system, which included attempts to increase the use of community-based alternatives to imprisonment and to limit the use of custody (by measures such as those introduced in the Criminal Justice Act, 1982 and subsequently extended by the Criminal Justice Act, 1988) and measures to reduce the amount of time spent by defendants in custody awaiting trial (through the provisions of the Prosecution of Offences Act, 1985), were not having the desired effect. It was also becoming evident that there were specific problems relating to the remand population which had come about because of the post-war emphasis on the training of prisoners and the fact that 'the system was geared to the custody and treatment of sentenced prisoners' (Morgan, 1994: 148). This effectively relegated those who were regarded as unlikely to benefit from training and unsentenced prisoners to local prisons which, with the rising number and proportion of prisoners remanded in custody (from 7.7 per cent of the average daily population in 1960 to 21.4 per cent in 1989), together with the lack of adequate statutory safeguards or management incentives to address the resulting problems, resulted in progressive overcrowding and consequent deterioration in their living conditions (see also Casale and Plotnikoff, 1990).

The prison building programme launched by the Conservative government in 1979 reflected this emphasis and the fact that in spite of the appalling conditions in local prisons, there had been no new local prisons built for over a century. As Morgan has argued, however, 'by the mid-1980s it had become apparent that if the building programme was not accompanied by a vigorous reductionist policy, there was a distinct possibility that the additional prison places would do little more than keep pace with the rising prison population' (Morgan, 1994: 149). In addition, in spite of the recognition that 'the integration of the convicted and the unconvicted invariably signals the disadvantage of the latter' (Morgan, 1994: 154), it was also becoming apparent that the physical separation of the convicted from the untried could not be achieved without further expansion of the prison system.

Pressures in Parliament

Secondly, the Home Affairs Committee of the House of Commons, with its responsibility for monitoring the operation of the prison system, was becoming increasingly concerned about such issues, following their inquiry into the state and use of prisons (House of Commons, 1987a) and although the Public Accounts Committee of the House of Commons (House of Commons, 1986) was given explicit reassurance in February 1986 that no work was being done within the Home Office on the privatization of prisons, within a few months, the Home Affairs Committee of the House of Commons had produced what transpired to be a highly influential majority report (House of Commons, 1987b), described by Rutherford as 'one of the briefest and most superficial reports ever made by a select committee of Parliament' (Rutherford, 1990: 47) and from which Labour members of the Committee dissented, on the impressions of some members of the committee formed during the course of a trip to the USA to observe two privately operated prisons.

The Committee prefaced their report with the observation that '[t]he present state of our prisons, blighted by age, severe overcrowding, insanitary conditions and painfully slow progress in modernisation make it necessary to consider urgent new ways of dealing with these problems which at present seem almost insoluble' (House of Commons, 1987b: para.1). Accordingly, they recommended that, as 'an experiment', private-sector companies should be allowed to tender for the construction and management of custodial institutions and in particular of 'new remand centres, because it is there that the worst overcrowding in the prison system is concentrated' (para. 15). Significantly, in the light of the discussion in the first part of this chapter, the Committee argued that whether contract provision of prisons in England and Wales was applicable 'is a matter to be decided on practical and political grounds' (para. 8), with no reference being made to moral or ethical considerations.

The Committee based the case for contract provision of prisons on two grounds. The practical ground was the failure of the existing system to overcome the problems of out-of-date and overcrowded prisons. The theoretical proposition, they argued, was 'that the state should be the sole provider of a service only when no-one else exists who can provide the same service at less cost or can provide a better service' (para. 9), subject only to the principle 'that the private contractor must be accountable to the state for the service he provides but need not be directly employed by the state' (para. 14). They therefore proposed that 'commercial companies should, as an experiment, be allowed to demonstrate the types of custodial services they could provide and at what cost' (para. 10).

Other Sources of Influence

It is also clear, from the first part of this chapter, that there was a considerable amount of pressure from a range of sources being brought to bear on the government and the Prime Minister, partly through the Number Ten policy unit, to give serious consideration to prison privatization as a policy option. In addition to the ideological and corporate pressures, however, individual politicians were also extremely active, from a variety of different motivations.

Among these, Lord Windlesham was a particularly active political proponent of private-sector involvement in the remand system and he offers an extremely interesting and informative account of the development of policy and his contribution to this (Windlesham, 1993). His concern and involvement was based on the contention that 'a fundamental distinction exists between the punishment of convicted offenders and the pre-trial detention of persons accused of a criminal offence' (1993: 257) which should be reflected in the conditions in which they are held. Consequently, he argued, 'If we accept as a fundamental principle of the English system of criminal justice that anyone who is accused of crime is entitled to be treated as innocent until he [*sic*] is proved guilty, it follows that only such limitations on normal rights and freedoms as are unavoidably necessary should be imposed' (1993: 260). (See also Casale and Plotnikoff, 1990.)

In deploring the conditions under which remand prisoners were being held, Windlesham recognized that a major reason for this was that 'Since most unconvicted prisoners avail themselves of *the right not to work*, the opportunities for work and training have been reduced gradually in the interests of economy until they have become virtually non-existent' (1993: 268, emphasis added). Importantly, for the purposes of this discussion, he argued that the moral and political arguments against privatization applied with less force to remand prisoners by virtue of their special status, which argument he put directly in a letter to Mrs Thatcher in July 1987 and copied to Douglas Hurd, the then Home Secretary.

In August 1987, Mrs Thatcher replied, making it clear that, as Douglas Hurd had told the House of Commons in July (see above), 'At present the balance of the argument seems to be against moving in this direction' (Windlesham, 1993: 278), although she indicated that she was awaiting the outcome of the tour of American prisons to be made by the Earl of Caithness in September which had been arranged following the recommendations made in the report of the Home Affairs Committee. By the following year, however, the overcrowding in the prison system was becoming an increasingly pressing problem, the population having reached a record level of 50,474 (including 11,067 unconvicted and unsentenced prisoners, over 1,000 of whom were being held in police cells) in March (Home Office, 1988a), prompting Douglas Hurd to make detailed proposals to the House of Common for dealing with the situation. It was apparent from this, and from his subsequent response to the Home Affairs Committee's recommendations, that he was still not minded to move towards private-sector involvement more generally but it was also clear that he was increasingly favourably disposed to private-sector involvement in the remand system (Windlesham, 1993: 286–7), a shift which was evident in the Green Paper (Home Office, 1988b) published in July.

Consultation and the Consultants

The consultation paper outlined the crisis of overcrowding in the prison system, the particular problems faced by remand prisoners and the steps which the government had taken to address these, but it also observed, in the light of the recommendations of the Home Affairs Committee, that 'it would be wrong to ignore the possibility that further private-sector involvement could make a speedier and more cost-effective contribution' (Home Office, 1988b: para. 12) to solving the problems.

Significantly, in view of the arguments put forward by Lord Windlesham, the Green Paper argued that '[b]ecause of the different purposes of remand, as opposed to the sentence of imprisonment, and the character of the remand regime, the running of a remand centre by a private company would raise fewer difficult operational questions or issues of principle' (1988b: para. 27), particularly in the light of the role of the courts in determining the time spent on remand and the relative absence of other means whereby this can be increased by executive decision-making. In terms of the character of the remand regime, the Green Paper also argued that because of the comparatively short periods of time spent on remand, 'the scope to develop educational and work opportunities is limited' (1988b: para. 30) whilst regimes for convicted prisoners should make much fuller provisions for these. Importantly, the Green Paper argued that:

> The government is mindful of the state's special responsibilities towards prisoners, but does not accept that this means that prisoners must

necessarily and at all times be looked after exclusively by Crown servants
or police officers . . . It is not at present inclined to accept that there is any
over-riding difficulty of principle which ought to rule out private sector
involvement, *provided that sensible practical safeguards are built into the
arrangements*. (Home Office, 1988b: para. 49–50; emphasis added)

It therefore proposed that '[s]ome form of monitoring or inspection
system would be needed to enable the Home Secretary to discharge
his accountability for the security and well-being of prisoners placed
in the hands of contractors' (1988b: para. 63). The Green Paper also
identified two important preconditions which would have to be met
before private-sector involvement could proceed – the arrangements
would have to ensure adequate security, and 'that prisoners were
treated no less humanely than in the normal prison system and that
their rights were properly safeguarded' (1988b: para. 52). It concluded that:

> The government is committed to achieving real improvements in condi-
> tions in the Prison Service as quickly as possible and to improving value
> for money in the remand system. It is important to establish whether the
> private sector could play a greater role in securing these improvements.
> (Home Office, 1988b: para. 100)

The Green Paper therefore proposed engaging a firm of management consultants and Deloitte, Haskins and Sells were accordingly
appointed, producing their report the following year (Deloitte,
Haskins and Sells, 1989). The report emphasised, *inter alia*, that:

> Contractors would not be in a position to control fluctuations in the
> number of prisoners committed to their care. However, a large proportion
> of operating costs would be fixed in the short-term. This implies that
> payment terms should have a substantial fixed component, and a limited
> variable element to allow for fluctuating numbers. (Deloitte, Haskins and
> Sells, 1989: Appendix V, Sheet 2)

Consequently, the report also asserted that 'there would need to be
strict limits on the prisoner numbers contractors would be obliged to
accept. Without such limits contractors could not be held responsible
for standards . . . and many of the existing overcrowding problems
would be likely to be replicated' (1989: 29) and recommended that
safeguards should be put in place to ensure that contractors could not
refuse to accept certain high-cost prisoners by claiming that they are
full (1989: 30). The report also emphasized the importance of the
monitoring of contractors and the need to appoint a Monitor to ensure
contract compliance, whilst also stressing 'that the Monitor should
not be involved in the contractor's day-to-day management of the
centre' (1989: 41).

As part of their study, Deloitte, Haskins and Sells sought information from potential contractors about estimated costs. It is interesting

to note in passing, especially in the light of the discussion above about the role of the private sector in lobbying for such developments, that those firms consulted 'provided more information for the design, construction and operation of remand centres than for court and escort duties, *as their preparation is more advanced for remand centre tasks*' (1989: 9; emphasis added). The consultants reported, however, that:

> All potential contractors claim they could operate a remand centre more efficiently than the Prison Service for a given level of service. In particular they propose to make savings by reducing staff numbers and by rationalising the management structure. Specifically, they see *the opportunity to reduce staff numbers by introducing more flexible working practices*, and by the greater use of improved technology. . . . Almost all the potential contractors proposed having a higher inmate to staff ratio: on average three inmates per uniformed member of staff. This compares with the current public sector average of 2.25. (Deloitte, Haskins and Sells, 1989: 10; emphasis added)

On the basis of their analysis, the consultants concluded that there was:

> a reasonable prospect of improvements in cost-effectiveness, outweighing the additional costs that contracting out would cause in contract administration and monitoring. . . . The Government would need to undertake significant further research to inform these decisions. A very critical area would be to quantify likely cost savings and to analyse the way that trade-offs between the making of those cost savings and raising levels of service would operate in practice. (Deloitte, Haskins and Sells, 1989: Report Summary)

During the course of their consultations, contractors emphasized the economies of scale which would result in areas such as management and accounting functions if they were able to operate more than one centre. The report identified the main disadvantage of this as the probability that a smaller number of companies might then dominate the market and therefore reduce competition. With this in mind, the consultants commented on the need 'to encourage diversity of supply with respect to the early new centres, since effective competition at later tenders would be sharper if a number of companies were to have gained early operational experience' (1989: 19), stressing that 'Improvements in cost-effectiveness from contracting-out services to the private sector can only be realised *if a market is created in which monopoly powers cannot be established and abused*' (1989: 3; emphasis added). In other words, the success of contracting-out in terms of both cost-effectiveness and guarding against anti-competitive practices depended upon the contracting-out of more than one prison to more than one contractor.

By March 1989, the Home Secretary had indicated to the House of Commons that he was prepared to experiment with private-sector involvement in the remand system because of 'the importance of experimentation in trying out alternative arrangements which could result in improved standards' (Windlesham, 1993: 291). Indeed, when the Report was published and in anticipation of the opposition, he argued that:

> Some critics have overlooked one point of principle, that prisoners should be accommodated in decent conditions which respect their dignity as well as ensuring the protection of the public. If the private sector can contribute to achieving this, that must be to the good. . . . My accountability for the treatment of prisoners and the safety of the public would need to be maintained. To achieve this I would propose that . . . each contract would be subject to permanent on-site monitoring by a Government official appointed by me. This official would also have under his [*sic*] direct control the exercise of disciplinary sanctions over prisoners and the hearing of complaints. (Home Office News Release, Private Sector Involvement in the Remand System, 1.3.89)

The Political Impetus Renewed

By this time, however, the remand population had begun to fall once more and the prison building programme was beginning to make an impact, which meant that the urgency of the argument was much reduced and, as Windlesham observed, 'Had the prison population not begun to decline, it is probable that the debate would have been less politicized' (Windlesham, 1993: 293). The impetus was maintained, however, by two factors in particular, both of which ensured that the issue would be politicized. The first was the re-election of the Conservatives in 1987 on the basis of a manifesto containing a controversial set of ideas designed to reconstruct the state and to 'renew the radical momentum of the Thatcher project in the third term' (see Gamble, 1994, above). The scene was therefore set for the introduction of radical policies.

The second was the continued pressure of the Adam Smith Institute (Young, 1987; also Elliott, 1988), which was making representations to the Home Office and holding seminars promoting the idea of private-sector involvement in the prison system (Windlesham, 1993: 292). In particular, Young launched a powerful critique of government policy on prisons, criticizing the government's 'passive, unimaginative attitude to our disintegrating prison system' which he depicted as a typical case of 'a state service being run to benefit the producers of the service, the employees, rather than the inmates and the taxpaying public' (Young, 1987: 4).

On the basis of his research into private jails in the USA, Young
enthusiastically and less than dispassionately concludes that contracting-out the management of prisons 'has led to a dramatic improvement in conditions for prisoners' (Young, 1987: 38); that
privatization has not adversely affected prison employees in the
public sector; that it has resulted in cost savings of 5 per cent to 25
per cent; and that private companies are able to build new facilities in
a remarkably short time and provide significant innovations in design,
construction and management. In the course of extolling the virtues
of free enterprise, he also declared that:

> Competing private companies immediately introduced new techniques of
> running prisons which were found to be more conducive to the smooth
> running of a jail. It is interesting to note that all the private prisons have
> tried hard to create a more friendly, relaxed atmosphere. Out have gone
> the guns, militaristic uniforms, and harsh attitudes, and in have come
> relaxed dress codes, greater comforts and increased respect for inmates.
> As one might have expected, friendlier jails are more efficient jails.
> Treated more humanely and given better conditions, inmates cause less
> trouble. (Young, 1987: 32)

On the basis of his research, he threw down the gauntlet to the
government, declaring that:

> Private prison experience in America has been sufficiently extensive and
> positive to warrant a major experiment with prison privatization in
> Britain. Britain has led the world in most areas of privatization, yet in the
> prison field there is a danger that she will fall behind countries such as
> America and France. (Young, 1987: 39)

Nonetheless, when David Waddington became Home Secretary in
October 1989, as legislation was being prepared in the form of a new
Criminal Justice Bill, the government continued to waver on the
issue, which was noticeable by its absence from both the Green Paper
(Home Office, 1988c) and the White Paper (Home Office, 1990)
which had already been published. At this point, Lord Windlesham's
account becomes particularly informative, when he explains that in
1990:

> After being advised by the Department that a detailed study had con-
> firmed that no substantial savings in cost could be anticipated, and swayed
> by the falling prison population, Waddington eventually came down
> against including a power to contract out certain remand prisons in the
> forthcoming legislation. Before proceeding, however, he took the precau-
> tion of enquiring whether the Prime Minister assented to the conclusion
> which he had reached so hesitantly. The answer was emphatic: she did
> not. (Windlesham, 1993: 297)

Moreover, Windlesham expresses the view that when Mrs Thatcher
intervened, it was because of 'her conviction of the need for radical

reform outside the prevailing consensus; not for any reasons of penological principle or administrative practice' (Windlesham, 1993: 421–2) and because 'At the start of a new decade, the legislative precedent of one new remand prison operated outside the Prison Service, but accountable to the Home Secretary, was a symbol as well as an experiment' (1993: 307). As a direct consequence of her intervention, the Bill was amended and in May 1991, Kenneth Baker, who had been Home Secretary since the previous November, was able to announce that invitations to tender had been issued to nine potential contractors for Wolds Remand Prison (1993: 300).

However, Windlesham notes that the Prime Minister's policy unit at 10 Downing Street had kept a close eye on the proposals for the contracting-out of prisons because of what it regarded as Home Office indecisiveness on the issue (1993: 421) and as the Bill had progressed through Parliament, small but important changes were made to the clauses concerning privatization during both the Committee and the Report stages of the Bill in February 1991. These were supported by Conservative proponents of contracting-out, most notably John Greenway, who had visited the USA with the Home Affairs Committee, whose report in 1987 had been so influential, and Sir John Wheeler (who, as mentioned above, was former Director General of the British Security Industry Association, a member of the Home Affairs Committee in 1987 and was, by 1991, Chairman of the Select Committee on Home Affairs). These amendments led to s. 84 of the Act which made it possible to extend the power to contract-out any prison, not just remand prisons, by giving the Home Secretary the power to make an order by Statutory Instrument, a process requiring Parliamentary approval rather than further legislation.

This, according to Windlesham, left Parliament 'with the clear impression that ministers would not be returning with proposals for its extension until the experiment with the first contracted-out remand prison at Wolds had been thoroughly assessed' (Windlesham, 1993: 426). However, an announcement by the Home Secretary in December 1991 revealed that this power was to be used in order to invite tenders for Blakenhurst, introducing 'what was in effect a significant change in policy . . . which seemed to have been launched in advance of the necessary Parliamentary approval to extend the power to contract out' (1993: 426). As Windlesham comments:

> As in the early stages of privatization, pragmatism reigned supreme. Since a newly constructed prison nearing completion [Blakenhurst] was too large for remand purposes only, a decision was taken to fill up the rest of the space with sentenced prisoners. Little weight seems to have been given to the distinction of principle between the two categories, and it was frankly admitted by ministers in private that the relationship between the

Prison Service and the contract prisons had not yet been thought out. Carried away by the heady new wine, the Home Office . . . had laid itself open to the charge of acting first and thinking afterwards. (Windlesham, 1993: 427)

Thus, by Ministerial fiat, the process of introducing private-sector involvement into the entire prison system in England and Wales, and not just the remand sector, was now complete, and was to be extended to Scotland three years later by a minor provision of the Criminal Justice and Public Order Act, 1994.

Strangeways and its Aftermath

Whilst the legislative process was taking place, the prison system had been rocked by the most serious and widespread disturbances ever experienced in the English prison system, starting at Strangeways prison in Manchester and eventually involving some 25 other prisons in April 1990. This led to one of the most thorough reviews ever undertaken of the prison system, headed by Lord Justice Woolf, the report being published only ten months later (Woolf, 1991). It is worth noting in passing the significance of the fact that, as Morgan observes, 'of the many establishments which experienced disorder in April 1990, five of the six most serious disturbances on which Lord Justice Woolf's inquiry concentrated its attention, were remand establishments and that remand prisoners played a leading or contributory part in what happened' (Morgan, 1994: 150–1), the report concluding that these remand prisoners had good reason to feel aggrieved. According to Stern, expressing a view shared by many other commentators, the report 'was probably the most detailed analysis of what had gone wrong with the prison system ever to appear' (Stern, 1993: 254). The report concluded that:

the disturbances were part of a long history of trouble in Britain's prisons. They were not one-off events. They were symptoms of serious underlying problems. They occurred because the prison system was not run with any understanding of how people feel and react. . . . The analysis of the real causes of the disturbances was that . . . [t]hey were about the way people treated each other and the structures within which this took place. From this radical perspective . . . the way almost everything was done at that time was inappropriate and needed to be changed. (Stern, 1993: 254–6)

The Woolf Report identified no single cause for the riots and offered no simple solutions. Instead, it drew attention to serious and long-standing problems underlying the way in which British prisons were being run, and concluded that the stability of prisons depended upon there being a balance between three crucial factors – security, control and justice. The Report also outlined an approach to the future development and management of prison regimes, proposing, *inter alia*, that the Director-General should be able to run the service at a greater distance from government ministers; that Governors and prison officers should have more responsibility passed down to them; that there should be a national system of minimum standards; that each prisoner should have a compact or contract, a two-way agreement between prisoner and prison management setting out what the prisoner might legitimately expect of the prison and what was expected of the prisoner in return; that prisoners should have more visits and better access to their families; that prisons should be divided into smaller units; and that the different status of remand prisoners should be more clearly acknowledged. (For a full review, see Player and Jenkins, 1994.)

In addition to the profound impact of these disturbances, the government had to contend with the shame and embarrassment resulting from a report of a visit by the European Committee for the Prevention of Torture which had concluded that in at least three British prisons, 'the way prisoners were living amounted to "inhuman and degrading treatment"' (Stern, 1993: 268).

The combined effect of these various pressures led to the publication of a White Paper in September (Home Office, 1991a), which outlined the government's programme for change. In it, the government concluded that: 'Prisons are about people: the sort of prisons which are required depend on providing the physical security and conditions necessary to create an environment in which constructive relations between prisoners and staff can be established' (Home Office, 1991a: para. 1.30). Prisons were therefore required to be secure, stable, safe, just, caring, decent, productive and positive. Included in the twelve key priorities outlined in the White Paper are the need to recognize the status and particular requirements of unconvicted prisoners, to provide active and relevant programmes for all prisoners, including unconvicted prisoners, and to improve relationships with prisoners. These perspectives were reflected by the then Director General of the Prison Service, Joe Pilling, in his delivery of the Eve Saville Memorial Lecture to the Institute for the Study and Treatment of Delinquency in June 1992, entitled 'Back to Basics: Relationships in the Prison Service', in which he argued that prisoners should be treated with respect, fairness, individuality, care and openness. In short, the White Paper 'set out a programme of reform that would do credit to any prison administration in the modern world if it were implemented' (Stern, 1993: 259).

It should also be noted in passing that the passage of the Criminal Justice Act, 1991 during this time, and the context provided by the preceding Green and White Papers, had set a generally reductionist tone in penal policy which was broadly consistent with the message of the Woolf Report and was similarly radical in its thinking. The Woolf Report had also drawn attention to deficiencies in the management of the prison system, however, which, in the context of the spread of managerialism in the public sector and concern to achieve the economic, efficient and effective use of resources, together with the campaign by the Adam Smith Institute, added to the perception of the prison system as being outmoded and unable to achieve the desired economic and management objectives. It seemed, according to Stern, to be 'the paradigm of an over-centralized, old-fashioned, top-heavy bureaucracy which lived in fear of the pressure from its trade unions and could not deliver what it was paid to deliver' (Stern, 1993: 269).

It is perhaps not surprising therefore that the Woolf Report and the White Paper were followed by an inquiry by Admiral Sir Raymond Lygo into the management of the Prison Service which reported in December 1991 and in which Lygo commented that 'I am convinced that without a change in the managerial framework within which the Service operates, the chances of achieving the ambitious agenda set out in the White Paper will be significantly diminished' (Lygo, 1991: para. 4). The report concluded that the Prison Service needed to be more independent of direct ministerial control by the Home Office and that it should be given agency status, a recommendation which came into effect on 1 April 1993. Lygo recommended, concurring with the Woolf Report, that 'more authority should be devolved to governors . . . too often governors lack any real control over their personnel or their budgets. . . . Plans to devolve greater personnel and financial responsibility to governors should proceed as quickly as possible' (Lygo, 1991: paras 40–1).

The Lygo report also commented on the contracting-out of Wolds Remand Prison. In May 1991, invitations to tender for the running of Wolds Remand Prison had been issued to nine potential contractors, the accompanying Home Office document emphasizing the opportunity this presented for providing a constructive regime and for developing a fresh approach to the treatment of remand prisoners. Several months later, whilst he was conducting his inquiry, Group 4 (Remand Services) Limited was awarded the contract. In his view, this had been a helpful exercise in setting standards, although he commented that there was as yet no conclusive evidence justifying an extension of the process. He was, however:

> impressed by the extent to which the exercise of establishing conditions for the management of Wolds remand prison had contributed to the setting of standards for the management of the rest of the prison system, [although] I have not myself seen conclusive evidence either from this country or the USA to justify as yet a general extension of the principle. It

may well be that a single experiment will provide insufficient evidence on which to base a firm conclusion. If the Wolds and any subsequent contracted out prison meet their objectives, there seems to be no reason why the same approach should not be applied elsewhere, particularly to new prisons, whereas there might be more difficulty in doing so in existing establishments. (Lygo, 1991: para. 58)

At the time the proposal for the research around which this book is based was being negotiated with the Home Office, therefore, there were three factors of major significance in the context of the opening of Wolds as the first contracted-out prison in the UK: first, that this was an experiment to test the feasibility of private sector involvement in prison management; secondly, that this experiment was aimed exclusively at seeing if improvements could be made to the conditions in which prisoners remanded in custody were held; and thirdly, there was a renewed commitment throughout the prison service, in the wake of the 1990 prison disturbances and the vision offered by the Woolf Report, to address the fundamental issues of ensuring the effective provision of custody, care and justice in Britain's prisons, and particularly for remand prisoners. This, then, was the political and policy context in which Wolds Remand Prison opened in April 1992 and which provided the backcloth to the evaluation which we were commissioned to undertake by the Home Office.

Note

1 The Select Committee on Home Affairs has primary parliamentary oversight of the prison system and is one of several such committees introduced by the Thatcher government in 1980, the prime purpose of which was to strengthen parliamentary scrutiny of the executive. These committees 'often play an important role in forcing issues and problems onto the political agenda' (Ryan and Ward, 1989: 48).

4

Contracting-out at Wolds

As outlined in Chapter 3, a major political consideration in the decision to involve the private sector in prison management was the need to remedy the appalling conditions in the local prisons which were most affected by overcrowding (Windlesham, 1993), and privatization was seen as the best means of achieving this. This view was reflected in the tender documents for the contract to manage the first prison to be contracted-out:

> The contracting out of the remand prison offers a unique opportunity to establish this fresh look and approach to the way in which prisoners on remand are treated. (Home Office, 1991b: 7)

The tender specifications and contracts drawn up for the management of Wolds provided a unique opportunity for the Home Office to specify minimum standards of living conditions, facilities and regime delivery which were not only higher than those in the public sector but which were contractually enforceable. Wolds was therefore contracted-out to the private sector in an attempt to improve conditions, to introduce innovative approaches into the management of prisons and prisoners, and to break away from the constraints of traditional Prison Service values, attitudes and methods which were regarded by some as stifling progress.

Located near Hull and adjacent to HMP Everthorpe, Wolds Remand Prison opened on 6 April 1992, under private management on contract to the Home Office. Group 4 Remand Services (now Group 4 Prison Services Ltd) was awarded a five-year contract to manage Wolds which stipulated in detail the minimum standards which the company had to provide in return for a monthly fee. The contract was to be reviewed after the first year, with the possibility of renewal after the completion of the initial five-year period. When it opened, Wolds was a category B prison with Certified Normal Accommodation (CNA) for 320 adult male prisoners and was the first prison in the UK to hold only adult remand prisoners for many years.

Wolds was built to a new Prison Service design by the UK construction firms Mowlem and McAlpine at a cost of £35.4 million, with the original intention that it would be managed by the Prison

Service. It consists of three identical two-storey houseblocks, each containing two living units with each unit designed to house 50 men, accommodated in single and shared cells. The cells, all with integral sanitation, are located around three of the four sides of the unit and face on to a large communal area where there are tables for pool, table-tennis and a dart board, as well as a dining area. Each unit contains its own servery, laundry room, shower rooms, two TV rooms, and there is a Supervisor's office located on the ground floor, with other offices and ancillary rooms situated on the first floor between the two living units in each houseblock. The three houseblocks are located at right-angles to each other and face out onto the tarmac exercise yard shared, originally, by all of the houseblocks. When the prison was built, only one small building was allocated to provide workshop facilities.

Setting the Scene

When Wolds opened, it was considered by many as the penal experiment of the century. As a result of the intense interest generated by its opening and operation, Wolds was the focus of a great deal of media attention, both locally and nationally, with every type of incident – be it major or minor – receiving detailed and generally negative coverage. It was also under the microscope of many penal pressure groups, whilst being largely isolated within the prison system. Any operational assistance provided by the Prison Service was kept to the bare minimum, whilst the Prison Officers Association (POA) was publicly decrying the introduction of privately managed prisons. This hostility flowed over into the local community and often staff were on the receiving end of criticism and ridicule from local people, particularly after Group 4's much-publicized and initially problematic take-over of court escort duties for the Humberside and East Midlands region. This oppressive atmosphere often created frustration among the staff who felt they never had a chance to defend themselves or what they were trying to achieve at Wolds.

This hostile interest (and in the case of the Prison Service, exclusion) was mirrored by the equally intense interest of the proponents of private-sector involvement in prisons. To them, Wolds represented a major political investment which they were keen to see succeed, or at least to be seen to succeed, since when it opened, Wolds had been presented as a test case for privately managed prisons. Indeed, it had been categorically stated by Angela Rumbold, the then Prisons Minister, in the House of Commons in 1991, that 'If, and only if, the contracted remand centre proves a success might we move towards privatization of other parts of the Prison Service.'

As a result of these various influences, Wolds and its staff found themselves working in almost complete isolation during their first year. In organizational terms, Wolds received virtually no support from the Prison Service. Indeed, it was not even possible to transfer difficult prisoners to other prisons for a 'cooling off' period during its first year and there were also suggestions that delays in forwarding prisoners' files and belongings by some prisons may have been deliberate.

This externally enforced isolation was compounded by the isolation staff experienced whilst working in the prison. Over time it became apparent that a number of the working practices adopted at Wolds resulted in staff feeling cut off from other members of staff, leaving staff feeling they were alone and unsupported in their work (see below). This isolation, both professional and personal, was in many ways unique to Wolds and was to play an important role in the first two years of its operations, permeating many of the difficulties experienced by staff.

Thus Wolds opened under intense pressure from both sides of the debate about privatization. In addition to this, staff were working to a contract which required standards to be met which existed nowhere else in the prison system, including the provision for prisoners of 15 hours out-of-cell and conditions which reflected the presumption of their innocence. Thus whilst Wolds staff were presented with an unprecedented opportunity to do something new in terms of prison management, they also faced challenges which had not been faced before in the entire history of the penal system in the UK.

The Research Project: Monitoring and Evaluating Wolds

When we initially contacted the Home Office regarding an evaluation of Wolds, it transpired that it had not occurred to the Prison Department to undertake or to commission such a study. After discussions with the Home Office Research and Planning Unit, however, we were commissioned to provide independent and external monitoring and evaluation, the report of which has since been published by the Home Office (Bottomley et al., 1997). The research was initially seen to be of central importance in evaluating the long-term prospects for any substantial extension of the contracting-out of other prisons, a major aim being to identify what lessons might be learned which could be applied to publicly operated prisons and the extent to which these might shape further developments in penal policy.

Our particular objectives were to explore five main areas: institutional management and staff roles, particularly those of the Home Office Controller (an entirely new but crucially important role) and the Director; regime delivery; staff selection and training; value for money; and moral and ethical issues. Since we were particularly concerned to evaluate the *quality* of what was being delivered by Group 4 for both prisoners and staff, our research methodology involved a combination of quantitative and qualitative methods but was grounded in an ethnographic approach. This involved the team spending a considerable amount of time, particularly in the early stages, observing different aspects of the prison routine, attending all regular institutional meetings, and talking to staff and prisoners in order to become familiar with the running of the prison and identifying emerging issues.

In addition to this general observation, a programme of structured and semi-structured interviews (with staff at all levels, prisoners and other key people such as specialist staff) was carried out, in order to produce data which would complement the routine but primarily quantitative systems-monitoring data produced by the Controller for the Home Office. A total of 43 prisoners (plus a sub-sample of 10 prisoners seen during the induction process) and 54 staff members, 10 of whom were senior managers, were interviewed. Throughout the research we had full access to the prison and full co-operation from staff at all levels (for a more detailed description of the research, see Bottomley et al., 1997).

Given this context, several external factors had an important bearing on our research. First, it is important to acknowledge the enormous political sensitivity of the research, of which we have been conscious and continually reminded throughout the study in various ways. Secondly, and related to this political sensitivity, is the fact that the policy context was continually changing throughout the research project. When the research commenced Wolds was still conceived as an experiment, but even before Wolds had opened, the Home Office had announced that it was seeking to contract-out a second prison, thus compromising the experimental status of Wolds.

Thirdly, as a result of further changes in penal policy during the research period, a number of modifications were made to our original research proposal. Thus, in July 1993 we were informed that the Remands Contracts Unit (RCU) wished us to drop the cost-effectiveness and value-for-money elements in our original terms of reference on the basis that they had commissioned other studies to analyse the financial implications of contracting-out (Dunmore, 1996). Also, in the light of a progress report submitted to the Home Office, the recently formed Prisons Board suggested the research should be extended to include the study of one or more comparable new prisons in the public sector, in order to shed some light on the question of whether particular features of Wolds which were beginning to emerge from the research might be similar to those found in new prisons in the public sector. In fact, when the research had been first proposed, we had included a comparative element but, for a variety of financial and other reasons, the Home Office decided against this.

The Wolds Way

'Punishment for profit' and the perceived immorality of introducing both the dynamics and ethics of the market place into punishment have figured prominently in the often heated debate surrounding contracting-out. Possibly one of the more surprising things we found early on in this research was how little this element figured in the early days of Wolds' operations. The senior management team all shared a similar vision of what they were trying to achieve, with the original Director being the driving force behind this vision. For them, Wolds offered the opportunity to open a prison with no defining parameters, apart from those that Group 4 had chosen to incorporate in their tender to the Home Office; it offered the opportunity to experiment and innovate in ways which would have been impossible in the Prison Service, as it was then; and it offered an opportunity to incorporate the best practices of the Prison Service whilst, at the same time, allowing what were regarded as those undesirable aspects of Prison Service culture which hindered innovation (such as some of the more negative attitudes of staff to prisoners and management, of management to staff, and the excessive bureaucracy) to be left behind.

There was therefore a strong consensus among the management team about the aims and objectives of Wolds which was reflected in the principles of the regime, in the working ethos senior managers instilled in staff from day one, and perhaps most significantly in the introduction of direct supervision as their chosen method of prison management and prisoner control. Their aim was to produce a regime offering a much higher degree of freedom of movement for prisoners and to subject prisoners only to such restrictions as were an inevitable concomitant of their imprisonment. Wolds' objectives therefore included endeavouring to assist prisoners to maintain contact with their lives outside prison whilst at the same time encouraging prisoners to use their time on remand productively, by becoming involved in the activities offered by the prison.

The Principles of the Regime

The Mission Statement for Wolds Remand Prison states, *inter alia*, that it intends

> . . . by effective management of resources to provide for the prisoners committed to our care by the courts a just, safe, humane and constructive environment which always meets and, where possible, exceeds all applicable standards.

From the outset, Wolds management adopted a philosophy of fostering prisoner responsibility based on the idea that prisoners are adults who are responsible for their own actions and must accept the consequence of these. This was reflected in Wolds' regime and operations which were guided by five principles:

- the legal presumption of innocence in relation to remand prisoners meant that only those restrictions, the imposition of which were essential in order to hold remand prisoners securely, were justified;
- since Wolds' prisoners were presumed to be innocent, prisoners should be provided with an environment which was as normal as possible;
- control grounded in constructive relationships between staff and prisoners was more efficient and effective than control by coercion, a principle which they hoped to achieve partly through the recruitment of staff who had no previous prison experience;
- the frustrations of prison life should be reduced through the development of administrative procedures, of which both staff and prisoners needed to be aware, which facilitated the smooth daily running of the prison;
- wherever possible, the regime provided would exceed the minimum standards specified in the contract below which Group 4 could not go without incurring financial penalties, particularly in relation to areas such as the provision of visits, which was regarded as a key component in reflecting the first four principles.

There were four elements seen to be central in achieving these goals, the first of which was the contract. The Group 4 tender document, and subsequently the contract, defined the provisions which they intended to provide in the regime at Wolds, although it allowed Group 4 to structure the way that this would be provided. Prisoners were to receive 15 hours out-of-cell every day, 6 hours of education and gym per week, daily visits lasting a minimum of one hour, access to card-phones on the living units, etc. By providing an outline of the regime intended for Wolds, the contract provided management at Wolds with a clear foundation on which to base their efforts to achieve their goals, as well as a degree of protection. Because of the contract, it was argued, it would be more difficult to erode any aspect of the regime at Wolds than at a non-contracted-out prison, putting the management in a stronger position to resist the vagaries of the criminal justice system, such as sudden increases in the numbers of prisoners being remanded to custody, since any changes would require the Home Office to renegotiate the contract.

The second element was the employment of staff without previous experience of working in prisons. Although in reality Wolds had little alternative, the employment of such staff was seen by senior managers as essential since by employing such staff the management team, who were heavily involved in their initial training, were able to permeate the training programme with the philosophy and values they wanted to establish at Wolds:

> What we were going to avoid was the negative bits of the Prison Service, the negative attitudes of staff to prisoners, negative attitudes of staff to management and negative attitudes of management to staff – we were going to avoid organizing things in a way that put what was convenient to us first and what was convenient for prisoners [second]. (Senior manager)

The third element was the adoption of a flatter management structure than that normally found in public-sector prisons, with only three tiers of management – the senior management team, middle managers (who were involved in the security of the prison and the running of the living units) and Unit Supervisors and Prisoner Custody Officers (PCOs). It was envisaged that having fewer tiers would improve the communication among staff and that a less hierarchical structure would help to prevent the emergence of some of the negative attitudes that had evolved between staff and management in the Prison Service.

The fourth and final element which was central to the management team's goals for Wolds was the compact between the prison and its prisoners, a concept which had first emerged from the Woolf Report (Woolf, 1991) in which the prison and prisoner enter into an agreement which stated what the prisoner could expect to receive from the prison and what the prison expected in return. This concept was incorporated into their strategy for regime delivery and was seen as a potentially powerful tool for encouraging prisoners to conform to the standards of behaviour expected of them and for encouraging them to become involved in the activities available.

For the senior management, therefore, Wolds offered the prospect of starting afresh with new staff, based on a new way of perceiving and treating prisoners – as individuals to be respected and treated humanely who, given the opportunity, could respond positively to such treatment. In the first 12 months of the venture, the charisma and commitment of the original Director played a vital role in sustaining staff at all levels in the pursuit of these goals. He had collected around him a team who shared his goals and enthusiasm, and it was this enthusiasm which they tried to instil in staff. The original Director also attempted to develop a team spirit in the prison, stressing that the opening of Wolds was very much a shared venture of which everyone was an important part. To a great extent he succeeded in achieving this, particularly with the staff who helped to open the prison. They were equally enthusiastic about the goals of the senior management team and were committed to making Wolds a success.

The Philosophy of Direct Supervision at Wolds

At the time of its introduction at Wolds, direct supervision was an untested approach to prisoner management in Britain. Originating in America, it had been introduced into a number of prisons there largely because it was cheaper than more traditional approaches to prisoner management (Erikson, 1992). It was based on the view that by treating prisoners more positively, in the context of closer contact with prison officers, disruptive behaviour would be reduced and consequently, the cost of building prisons could also be reduced because they would not be required to withstand such high levels of destructive behaviour by prisoners and could therefore be built to lower specifications.

Although the main principles of direct supervision were adopted at Wolds, the American concept was not adopted in its entirety (Twinn, 1992). Modifications were necessary because of legal, practical and cultural differences between the American and British penal systems – most obviously, differences in the authority vested in American prison officers to deploy sanctions such as long-term pre-emptive segregation against disruptive prisoners; differences in the rights of prisoners; the potential threat of the use of firearms that exists in many American prisons; and differences in prison design. In short, the more coercive context of American prisons, in which direct supervision was developed and implemented and on which its effectiveness partly depends, does not exist in the British penal system.

At Wolds, direct supervision took the form of a single Unit Supervisor having responsibility for a living unit of 50 prisoners and being the focal point of his or her unit, to set the standards, to make it clear what behaviour was and was not acceptable, and to set the boundaries within the unit. It was intended that the Supervisor would thereby become responsible for meeting all prisoners' needs, making prisoners highly dependent on the Unit Supervisor and thus giving that officer a high level of control. It was also intended that as part of this process, and as a by-product of the relative isolation of the Supervisor, he or she would form even closer relationships with prisoners.

Effective control, supervision and communication were the cornerstones on which direct supervision was to be founded. Emanating from these core principles were other important objectives such as ensuring efficiency in operations, safety of staff and prisoners, risk identification, fairness and consistency. The success of direct supervision therefore depended on the existence of effective control, without which other organizational goals would be difficult to meet. Effective control and supervision were seen as the foundation for the safe and humane environment which Wolds management sought to establish in the prison. Only when the safety of the prisoners and their proper treatment by staff had been achieved could management and staff proceed to encourage prisoners to become involved in the prison's regime and to use their time on remand constructively.

Direct Supervision in Operation

The adoption and implementation of the American model of direct supervision at Wolds was successful in certain key respects, most notably in the quality of staff–prisoner relationships, although the importance of having a staff group without Prison Service experience or background also undoubtedly contributed to this. It was, however, less successful in terms of controlling or reducing the disruptive behaviour of some prisoners. This highlights areas of difficulty such as the initial lack of effective sanctions for dealing with such prisoners, the ineffectiveness of the initial compact system, and shortcomings in some aspects of regime delivery.

The implementation of direct supervision at Wolds was also hindered by the fact that the physical design of the prison was not ideally suited to direct supervision, since none of the living units was self-contained (they had no separate exercise or education facilities). Prisoners therefore had to move around the prison frequently in order to use its facilities, which affected the degree of influence Supervisors could have on the living units. This problem was compounded by the 'free-flow' movement of prisoners allowed when Wolds opened, which meant that prisoners could choose when and whether they would join in the prison's activities, whilst also allowing them to visit living units other than their own.

It gradually became apparent, however, that allowing prisoners the freedom to come and go at will was not conducive to effective control or the successful operation of direct supervision, since some prisoners took the opportunity to steal from cells on other living units and there were reports of prisoners bullying and taxing (extracting goods/money through threats) prisoners on other units. This also lead to situations where Supervisors might have more than 50 prisoners on their unit, some of whom they would not know, which increased the difficulties of maintaining control. As a result of this, movement between living units began to be restricted, with Supervisors controlling the living unit gates (which were electronically controlled from the Control Room) by radio. Eventually it was decided that access to other living units should be completely restricted so that prisoners were required to stay on their own units.

This change of policy, however, had an impact upon Supervisors' ability to supervise their unit effectively. Following the introduction of the new policy, Supervisors had to be able to see who was coming on the unit before opening the gate. This restricted their movements to a very small area of the unit, hindering their security cell checks and any other work they needed to do:

> The fact that we are always opening and closing gates and looking in and out to see who is coming in and out decreases our efficiency – we are always controlling access and exit. That is really what takes up our time. (Unit Supervisor)

The restrictions that controlling the gate put on Supervisors was often a source of extreme frustration to staff and the view was often expressed by Supervisors that they were in reality little more than highly paid gate-keepers:

> 'Gate, gate, gate!', that's all I hear and all I say. I'll be saying in my sleep – 'Alpha gate please, Alpha gate please'! (Unit Supervisor)

Another difficulty experienced with the operation of direct supervision was Supervisors' reluctance to be out on the unit for the full duration of their shift, a practice the management espoused in order to foster better relationships with prisoners and to ensure effective surveillance on the unit. Because of this, offices were not originally allocated for use by the Supervisors on the units. When Wolds opened, Supervisors had their desks on the floor of the unit and spent all their time there. However, Supervisors felt they needed somewhere which would allow them 'breathing space' from the prisoners and, that because of the amount of paperwork, much of which was confidential, an office was a necessity, particularly in view of the numerous attempts which had been made to break into desks.

In addition, prisoners agreed with staff, with a number expressing the view that an office provided a degree of privacy if prisoners wished to discuss a private matter with a member of staff. Consequently, not long after the prison opened, the room assigned for use as an interview room by probation staff and others was taken over by

Supervisors for use as an office. Despite a number of subsequent attempts by management to move Supervisors and their desks back on to the open unit, they were unsuccessful because Supervisors were reluctant to relinquish the space and privacy with which the office provided them.

In some ways, however, the introduction of the Supervisor's office interfered with the delivery of direct supervision as managers had feared, since some staff tended to use the office as a refuge, particularly if they were lacking in confidence and when this happened, units were not supervised so effectively. However, the level of demands by prisoners on Supervisors had a much greater impact on the amount of supervision that took place on a unit, since they were responsible for dealing with the requests from 50 prisoners and could spend a great proportion of their time making follow-up inquiries on the telephone. Supervisors were expected to be available to deal with any problems a prisoner might have, whether practical or emotional:

> How can you give your attention to a prisoner with a real problem if you've got prisoners coming in and out of the office collecting mail and other things? (Unit Supervisor)

> You're so busy trying to make sure everybody's all right on the unit, then you get tied to the phone. There was an instance where I made 12 phone calls to 12 different areas and there was no answer, and then you are stuck. (Unit Supervisor)

Another difficulty in implementing direct supervision was Supervisors' initial reluctance to confront disruptive behaviour displayed by prisoners on the units. A number of factors combined to create this reluctance, including staff inexperience, a sense of isolation and hence of insecurity among Supervisors, and the initial lack of effective sanctions for dealing with disruptive prisoners. During training, the need for staff to assert themselves and to confront and deal with inappropriate or aggressive behaviour from prisoners had not been given sufficient emphasis:

> We clearly didn't teach them enough about what to do when people don't respond like human beings . . . and we didn't teach them enough about the subterfuge and tricks that prisoners were going to get up to in pursuit of doing what they wanted to. (Senior manager)

The lack of training in how to deal with disruptive prisoners was compounded by the fact that if a Supervisor *did* confront a prisoner over his behaviour, there were, in practice, few sanctions available to deal with them. Although the majority of prisoners conformed to the prison's rules and behaved responsibly, the small minority who did not caused considerable difficulties and Supervisors found that a disproportionate amount of their time was being taken up by dealing with those who continually sought to take advantage of the fact that there was only one staff member on duty on a unit of 50 prisoners by engaging in illicit activities, or merely disrupting the normal running of the unit by making constant demands on the Supervisor.

However, the behaviour of such prisoners, although extremely disruptive, was not disruptive enough for them to be put on a charge or removed to the Segregation Unit on the grounds of 'good order and discipline'. This led to an unsettled atmosphere on the living units which prevented both staff and prisoners experiencing the benefits of direct supervision. It also placed the Supervisor in the position of trying to keep a balance between establishing and maintaining a quiet, smooth-running unit and being constantly involved in confrontations with such prisoners, creating the impression of weak supervision on some units:

> Staff are not assertive enough at times. They need to be a bit more assertive. Prisoners pick up on that and use it to 'bully' staff, or try to intimidate staff. (Senior manager)

In the light of the effect of such behaviour, management increasingly felt that Wolds lacked sufficient incentives and disincentives to encourage such prisoners to co-operate. When Wolds opened, the prison adopted a two-tier compact system with a basic and an upper compact. The basic compact offered all the facilities agreed by Group 4 in the contract, in return for which prisoners agreed to follow the standards of behaviour laid down in the prison rules, but the upper compact placed extra responsibilities on prisoners and staff. In agreeing to the upper compact, which the majority did, prisoners agreed to be available for work, for which they would be paid £1 a day. If no work was available, they would receive 50p a day unemployment pay. In addition to paying a 'wage', the upper compact gave prisoners extra benefits, such as longer visits and more access to sports and education, although these were not guaranteed. Failure to comply with the obligations of either compact could in theory lead to disciplinary action.

Although the compact at Wolds was designed in the spirit of the Woolf Report, no guidelines had ever been issued concerning the design and use of compacts and the Wolds scheme never gave the advantage over prisoners that management had originally expected, staff finding it hard to implement as it gave them little extra leverage over prisoners. Part of the reason for this was that the contract required very high basic standards to be provided for prisoners, in addition to which Wolds management was committed to exceeding their contractual obligations whenever possible – for example, by providing prisoners with generous visiting hours. In reality, therefore, there was no great difference between the two levels of compact and the system had little specific impact in encouraging conformity:

> There wasn't much in it for prisoners, a lot of privileges had become rights for them so there was nothing really to give them what they wanted in the compact. (Home Office Controller)

When asked 'What compact are you on?' the majority of prisoners replied 'What's a compact?' and those who were aware of the system related it to their employment.

In addition to this lack of incentives, management began to realize that some of the control and discipline problems being experienced resulted from attempting to apply the principles of direct supervision to all prisoners. It was therefore concluded, in the light of American experience that approximately 10 per cent of any prison population were not amenable to direct supervision, that other methods were needed for dealing with disruptive prisoners and that a different regime was required for up to 30 of the more difficult prisoners. Consequently, management decided in February 1993 that 'F' Unit should be converted into a combined Induction/Structured Regime Unit to relieve other units of trouble-makers. The structured regime operated in stages with the first stage being the most restricted, with the prisoner receiving the bare minimum and being confined to his cell for most of that period. Subsequent stages allowed progressively more activities and time out-of-cell. The unit was also to be completely self-contained, with its own visits room and exercise yard, and with higher staffing levels to correspond to its new role.

Both management and staff felt that the opening of the structured regime on 'F' Unit immediately had the desired effect on prisoners' behaviour which was reflected in the general drop in the number of adjudications in the period immediately after the unit opened (see Figure 4.1). The establishment of the structured regime on 'F' Unit also eased pressure on the Segregation Unit, which had increasingly been used to house the more disruptive prisoners. Locating the Induction Unit with the structured regime, so that new prisoners could see the restricted regime before they went on to ordinary location, was also part of management's long-term strategy for addressing unruly prisoner behaviour.

It is unclear how successful this part of the strategy was, however, since new prisoners still had contact with prisoners from other units and hence knew how other units operated. Some difficulties were also experienced with the introduction of the structured regime, since

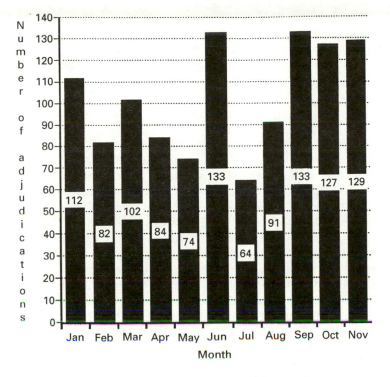

Figure 4.1 *Adjudications for 1993 (monthly totals)*

some prisoners preferred the structure it provided and would deliber-
ately misbehave in order to remain on the unit, which defeated its
purpose to some extent.

Although management and supervisors felt that the immediate
impact of 'F' Unit was positive, some of the staff on A/B and C/D
Units were unhappy with the detrimental impact 'F' Unit had on the
staffing levels in their units, since the additional staff needed to run
the structured regime had been taken from the other units. When 'F'
Unit opened, the pool of staff working on the other living units was
reduced from 10 to 8, which many staff felt was unacceptable
because of the consequent lack of flexibility for covering unexpected
sickness or staff absences and the resulting additional demands this
placed on them. Ironically, it had been intended to establish a
structured unit at Wolds from the outset, but because of the lack of
sufficient staff to operate such a unit safely, the original Director had
decided not to develop one but to try to run the prison without the
presence of such a sanction.

Staffing Levels at Wolds

The issue of staffing levels within the prison was one that was a source of continuing concern for management and staff throughout the research period. In their tender document for Wolds, Group 4 projected that it would require a complement of 153 to run the prison, of whom 100 would be operational staff. During most of 1992 approximately 25 per cent of staff were female, although this dropped to 16 per cent towards the end of the year. Five to six members of staff were from ethnic minority groups although again this figure fluctuated from none to between five and six. Adopting direct supervision meant that Wolds required a lower staffing level than would be found in an equivalent public-sector prison, although even when the prison opened managers acknowledged that they had 'enough staff, but it's tight' (Middle manager).

Within four to five months, however, it became apparent that although Wolds had enough staff to operate under normal circumstances, there was no 'slack' in the system to accommodate any unanticipated occurrences and as many as 80 per cent of the staff we interviewed were dissatisfied with the staffing levels. Although all staff were employed to work a 40-hour week, many found themselves working 60 hours a week from the time the prison opened. By December 1992, Unit Supervisors and Prisoner Custody Officers (PCOs) were owed a total of 1,260 hours time-off-in-lieu of hours worked (TOIL) and management decided that they had no option but to 'buy back' TOIL from staff since it would have been impossible for staff to take this amount of TOIL without causing serious staff rostering problems.

One area that caused particular difficulty was the number of external escorts (the majority of which were hospital bed-watches) that were found to be necessary. In their tender for the Wolds' contract, Group 4 had provided for one external escort a week, but this seriously underestimated the number of external escorts they actually found themselves supplying and each external escort required two members of staff, often for long periods of the day. This left management no alternative to either taking staff out of the prison, thereby leaving fewer staff to meet normal operational requirements, or calling staff in on rest days in exchange for TOIL.

Such difficulties had potentially serious implications for security and control within the prison. Wolds operated a five-person system of General Duty Prisoner Custody Officers (GD PCOs) whose remit was to escort people/items around the prison as required, assist Supervisors on the units at certain times, and perform other miscellaneous tasks. Three of the five GD PCOs also made up the First Response

Team, which was responsible for responding to any calls for assistance from staff anywhere in the prison. Due to this requirement, they were not supposed to be allocated tasks which could not be dropped at a moment's notice (such as supervising visits) so they could respond to any emergency calls.

It became a regular occurrence, however, for two or more of these GD PCOs to be allocated to external escorts, leaving the prison with only three or less GD PCOs on duty. This seriously weakened the First Response Team, particularly in terms of response time and also meant that the Second Response Team (made up from any other available staff) was often non-existent. Under such circumstances, Unit Supervisors felt increasingly vulnerable, particularly in relation to confronting inappropriate prisoner behaviour, and reluctant to confront disruptive prisoners, especially if they were aware that few GD PCOs were available to assist if required:

> The amount of times we're short of staff! They're short everywhere – mainly its PCOs and GDs. . . . Supervisors would like to feel that if anything went off and they pressed the button, 8–10 staff could come running. It doesn't always happen and the quality of staff who do come running doesn't always inspire you with confidence. (Unit Supervisor)

> Sometimes they're struggling to get first response, three people above the staffing level of units. And sometimes they run without. (Unit Supervisor)

> Obviously because a supervisor is left for hours and hours on end, I can understand why they turn a blind eye on things. The main thing [is to have] an easyish shift and not too much hassle because the following day, you've got to go back on the unit. (PCO)

Many staff therefore felt that there were generally not enough staff for the prison to operate effectively and 71 per cent of staff interviewed thought there were not enough staff to run the prison safely. A shortage of GD PCOs affected the whole prison since this meant there were insufficient staff to bring or collect items for Unit Supervisors, to escort individuals within the prison (for example, Vulnerable Prisoners, who required an escort in order to use the prison's facilities). Staffing levels also had an impact on the delivery of direct supervision, since Supervisors were often called in to provide cover on other units, which went against the idea of establishing close working relationships with one particular group of prisoners and developing a sense of unit 'ownership'. Prisoners on other units were not known, which made the job harder, more time-consuming and placed Supervisors under additional pressure – for example, because of the need to identify prisoners before giving out mail or medication. As one Supervisor commented: 'If you know them you can keep some order, if you don't it's a nightmare.'

The dynamics of direct supervision meant that working on their own units did not necessarily cause Supervisors anxieties about their safety since they were able to build up a rapport with prisoners, but some staff expressed concern for their safety if they were required to work on units where they did not know the prisoners:

> On this unit, I've got no qualms, no worries. If I go to another unit, then yes, I do feel uneasy. It states in the policy for direct supervision, it won't work if prisoners don't know the staff and vice versa. (Unit Supervisor)

However, some staff expressed concern about working alone on any unit. They felt this left them vulnerable and exposed, and that they always had to 'watch their backs'. Of the staff interviewed, 23 per cent expressed concerns for their safety at all times with 46 per cent being sometimes concerned for their safety, and as many as 91 per cent of staff interviewed said they experienced work-related anxiety and stress.

Wolds faced increasing pressure over staffing levels the longer it was open. Staff found they were continually being asked to come in on their rest days to cover staffing shortages. For much of 1992, staff did not object overtly since there was a real sense of shared ownership, a commitment to making Wolds a success, and a sense of being pioneers which was initially an energizing force. However, with the passage of time and with no decrease in the pressure on staff, they began to feel the strain and that their commitment and goodwill were being exploited, whilst middle managers were finding that most of their shifts were being spent trying to ensure that enough staff would be available to cover the next shift:

> I'm spending a lot of time ringing staff. Because of the pressure of the job there are staff who are becoming ill over it and that then puts pressure on the remainder of the staff to cover those shifts. And to keep ringing possibly the same people all the time, it's just going to end up with maybe them going sick and it's just a vicious circle. (Middle manager)

From April 1993 onwards, Supervisors began to argue that more than one member of staff was necessary to ensure the efficient and smooth running of a unit and that there should be at least two members of staff on duty at all times, not only to provide mutual support, both emotional and physical, but also because of a growing view that, in reality, one person could not do the job properly. Some Supervisors felt that direct supervision left them far too dependent on prisoners when it came to maintaining control. They were unable to concentrate fully on tasks such as cell checks because of what might be going on elsewhere in the unit, and felt that whenever a prisoner engaged them in conversation, it was in order to distract their attention from illicit activities elsewhere in the unit. This fear was not without foundation as on one occasion when the prison shop had been robbed, prisoners had started a 'fight' in the yard as a diversion:

> Like last time, a group of lads would get together and decide he was going to get a good hiding, so the softest person would go on and divert the screw. (Prisoner)

Staffing levels therefore became an increasingly important issue for the staff. A number of ways of improving the situation were explored, such as PCOs joining Supervisors on units at times of potential difficulty like meal-times, and during the research period rostering systems were reorganized on several occasions in an attempt to alleviate difficulties. Despite these efforts, however, Wolds continued to experience staffing problems and throughout our fieldwork the question of what were appropriate staffing levels for the prison and, in particular, the living units, was constantly under review. Staff perceived this issue to be directly related to the amount of profit Group 4 would be making from the prison:

> It's the profit margin that determines these low staff levels. (Unit Supervisor)

> All the staffing problems are really to maintain Group 4's profits. (PCO)

> It's not that we can't spend more but if we do, it comes out of profit. (Unit Supervisor)

This widespread perception of the cause of what was seen by many as a significant staffing problem had a negative impact on staff morale and the experience of repeatedly being called in on rest days and having shifts changed, often at very short notice, resulted in staff beginning to feel exploited by management – many spoke of being nothing more than numbers to management at Wolds – which resulted in staff developing an increasingly negative view of management. The reluctance of management to provide staff with information on the contractually specified staffing level because it was 'commercial-in-confidence' further added to staff misgivings over staffing issues.

There were also mixed views among the prisoners about the number of staff needed to work on a living unit. Some felt that one Supervisor was adequate and argued that although it was fairly pressurized for one person, it was the most effective way of managing a unit:

> It's a lot for one person to take on, but you get the same result in that nobody's going to get 'tret' differently. It's a good idea really.

> I would say that one person running 50 inmates shows that they are winning. It's when they have to start getting 5 or 6 Supervisors to a unit that there is a problem.

However, other prisoners expressed reservations over the ratio of 50 prisoners to one member of staff. A small majority (51 per cent) of the prisoners interviewed felt that with only one Supervisor in charge of a unit, they actually missed a lot of what was happening and that it was relatively easy to distract the Supervisor's attention whilst something went on elsewhere. The principal reason for prisoners feeling the need for more staff on the units, however, was in relation to incidents, with a small majority of prisoners feeling that a single Supervisor was insufficient to deal with a number of prisoners fighting or intent on causing trouble:

> Just in case something does kick off, like if there is only one on and something does kick off, someone could be seriously damaged by the time the rest came.

Prisoners did not want a large increase in staff on the living units, however, and a maximum of two or three staff was considered sufficient to allay many prisoners' concerns. Indeed, it was felt that any more staff than this would undermine staff–prisoner relations.

It was only after the appointment of the new Director in April 1993, and after consultation with Group 4, that funding was authorized to enable management to recruit a substantial number of additional staff, including part-time staff and security guards (who were restricted to working in the Control Room and reception areas), in an attempt to alleviate these difficulties. The recruitment of new staff seemed only temporarily to ease the situation, however, since each time additional staff were recruited it appeared in the end only to maintain existing staffing levels and the prison never seemed to experience a net gain in staff after such recruitment drives. Indeed, only once did Wolds accumulate a surplus of staff (in anticipation of Group 4 succeeding in their bid for the contract to run Doncaster Prison) and a number of these subsequently left to work at Doncaster for Premier Prisons Ltd.

Staffing therefore remained a central issue for staff from the time Wolds opened and its significance was reflected in the considerable attempts management made to deal with the difficulties experienced by rearranging shift systems and recruiting additional staff, some on a part-time basis. The contract for operating Wolds stated that 'the Contractor shall maintain sufficient Staff to carry out the provision of the Agreement, including the provision of cover for annual and sick leave and other emergencies' (s. 18.8, Sch. 1, Contract Ref: HOPU/ 91/RCU/02). Our evidence suggests, however, that there is room to question whether staffing levels were, indeed, 'sufficient . . . to carry out the provisions of the Agreement' during the period covered by our fieldwork.

Experience vs Inexperience: Living and Working at Wolds

Experienced Prisoners and Prisoners' Experience

In contrast to the staff, the large majority (84 per cent) of prisoners interviewed had been in prison before and had experience of over-crowded local prisons such as Hull and Leeds, where regimes had been relatively impoverished and prisoners routinely spent most of their time locked in their cells. Many, therefore, found difficulty in adapting to the degree of freedom available to them at Wolds, including the amount of time out of their cells, and expressed a sense of 'culture shock' on their arrival at Wolds:

> I was taken aback by it. I'm used to being banged up and not so much respect, you know. I mean, say Hull's all right, I wouldn't have minded Hull before I came here. Until you come here it's all right – then it's the pits! (Prisoner)

What was greatly underestimated, however, was the impact of *prisoners'* previous experience of prison life and the extent to which this would influence their behaviour and relationships with staff. Consequently, one of the problems staff had to struggle with was that many prisoners made a number of important assumptions about prisons and how they were run based on their previous experience of prison, whilst some of them held considerable resentment and anger against the system, or had simply absorbed the prevailing ethos of public-sector prisons. Finding themselves treated so differently at Wolds, some could not adjust to it and sought to exploit it, or to test its regime and ethos, resulting in a range of abuses such as excessively intimate contact with spouses and girlfriends in the relatively relaxed visits hall.

Although some senior managers felt that such abuses would eventually disappear as prisoners adjusted to the different prison culture at Wolds, there were strong pressures to change the regime rather than wait for prisoners to adjust (see below):

> I think there is no doubt that the thing could move around and the predominant 'self-culture' amongst prisoners could change but I think you're talking about two or three years of very, very intense and difficult work. (Senior manager)

Prisoners' Views on Wolds

General conditions. The majority of prisoners interviewed felt that Wolds was generally a better prison than the public-sector prisons they had experienced and praised the living conditions – for the amount of freedom available to them; for the facilities available in the prison; for the amount of access provided to facilities such as education and sports; and for the amount of visits prisoners were able to receive. Indeed, 58 per cent of the prisoners interviewed felt that the facilities on offer at Wolds were better than those for remand prisoners in a public-sector prison and 79 per cent thought it was a better prison overall:

> Yes, it would have to be. If you had the choice between two evils, it would be this evil.

> You come out of this prison into the world normal again I think, but you come out of the state prison you are so full of hate and aggression.

> I'm sure it would have been a damn sight easier state-side with the fact of being shut behind the door and kicked out one day. Whereas here, it's made me think a lot and that hurts. It's made me re-evaluate my life.

In addition, despite all the pressures on staff and Unit Supervisors in particular, the genuine respect and concern for the prisoners in their care – a feature of the prison commented upon by the Board of Visitors in their first Annual Report (1993) and Her Majesty's Chief Inspector of Prisons (HMCIP) in his first report on the prison (1993) – was also appreciated and reciprocated by a large majority of the prisoners at Wolds. Thus it was the combination of the staff, the facilities and the atmosphere within Wolds which was identified by prisoners as making it a better prison. Very few expressed any concerns about its being run by a private company – it was the conditions in which they had to live and the way they were treated that concerned prisoners rather than who was running the prison:

> I don't see it as being a problem on the privatization side – I see it as the inmates respecting what they've got and appreciating it.

> It doesn't matter if it's run by a private company or POA, as long as it's run correctly. So long as they take a look at this jail and take a lesson out of Group 4's book. Run it fairly, talking to you as an adult and giving respect, and they'll get it back.

On the whole, prisoners' comments suggested that relationships with other prisoners were also good. Some prisoners found the openness of the living units and the constant contact with other prisoners difficult to deal with, since they were unaccustomed to having to interact with large numbers of prisoners for long periods of time. This also occasionally led to tensions and outbursts of aggression, but quite often prisoners would attempt to intervene and to calm others down in such situations. This type of intervention was actively encouraged by some Supervisors, who identified such behaviour as being part of the ethos of Wolds and of prisoners accepting responsibility for their behaviour. This was, however, not always the case and prisoners were sometimes left to intervene in such situations because

Supervisors were not confident enough to intervene themselves or because they were occupied elsewhere on the unit.

Time out-of-cell.   There was, however, a range of views among prisoners about the benefits of the time out-of-cell provided at Wolds. Some identified the 14 hours out-of-cell as a positive thing, enabling prisoners to live a more civilized and humane existence. Such prisoners felt that the amount of time out-of-cell, in conjunction with the facilities available and staff attitudes at Wolds, provided prisoners with opportunity to maintain contact with their lives outside and made their time on remand easier to contend with:

> It's not like being in prison, it's like being kept away from society. You seem to be imprisoned by the four walls, but not mentally.

> It's a lot freer, you've got more chance of sorting your problems out in a mature way, rather than being locked up 23 hours a day.

However, other prisoners felt that the time out-of-cell provided was too long and some individuals struggled to cope with it:

> The only difference here is that you get more association. You're open 14 hours a day. But you still get bored.

> This place is totally boring. In here you have so much freedom. The self-discipline for someone who is used to prison is too much of a burden.

Life on the units for many prisoners tended to consist of staying in bed until late in the morning or even lunch-time, congregating in the TV room, playing pool, visiting each others' cells and occasionally going to education, sports and visits. A number of prisoners expressed the view that after two or three weeks at Wolds, all avenues of interest had been exhausted: 'After say being in two or three weeks, a pool table will make you start banging your head off the wall.'

Both staff and prisoners felt there was a considerable amount of boredom among prisoners (60 per cent and 56 per cent respectively). For many prisoners, getting up late was a way of making the long day more manageable. Some prisoners felt that Wolds did not offer enough activities to keep them occupied, particularly in the area of work: 'I think they give us too much time – they give us that much time they can't provide us with enough activities or something to do for that time.' Others felt that there was quite a lot available but that it was up to prisoners to involve themselves. Those who had experience of public-sector prisons, and particularly local prisons with poor regimes, found it difficult to adjust to making their own decisions about what to do:

> There are several things you can do – it's just a matter of self-motivation to get yourself to do it.

I think they've done all they can really, the rest is up to us, isn't it? But if you're only on remand for a few months, then you think 'I'll just sit it out, no point in getting into things.'

Bullying/violence and drugs.   Prisoners' views on the nature and extent of bullying at Wolds varied. Some felt that the amount of bullying was the same as in any prison, but that the design of the prison and its regime meant that violence was more visible. Some prisoners also explained to us that much of the violence was not bullying as such but quite often it was a group of prisoners 'reprimanding' others who had, in their view, stepped out of line. In many such cases, these prisoners regarded the violence as a form of 'justice':

It's not so much bullying – it's just if one steps out of line, comes down and steals out of another cell, he deserves a beating for it – if you don't look for trouble, you won't get it.

It's not bullying – they owe something and they get slapped. It's not that they're getting bullied, it's because they screwed up themselves.

However, not all prisoners shared this view, some feeling that the degree of freedom available to prisoners, coupled with the low staffing levels on the units, left prisoners vulnerable to bullying and violence:

I think if you were to get attacked in a prison like this, they could cause more damage to you with it being open, as well you can get weapons more easily because of the prisoner contact – you can't get it so easily if you're locked up for 23 hours.

If there were an outbreak on here it could be over and done with and a lot of people injured before there's many staff here.

It would seem that much of the violence which did occur was related to prisoners getting into some kind of debt, often associated with drugs. The majority (63 per cent) of the prisoners interviewed felt that staff were aware of the bullying which took place and did their best to prevent it from happening, whilst some prisoners indicated that bullying was something they did not tolerate and often dealt with swiftly themselves:

There is no bullying at Wolds, it's not tolerated by the inmates.

The lads prevent it not the staff – [they've] not got the staff to do it.

The view of 65 per cent of the prisoners interviewed was that it was easy to get drugs in Wolds and a wide range of drugs was reported to be available, including Class A drugs such as heroin. A number of reasons were given by prisoners to explain why they used drugs – boredom, coping with prison, and maintaining an existing habit being those most commonly cited. Prisoners believed staff were aware of the problems although some questioned whether they were fully aware of the scale of drug use in the prison. However, most felt there was not a great deal more staff could do to prevent drugs from coming into the prison. Although prisoners claimed drugs were easily available in Wolds, less than a quarter of those interviewed thought they were more readily available in Wolds than in public-sector prisons of which they had experience. However, many felt that the open design of the prison, the free movement of prisoners and the hours out-of-cell resulted in more awareness of the availability of drugs and much greater opportunity to make deals.

Staff–Prisoner Relationships

Both staff and prisoners identified the quality of staff–prisoner relationships as being one of the most important aspects of Wolds. Many of the prisoners felt that staff were different from those in public-sector prisons, just over half identifying the main difference as the greater respect shown to them by the staff at Wolds. For many, this made a major difference to the experience of being in prison and many said it was the first time they had maintained their dignity whilst in prison:

> Here they see in me and the other prisoners a person – in state prisons, you are a number, an animal and that is it. They don't care what has been happening with you.

> Their attitude in the state prison, you're under them you're not an equal. In here, they treat you as you are and if you mess up that's when the bad things come in here.

The majority of prisoners interviewed and spoken to during the research period spoke highly of the staff working at Wolds. Prisoners felt that staff were genuinely concerned about prisoner welfare and were willing to help prisoners whenever it was possible, which was an extreme contrast to their experience in other prisons. Although this did not stop some prisoners from exploiting the situation, it did allow for a more relaxed atmosphere to develop for the majority of prisoners and staff within the prison. The majority of prisoners (63 per cent) described relationships with staff as 'mostly good' or 'very good', attributing this mainly to the respect shown to them by staff and the fact that staff gave their time to talk to prisoners. Staff were seen to spend most of their time on the units interacting with prisoners:

> They mix in, get on with the guys. Basically they've got it right. But you've got to train the lads as well. Sort out the prisoners as well so they accept it without looking for ways of exploiting it too much.

A lot of time is spent dealing with people's problems in the office . . . Any time the officers aren't busy with paperwork they mix with the inmates, make sure everybody's happy with what's happening.

Staff were also very proud of the positive relationships they had established with prisoners and despite some of the problems they experienced, staff endeavoured to see that these did not have a negative impact upon these relationships. Indeed, they identified this as being one of their main achievements, with 52 per cent of staff interviewed describing relationships with prisoners as being 'mostly good' and 39 per cent as 'very good'. Staff thought being available and talking to prisoners was the most effective way of maintaining good relations:

Being open with the prisoner, having a quite friendly disposition with him. Getting out and talking to him. (Unit Supervisor)

I don't think you have to be very authoritarian to do this job, not to do it well, because now the units are established they run themselves very much. As long as you get yourself about and notice when somebody has got a problem and you deal with it, as long as you don't get bolshy, you're alright. (Unit Supervisor)

Although most staff would describe the staff–prisoner relationships as being good, there were reservations expressed concerning the reasons for this. Some staff felt that the practice of direct supervision left them far too dependent on prisoners when it came to maintaining control:

I would say exceptionally good. Mainly because if someone is awkward, then they would be making the job awkward for themselves and the rest of the people around them. So we're polite and smile to their faces and when they're gone we tear them to pieces. That's why – we've got no option because they've got so much freedom. (Unit Supervisor)

On the whole I think they're quite good . . . I think part of the reason behind the good relationship is because we need the co-operation of the prisoners to run the prison, because of things like staffing levels and obviously the design of the prison. (Unit Supervisor)

Unit Supervisors felt that those staff who were most successful at applying the philosophy of direct supervision were those who could keep the majority of prisoners on their side by 'jollying them along' and being flexible with the rules. There tended to be few Supervisors who were willing to enforce the rules rigidly since this caused too much conflict and friction with the prisoners.

Staff Inexperience and the Experiences of Staff

With the exception of three senior managers and two middle managers, none of the original staff at Wolds had any prior experience of working in prisons. The initial training courses took place in an empty prison and the vast majority of staff had no contact with prisoners until the day Wolds opened. This lack of experience contributed to many of the problems which emerged, particularly during the early months of the prison's operations. When experienced senior managers issued instructions to staff, they tended to overlook the need to give precise details and to explain the thinking behind the instruction, often failing to recognize that staff did not have the background knowledge necessary to ensure full comprehension and compliance:

> In some ways staff don't always have the experience to sort of be able to understand what a communication fully meant . . . it is possible to make an assumption that people may know something when they don't, because something will happen and you will think 'How on earth could that possibly happen?' and then you find well, because I never told them it was a possibility. (Senior manager)

Initially, because of lack of experience and confidence, staff frequently referred decisions to senior managers, who therefore found themselves being called upon to make most of the decisions at every level of management and consequently dealing with a multitude of issues related to the day-to-day running of the living units. Thus the chain of command at Wolds initially did not function as planned because senior managers were reluctant to establish an inflexible hierarchical system in the light of staff inexperience. Four months after it had opened, a senior manager commented: 'We haven't drawn any hard and fast guidelines for staff in what they can decide and cannot decide. Our reluctance is because of staffing experience.'

The senior management team therefore found themselves in a position where they were reluctant to hand over responsibility completely to prison staff, who in their turn were reluctant to shoulder responsibility because of their inexperience. Senior managers therefore took on far more work and worked longer hours than had been envisaged. In particular, since at that time the Director and Head of Custody were the only two members of staff who had worked as governor grades, much of this additional burden of work fell to them. This also meant that their time was taken up with managing the minutiae of prison life rather than taking an overview of how the prison was operating and in developing longer-term strategic plans. The lack of experience at middle-management level was particularly significant here since middle managers were unable to give the support and guidance needed by Supervisors and PCOs, and thus this additional responsibility fell to senior managers.

This lack of hard and fast guidelines also lead to inconsistent decisions among Supervisors, or instances where Supervisors' decisions were over-ruled by a manager, because decisions were being made on an *ad hoc* basis. This lead to a considerable degree of frustration among staff and prisoners. Supervisors felt that having their decisions over-ruled undermined their position of authority in the eyes of prisoners and undermined the delivery of direct supervision on the units. Prisoners were also frustrated by the lack of consistency and the sense that what they were allowed to do by one Supervisor one day would not be acceptable to another Supervisor the next day:

> One day they put rules on you and the next day they take them off. One day you get out of bed and they allow you to do something. Then they change staff and say 'No, you can't do it'.

Over time, senior managers recognized that this general problem of staff inexperience was compounded by the fact that the initial training courses had given staff an unduly optimistic view of prisoner behaviour. As noted above, senior managers consciously adopted this approach in order to foster positive relationships between staff and prisoners. Initial training had, however, failed to emphasize that some prisoners could sometimes be manipulative and aggressive. Therefore, the need for staff to be able to assert themselves also tended to be overlooked and insufficient emphasis was given to confronting and dealing with inappropriate or aggressive prisoner behaviour. When staff subsequently faced such behaviour from prisoners, therefore, they did not always have the confidence or skills with which to address it.

Consequently, particularly during the first year after Wolds opened, prisoners were given a good deal of leeway because staff were reluctant to deny prisoners' requests, even when these were sometimes clearly unreasonable, or to confront difficult and disruptive behaviour. Of the staff interviewed, the majority of whom were trained on one of the first two courses organized, 80 per cent felt that their initial training did not fully prepare them for their work or did so no more than adequately. The general opinion of staff was that prison work was not something which could be easily taught, however, and that it could only be learned by doing it:

> It gave us the basics on how to handle situations, but it's not really something you get out of textbooks, you have to learn to manage people. (Unit Supervisor)

> At the end of the day, it's how you deal with these people. It's personal contact and how these people are that is the job, how you deal with these people and do you let them get to you? All these things go through your head – and training, yes, we heard what these people are like, dealing with

anger, suicide, but at the end of the day, training is one thing but to me this job is hands-on experience – you need to work with these people. (PCO)

Once the prison opened, practical work-based exercises and tests (including new staff shadowing Supervisors and PCOs as they worked) were incorporated into the training. The majority of new staff felt that they benefited from the 'hands-on' experience as it helped them understand how the philosophy and theory they were being taught was put into practice.

Staff isolation. Many staff found working in Wolds was a lonely experience and often spoke of a feeling of isolation within the prison, which appeared to be experienced at three levels: the physical isolation of Supervisors on their units; the isolation of PCOs in terms of knowing what their role was within the prison; and the isolation both Supervisors and PCOs felt from their line managers.

Senior management, following the tenets of direct supervision, felt that limiting the number of staff on living units encouraged staff to interact with prisoners. In addition, during the initial training course, Supervisors had been led to believe that there would be a constant stream of communication between them and unit managers since originally it had been planned that Unit Managers would be located in the office which overlooked the living units. However, because of Unit Managers' workload, in practice this did not happen and Supervisors rarely saw them unless they had specifically requested it. The isolation of Unit Supervisors and the pressure that went with it became apparent as early as October 1992, when many started to make requests for 15-minute breaks to be introduced into their shifts, in order to give them a complete rest from the prisoners and a chance to see other members of staff:

> During our training we were given a short story to read. The title was 'Alone, but not by myself'. As a Supervisor on a living unit I would term it 'Alone and by myself'. (Wolds staff attitude survey, March 1993)

> [There is a] feeling of isolation inasmuch on an 8 or 12 hour shift, or whatever, you are locked away – the mere fact that somebody comes in and spends an hour with you is reassuring. (Unit Supervisor)

As a consequence, some Supervisors asked to be demoted to PCOs because they found it difficult to handle the stress and isolation of the Supervisor's job.

The isolation experienced by PCOs, however, was largely related to their lack of a clear sense of identity within the prison. In one of a number of staff surveys carried out at Wolds, they complained of a lack of identity and a need for job-enrichment. There was a feeling among these officers that they were regarded as just general dogsbodies. To address this problem, management implemented a 'squad system' to link groups of PCOs to a specified duty Security Manager. This manager was to be responsible for the appraisal of the officers in his or her squad and to be available to them for consultation. However, because of the demanding work-load of duty Security Managers, the system was not very successful. Moreover, management's decision to use PCOs to provide cover for Supervisors on units as a way of tackling the staffing problem failed to win their support and there remained a sense among PCOs that they were undervalued and that little thought was given to the tasks they were given:

> It's when you're on your own, especially when you're GD-ing it. Because prisoners laugh at you when you're out on [the] yard especially in winter. (PCO)

> I was GD – just your General Dogsbody. (PCO)

There was also a feeling among many Supervisors and PCOs of a more general isolation from management and management decisions, since Supervisors and PCOs rarely came into contact with either middle or senior managers. Supervisors found this especially frustrating since the senior managers who made decisions affecting the Supervisor's job had no first-hand experience of operating direct supervision. This problem was compounded by the fact that managers came on to units less frequently the longer the prison was open, which deprived them of information about the difficulty of implementing direct supervision. The methods of communicating were recognized by both sides as lacking in a number of ways:

> At times it's appalling. It's all dependent on actual individuals – some managers are really, really good, they communicate really well. (Middle manager)

> I don't think it's a 100% right. There are occasions when things are happening and we're not getting the information soon enough. (PCO)

Improved communications and more staff consultation were highlighted as areas needing improvement in a Wolds staff attitude survey in March 1993. The feeling among most of the management and prison staff was reflected in the view expressed by one middle manager that:

> There should be more meetings at all levels. I mean this Team Briefing we have, you really don't see the staff, it's a paperwork exercise. Staff should be in groups more often and seen by their line manager.

Organizing these group meetings proved to be a problem, however, since there was not enough slack in staffing levels to allow large numbers of staff to get together.

Staff morale. Although the Personnel Officer attempted to tackle the problem of staff morale by trying to get around the prison on at least two afternoons a week in an attempt to support staff and in order to hear their views, this sense of isolation was one of the main factors that affected morale at Wolds in the early months. Of the 44 main grade and middle-management staff interviewed, 73 per cent felt that staff morale at Wolds was poor to moderate, with those being interviewed towards the end of the fieldwork period being only marginally more positive. When the prison opened, morale had initially been extremely high. There was a strong team spirit among all levels of staff with a real sense of belonging to a pioneering enterprise and staff invested a great deal in ensuring that the prison succeeded. During the period of the research, however, morale fluctuated and issues such as staffing levels, isolation and critical opposition to the prison from outside, particularly from the news media, all contributed to the fluctuations in morale.

The impact of constant criticism of the prison in both the local and national newspapers was considerable. Staff felt unfairly criticized by such publicity, often having to tolerate inaccurate descriptions of, and allegations about, what was happening in the prison, in addition to a sense of injustice because some of the issues reported by the press were common to all prisons, yet attention was never drawn to this. Staff also often felt that the coverage was biased and that few good reports were published, in spite of what they were achieving. As a senior manager observed:

> It's a more emotional prison than anywhere I've worked before, in the sense that staff are conscious of everything that is in the paper. They bleed a lot, and when they're bleeding they think everyone has forgotten them.

Accounting and Accountability

Controlling Contractors

Several issues have remained high on the agenda in the debate surrounding contracted-out prisons, including the need to safeguard not only public and political accountability, but also crucially the rights and interests of prisoners, the need to ensure the proper monitoring of the use of authorized force by private-sector employees, and questions surrounding the introduction and interpretation of the term 'commercial-in-confidence' and the extent to which information should be so regarded. Thus the mechanisms for ensuring the accountability of private-sector prisons, through the contract and the role of the Home Office Controller, needed to be effective in order to assuage any fears of a 'cover up'. It is to this issue of accountability that we now turn.

Group 4 and Wolds management were originally accountable to the Remands Contracts Unit (now Contracts and Competitions Group) for adhering to the terms of their contract. The on-site Home Office Controller was the 'eyes and ears' of the RCU and the way in which this role was interpreted and implemented had important ramifications for the delivery and enforcement of the contract. The creation of this post was an important part of the 'experiment' of managing a contracted-out prison, but it created an entirely new role in the prison system and therefore one for which there was no directly comparable experience on which the appointed person could draw. Under such circumstances, and in the absence of a clear job description, it is perhaps inevitable that the personality, skills and experience of the Controller also played an important part. In many ways, whether the conditions of the contract were deemed to have been met or not was dependent on the Home Office Controller and the way in which this judgement was made, and in which failures to deliver the contract or meet any of its requirements were dealt with, had an important impact on the running of the prison.

The original Controller at Wolds was a Prison Service Governor 3, with a Governor 5 as Deputy and a full-time Personal Secretary. The Controller's statutory responsibilities involved monitoring and reporting at appropriate intervals to the Home Office on all aspects of the running of the prison. To assist this process the Controller received monitoring data from Group 4 on a monthly basis covering the main aspects of the prison's operations, such as number of admissions, discharges, number and type of incidents, number of adjudications, exception reporting on the regime (for example, if the agreed hours of unlock were not achieved for prisoners, this fact and the reason for it had to be reported to the Controller) and related prison matters, although these data were not always complete.

An essential component of the Controller's role was being able to get around the prison in order to keep in touch with developments. However, Wolds' first Controller found that much of her time was taken up with the statutory obligations of the post, such as adjudications for which the Controller was responsible, and the high number of these (1,131) between January and November 1993 made much heavier demands on her time than had been anticipated. Although a Deputy Controller was subsequently appointed, nevertheless the statutory obligations of the post continued to take up a large amount of her time

The importance of the personality, skills and experience of the Controller was highlighted when she had a three-month leave of absence due to illness. During this time her post was filled by several Governor Grades from the RCU, each being there for only a short period, some of whom experienced difficulties in adapting to the role. They were aware of their statutory obligations and the need to avoid becoming directly involved in the running of Wolds but, in practice, this sometimes proved difficult, especially when faced with the temptation to help with problems and particularly when approached by inexperienced staff seeking advice. Such 'over-involvement' posed a dilemma for senior managers and produced mixed responses from staff, some feeling that the temporary Controllers had over-stepped the mark whilst others welcomed it, feeling they were not getting sufficient support from their own management.

These problems were exacerbated by the fact that during this period, the Deputy Controller became responsible for monitoring the Court Escort Services contract which Group 4 had won. The intention had been that the Deputy Controller would divide his time between the two posts but because of the problems initially experienced by Group 4 in providing the Court Escort Service, most of his time was taken up by this contract. Consequently, there were several months when the Controller's secretary was the only 'representative' of the RCU who had a working knowledge of Wolds, which may have weakened the Controller's position at Wolds, a point highlighted in Her Majesty's Chief Inspector of Prisons' report on Wolds (1993).

The responsibility for adjudications and prisoners' punishment was retained by the Controller as the state's representative at Wolds. Consequently, the disciplinary and management responsibilities, which would normally be combined in the role of Governor in a public-sector prison, were split. Although many of the staff and management acknowledged the importance of a private company not being involved in allocating punishment to prisoners, there was some concern about the prison's Director being deprived of a useful management resource since, in public-sector prisons, adjudications are regarded as an important means of gauging the mood of the prison and the feelings of prisoners and staff alike:

> As a Prison Governor, part of managing prisoners, difficult prisoners particularly, can be done through adjudications in that you can say things, as well as deal with adjudications as such ... you know that if you can say [something] to a prisoner, as a prison manager you can deliver – you [can] say to a prisoner that 'If you misbehave in my visits area again, I will make you sit at table No. 6 which is next to the staff when you come in.' The Controller can't do that because sitting at table No. 6 isn't a punishment award, it's an administrative act, and so there are ... some difficulties with the Controller doing adjudications. (Senior manager)

The original Controller at Wolds shared this view:

> I think [adjudications] ought to be part of the management of the prison with the Controller monitoring how they are doing it, making sure there are not any abuses. . . . The discipline part of it is so much about the way the Governor would run the prison and the sort of messages you are trying to send to your staff and prisoners about what is acceptable and what isn't.

There was not, however, a consensus among staff about the Controller's role in adjudications, some staff arguing that the Controller brought impartiality to the proceedings and protected Group 4 from possible accusations of bias or disciplinary impropriety:

> It should be the Home Office Controller – it's the correct authority. If it was the Director, you would have all sorts of comeback. (Unit Supervisor)

Many of the prisoners themselves seemed unaware of the Controller's role. Since prisoners' main contact with the Controller was during adjudications, they made the assumption that, since in public-sector prisons it is the Governor who carries out adjudications, the Controller was in fact the Governor.

During our research, we became aware of few inherent problems and no major areas of conflict or tension between the Controller and the Director, although there were divided views about whether it would be desirable for adjudications to become the responsibility of the Director and it is clear that careful consideration needs to be given to the most appropriate background, attitudes and experience for those appointed as Controllers. However, apart from an unmanageable workload and the risks and pressures this generated, this innovation seemed to work well at Wolds and it was clear that the Controller was active and generally successful in monitoring the terms of the contract.

The Contracting-out Process

Neither the Remands Contracts Unit (RCU) nor Group 4 had any prior experience of the process of contracting-out the management of a prison and the final contract reflected that inexperience, with important issues remaining unclear, particularly in terms of finance. For example, there was continuing uncertainty about whether Group 4 or the Home Office would be financially responsible for any damage done by prisoners to the fabric of the prison. There were many times during our fieldwork when senior managers were negotiating with the RCU/CCU to establish who should pay for such damage and although when our fieldwork ended Group 4 had replaced and repaired any damaged equipment, they continued to seek reimbursement for this. Although this was an area that caused difficulties at Wolds, we understand that it has been addressed and largely clarified in subsequent contracts.

In addition, it was acknowledged that in practice, some of the standards set down in the contract and agreed to by both parties – for example the 1,800 hours a week that the Education Department were contracted to deliver – could not be delivered by Group 4. As a result it was necessary for Group 4 to refer to the RCU to clarify or to negotiate over a number of issues, which also meant that some senior managers at Wolds had to take time from their operational responsibilities to deal with such contractual issues.

Group 4 sub-contracted some services within the prison, such as medical and catering services. We gained the impression that, because Wolds was the first contracted-out prison and the contracting-out process had been so competitive, emphasizing value for money as well as quality, companies had submitted the lowest bid possible, leaving them struggling to provide the services for which they had tendered:

> When AMI put the bid in [for the provision of medical services], they put in a bottom line of course to get the first contract. Their next bid will be higher, much more realistic. They didn't know what prison work was like when they put in the bid. So we are struggling. I would say that our staffing is only just adequate . . . and AMI and Group 4 cut it very fine the first time. (Member of AMI staff)

The Contract in Operation

Paradoxically, in certain respects the contract arrangement proved to be less liberating than senior management had anticipated. It was intended that the contract would ensure certain standards were maintained whilst allowing flexibility in how they were achieved. However, although the contract did not specify requirements for the day-to-day running of the prison, Wolds' management did find that a number of proposals for changes in the way they ran the prison required clearance from the RCU before they could be implemented, and on occasions, this caused considerable frustration.

For example, any changes to the fabric of the prison required the permission of the RCU, since the buildings remain the property of the Crown. Permission therefore had to be sought when Group 4 decided to create a more secure parking area for staff cars outside the perimeter wall of the prison, and when they developed the structured regime on 'F' Unit, since this required part of the exercise yard to be fenced off in order to create a separate exercise yard for the unit. In addition, if changes were proposed to any aspect of the prison regime which was covered by the contract, prior permission had to be obtained from the RCU. Such negotiations often took a considerable time and sometimes delayed innovations (such as the introduction of the structured regime on 'F' Unit), preventing a quick response being made to operational problems that had emerged. In addition, sometimes to delaying possible solutions to difficulties, this also gave staff the impression that Wolds' management were lax or slow in tackling problems, or did not appreciate the difficulties staff faced.

It would also appear that Group 4 was unable to meet some of its contractual obligations. For example, Wolds provided prisoners with 14 hours out-of-cell a day, but the the contract (para. 10 (i) of Schedule No. 2) refers to a provision of 'a total of 15 hours on seven days a week' time out-of-cell. Some of these, however – for example the initial failure to provide library services for a year; to provide the required number of education hours for prisoners; to meet annual requirements for five days staff training; and the failure to provide a Bail Information Officer for over a year – were comparatively minor and sometimes due to circumstances beyond their control. However, both the problems in providing library services and a Bail Information Officer highlighted some of the difficulties in the contracting-out of service provision, since both these services were delayed because of difficulties that arose during the negotiations which were beyond the control of Group 4.

It is clear from the experience at Wolds that much has been learned, both by potential contractors and the Home Office, not only about the process of tendering for and drawing up contracts, but also about managing them, and subsequent contracts will have undoubtedly benefited from this. At Wolds, however, in the absence of any previous experience on which to build, both the Home Office and Group 4 had to learn in the process of dealing with problems as they encountered them and this, also undoubtedly, exacerbated some of the difficulties encountered during the first two years of running the prison.

The Context of Compromise

As we have already observed, since Wolds was the first contracted-out prison in the UK it was under close scrutiny, as well as considerable pressure to succeed. This meant that in many ways, Wolds' management often felt unable to take a long-term view on some issues. So, for example, they could not simply ride out the initial difficulties experienced with prisoners whilst they adapted to the new ethos at Wolds, since this would have attracted too much negative publicity. Increasingly, therefore, and particularly after the departure of the first Director, whose replacement had a more traditional approach to managing prisons, Wolds began to move away from certain elements of its original ethos. More structure and restrictions were built into the regime in an attempt to encourage prisoners to become more involved in the life of the prison, by making it less comfortable for those who did not.

Part of this was a response to weaknesses in the direct supervision model as applied in the UK context. However, it also reflected a change in the general approach to prison management which began to appear on the political agenda in late 1992 (see Chapter 7), as well as a specific response to criticisms of the lethargy among prisoners made in HMCIP's report on Wolds and the report's main recommendation that 'a more active regime should be required in which the participation by all inmates is strongly encouraged' (HMCIP, 1993: 117).

During the closing stages of our fieldwork, therefore, management were attempting to tackle this issue, with changes being made to the induction procedure and the introduction of a new compact system. Both education and workshop provisions were being enhanced and it was hoped that reducing prisoners' basic entitlements, whilst also increasing the privileges which could be earned as an incentive for their compliance and participation, would lead to fewer problems in running the prison and a more constructive and active regime. During this time Wolds was also facing up to the difficulties of the increasing prison population and in March 1994, the Wolds' contract was renegotiated to allow for 10 per cent overcrowding in the prison, resulting in the multi-occupancy of some single cells, a development to which both prisoners and staff were opposed.

There were also considerable internal pressures leading management to re-evaluate the original ethos of the prison and to tighten the regime, since one of the problems that staff had faced from the outset was dealing with the effects of the unreasonable behaviour of a small minority of disruptive prisoners on others:

> The difficulty of course is protecting prisoners from the consequences of other people's stupid decisions all the time and that's one of the strongest things – you see pressures arising that will drive you back into an absolutely recognizable state sector prison. (Senior manager)

These and some of the other factors which led to compromises being made to the original Wolds philosophy and pressures to resort to more familiar public-sector practices (such as the increasing restrictions over prisoners' movements, the introduction of more sanctions for non-co-operation, tightening up the Segregation Unit and the regime, and reducing some of the standards originally set, such as length of visits, which had exceeded the minimum contract requirements), serve to highlight issues which are intrinsic to the management of prisons rather than being a function of whether they are managed by the private or public sector.

Wolds was contracted-out at least in part to encourage the introduction of innovative approaches to the management of prisons and
prisoners. However, the impact of both external and internal pressures on Wolds, which were similar to those faced by *any* prison,
meant that some of the most significant innovations had to give way
to the need to run an orderly prison. As a result of the Prison Service
acquiring agency status in April 1993, and the recommendations of
Judge Tumim and the Director General, Wolds found its isolation
diminishing and the Prison Service began to play a more active role,
since part of its new remit was to take forward government policy on
the involvement of private-sector management in prisons.

This closer involvement with the Prison Service, although bringing
benefits to Wolds, also exposed it to the vagaries of the criminal
justice system. As a consequence, Wolds sacrificed one aspect of its
hitherto unique status, of which many local prisons had been envious
– the ability to resist overcrowding. For many public-sector prisons,
Wolds represented what they had been requesting for over a decade –
a set of minimum standards which were legally enforceable, to assist
them in their attempts to manage prisons humanely – and yet without
this, or the other advantages of contractual protection, they had been
asked increasingly to 'compete' with prisons like Wolds. The impact
of such pressures on public-sector prisons will be considered in the
next chapter.

5

Responding to the Challenge in the Public Sector

Proponents of private prisons maintained that the 'stimulus' of privatization would serve as a powerful (albeit painful) force for change and that the introduction of competition would provide a new benchmark against which public-sector prisons could be measured and compared. How far changes that have occurred in the public sector in recent years have their origins in such competition, or how far such changes, to industrial relations, regime delivery, management style and the use of technology might have taken place without it, we cannot judge conclusively. This chapter outlines the origins and findings of the comparative element of our research which was carried out in order to explore some of these issues. We look in detail at the life of a new public-sector local prison, selected because of its broad resemblance to Wolds in terms of its architecture, time of opening and innovative approach to regime provision for remand prisoners. We conclude this account of the response to the challenge of privatization by the public sector by drawing together the main findings from all six new local prisons studied in this research.

The Comparative Research

The important comparative element of our research was not introduced until we were already one year into the research at Wolds. We had, as a research team, wanted there to be a comparative element built into the research from the beginning, but for financial (and political) reasons, this had not been possible. The key factor which reversed this decision was the interest expressed by the Prisons Board as to whether some of the issues we were identifying at Wolds were also likely to be evident in public-sector prisons, or whether they were a direct or indirect result of the prison's private-sector status. Consequently, we were invited to incorporate a comparative dimension into our research, by selecting an appropriate public-sector local prison, for detailed comparison with Wolds, and to make a briefer study of four other newly opened prisons.

However, because of the unique nature of Wolds as the only dedicated adult remand centre in the UK, there was no prison which was directly comparable. After consultation with the Remands Contracts Unit (now the Contracts and Competitions Group), it was agreed that the main comparator prison would be HMP Woodhill, at Milton Keynes. Woodhill was selected because it was considered by our Steering Group to be similar to Wolds in some key respects, and provided an example of good practice in the public sector. The main comparator prison was not therefore identified at the beginning of the project, but instead one year into the life of Wolds, and against which data emerging from our fieldwork at Wolds could be compared.

Woodhill had opened one year before our approach to its senior management team with a request for research access. To that extent, we had missed its early life and were introduced to it at an arguably more stable period of growth and consolidation – unlike at Wolds, where our fieldwork began at a much earlier stage. Despite these methodological limitations, and the inevitable problems of comparing any two prisons, we conducted a broadly similar programme of observation, interviews and other data-collection in order to make the comparison as valid as possible in the circumstances. We concentrated on the experiences of the remand population at Woodhill, so far as this was possible, spending most of our time on the remand units and selecting our sample of interviewees accordingly. A total of 38 staff and 39 prisoners were formally interviewed, with a small additional group of 10 prisoners interviewed at the induction stage. Time was also spent attending meetings, observing life on the wing and participating in aspects of Woodhill's regime. Given the purposes of our research at Wolds, most of what we have to say about Woodhill relates primarily to provision for adult remand prisoners, although inevitably, life for them was to some extent dominated by the existence of sentenced prisoners. Woodhill saw itself as a 'post-Woolf community prison', catering for the multiple needs of prisoners remanded into custody, those awaiting sentence or allocation, and those with short sentences to serve. Little distinction was drawn at Woodhill between remand and sentenced prisoners, except in terms of accommodation: remand prisoners were concentrated on two of the houseblocks.

In order to broaden the comparative element, additional short but intensive and highly organized two-day visits were made to four other new local prisons (Belmarsh, Bullingdon, Highdown and Blakenhurst – three public-sector and one privately managed new prison, respectively). The following account will focus primarily on the research carried out at Woodhill, with our final conclusions drawing upon our observations from the other newly opened establishments.

Woodhill: New Generation Management?

HMP Woodhill opened in July 1992. It was the first 'new generation design' prison (see National Audit Office, 1994a), built at a final cost of £117.8 million (£203,000 per prisoner place). The main prison consisted of four main houseblocks on an open campus site, each containing two separate but adjoining wings. Each wing housed 60 prisoners in single cells equipped with full integral sanitation. The 60 cells were divided into three landing areas of 20 cells each, along two sides of a triangle. Each wing had two television rooms, a large and well-lit 'atrium' or association area containing table tennis and pool tables, and seating for dining. The large atria windows faced either east or west across a green, allowing an unusual amount of daylight into the association area. No cell faced either the central green or into another cell. This was to prevent prisoners from observing staff movements across the green or from shouting to prisoners outside or in other cells. Each of the four main three-storey house units had a central core with office accommodation uniting the two wings:

> Staff are able to observe all the cells without having to move about in an obviously patrolling manner. The overall design of the wings is geared to create a positive sense of group identity with manageable numbers and close staff/inmate interaction. (Clark, 1992: 1)

The benefits of this design were good control (arising from the discrete small units), the generation of closer staff–prisoner relationships, the facility to hold different types and categories of prisoner, and the general impression of space and light. The 'New Generation' design was imported into the UK from the USA.

Woodhill accommodated 550 prisoners including 60 young prisoners. It held remand and convicted prisoners and a small number of prisoners with behaviour problems. Convicted prisoners made up about 60 per cent of the population. At the time of our research, there were five prisoners in the Control Review Committee (CRC) units complex and six prisoners in the protected witness unit.

Opening Woodhill

Woodhill received its first staff members in December 1991 – the commissioning team. Woodhill was a far larger and more complex prison than Wolds, performing a number of very different functions (including the resource-intensive Special Units for disruptive long-term prisoners). Although (as in all newly opened prisons) a large proportion of the staff were new to the service (55 per cent), the Commissioning Team were also able to recruit a core of experienced staff at middle-management level for the residential units, in a way that had not been possible at Wolds. It had also managed to build up its population in a very controlled way.

The prison, its purpose, direction and 'ethos' had all been carefully planned. The establishment's statement of purpose was 'to provide a secure and caring environment with a positive regime; to encourage the development of all staff and inmates and provide support within a safe, civilised and orderly work culture; to provide support to the families of staff and inmates; to assist inmates to make a positive contribution to their community; and to look to the community and share mutual resources and develop a greater understanding of the work we do'. (HM Prison Service, 1992a) The values to which all staff were expected to work were clearly stated in many publications and in a separate booklet for staff: to respect human dignity; to behave with integrity and without prejudice; to maintain professional standards, valuing fairness, sensitivity, restraint, civility and dedication; and freedom to express views to improve the quality of life in the prison.

The challenge facing the prison, as stated in the staff booklet, was to be united, purposeful, open, stable and innovative, always working towards a positive staff and prisoner regime, and always looking for improvements in quality of life. The Governor's statement in the Business Plan began with an acknowledgement of the need for continual self-evaluation and improvement. The senior management team (assisted by the specially formed QUIT team – see below) sought ways of controlling costs, maximizing the use of accommodation, enhancing and reviewing the regime, refining the management structure, and planning ahead. All of these concerns were aimed at achieving a clear 'end product' to fulfil the 'vision of Woodhill as a positive and "leading edge" establishment' (HMP Woodhill, 1994a: 3).

The main conclusions from our observations of Woodhill were two-fold. First, it had more in common with Wolds in terms of its innovative management style and ethos than it had with most other public-sector local prisons, at that time. Secondly, it opened in an era of competitive tendering: its managers and, to a slightly lesser extent, its staff, were achievement and 'performance-oriented'. The threat of market-testing was used 'as a tool' by the management team, who pointed to achievements at Wolds (in so far as they were known about) as a spur to their own staff. The Governor of Woodhill and his senior management team were imbued with the commitment and drive to deliver a 'high-quality service', and were able to communicate their enthusiasm and dedication to the staff groups as a whole.

Senior management and staff had half an eye on developments in the private sector, and were determined to 'out-perform' Wolds. This ambition was not wholly determined by the competitive environment – as we were to discover. Personal pride and ambition, and a very real urge to deliver a high-quality regime existed among many senior managers in the Prison Service before the introduction of privatization. However, the new competitive era concentrated the efforts of senior managers around a private/public divide. The presence of our research made this competitive edge more obvious, as staff asked us continually, 'How are we doing compared to Wolds, then?'

The senior management team felt that they were doing everything they could to motivate staff and give direction. They self-consciously ensured that they had a real 'presence about the place'. Woodhill was praised by several members of staff (and by the Inspectorate when they visited) as having the best communication structure of any prison where they had worked:

> I think from the top, certainly downwards it's one of the best I've ever come across. Sometimes I've thought it is overkill . . . there is everything . . . even on a day-to-day basis, the morning briefing sheet, things like that. I'm quite impressed by it really. It's there if people want to find it. (Principal Officer)

A Quality Improvement Team (QUIT) was set up at Woodhill, 18 months after opening, which consisted of a Principal Officer, a Senior Officer, a Governor grade and a psychologist. The team was charged with reviewing several aspects of the prison's management and functioning, and was to make recommendations. They were asked to consult widely with staff and to concentrate on developing specific proposals:

> Their job is threefold – one is to turn over those stones that we put in place a bit hastily in the early stages and see if the stuff underneath is cleaned out and placed neatly back, two is to set up a system of monitoring and review of Woodhill so that it can review itself effectively and three to make some preparations and assist the process of the strategic planning bit that we want to take ahead. (Governor grade)

Staff reported a considerable level of confidence in senior management at Woodhill – significantly more than reported by staff at Wolds at the time of our research. Forty-five per cent reported 'quite a lot' of confidence and 17 per cent reported 'a great amount of confidence' in senior management (compared with 48 per cent reporting 'quite a lot' of confidence at Wolds and none reporting 'a great amount'). Reasons for this level of confidence were varied, but a theme which emerged often was their ability to be co-ordinated and united, despite often quite different personal styles and beliefs. All were striving for the same goal and seemed clear about what that goal was: to put

Woodhill on the map as the 'best new prison'. They gave staff the impression that they knew what was going on in the prison and that they were 'in control' – in contrast to the first year at Wolds, where teething troubles and changes in direction were relatively frequent.

Both Wolds and Woodhill opened under the leadership of strong and charismatic Governors, but at senior and middle-management level Woodhill had more experienced and effective staff. The Governor's chosen style of management at Woodhill was one of 'consultation':

> I think no one can underestimate the impact this governor has had on Woodhill, and no one should underestimate it. He has been a driving force, a great motivator, with very clear cut ideas on what he wanted to achieve. I just feel it could have been a different prison – not a better prison – with another governor. (Senior manager)

He was described as forward-thinking, innovative and highly determined, being fully aware of the significance (and the limitations) of the Governor's role in an establishment:

> I think it's very important – it's very important in determining the extent to which you can capture the strengths of your staff. I think at Woodhill we have tried to allow staff a bit of room to breathe and develop themselves and take to forward areas and to have a bit of power – that's the word that's going around – to have a sense of ownership of various areas within the establishment – and I think that Governors to a greater or a lesser extent, can affect that. . . . There's far more to what a Governor can bring or might not bring to an establishment than just that, there's a whole sense of organization, there's a whole sense of how the senior management group works together – it's a big issue. (Governor grade)

In addition to the quality of its senior management, Woodhill had other advantages – it was, architecturally, the most modern, expensive (per prisoner place) and carefully designed prison to have been built in the UK. Disentangling these features in order to explain its relatively successful opening is difficult. Woodhill was a dynamic and forward-looking prison in terms of its architecture, its regime and its management. It provided decent conditions for prisoners, it was clean, secure, ordered and relatively active. Its staff and management were committed and hard-working and the atmosphere was very positive, particularly among the senior management team. This was not the whole picture, however, as we shall see below. There were occasional suggestions, both by staff and prisoners, that the management team and their style were verging on the dictatorial, and that their expectations were exceedingly high. Their result-oriented approach was successful in securing high standards, but it seemed that almost everyone in the prison was working at his or her threshold, and that the painfulness of constantly 'delivering the goods' was acute.

This mixture of dynamism and innovation at management level, together with the difficulties of translating such effort into a real change in the 'quality of the regime' for staff and prisoners, resulted in apparent contradictions. Woodhill seemed impressive by any standards, both at management level and in terms of meeting its 'key performance indicators' (KPIs). Underneath the senior management layer, on the house units, and among staff and prisoners, the picture was more complex (as to some degree, the senior management team were only too well aware). Achieving positive, cost-efficient regimes turned out to be an arduous and uncertain task, the difficulties of which were not always reflected adequately by KPIs. Assessing the regime, from different and more qualitative perspectives, was difficult. Drawing comparisons with our experiences of Victorian local prisons was unavoidable. It was fortuitous that one of the two main fieldworkers had no prior experience of prisons before Wolds and Woodhill – in this sense, her reactions to each establishment were unsullied by prior expectations. For the other fieldworker, responses to both Wolds and Woodhill were 'comparative' in many respects. For both, after Wolds, it felt like there were a lot of staff at Woodhill! But compared to a public-sector benchmark (pre-1992), Woodhill was staffed relatively leanly. We now look in more detail at life in Woodhill for 'new generation' staff, at 'new generation' regime delivery, and the experiences of 'new generation' prisoners.

New Generation Staff?

Both Wolds and Woodhill had highly motivated staff who were committed to working within a positive and successful regime. The major difference between the two staff groups was the number: Wolds had significantly fewer, with less previous experience and less day-to-day contact with each other. These differences are important in terms of the views we heard from staff in each prison about their work. Far more of the staff at Woodhill reported enjoying their work (79 per cent, compared with 50 per cent at Wolds). More at Woodhill felt the most was being made of their skills (52 per cent, compared with 18 per cent) and that there were good promotion prospects ahead of them, whereas very few staff at Wolds saw promotion ahead of them. Staff at Woodhill were more positive in their assessment of staff–management communication and confidence in management.

Most of these differences could be accounted for by the significant difference in previous prison experience at Woodhill and the more radical departure from traditional Prison Service management ethos at Wolds. Woodhill could boast an unusually integrated and powerful management team, however, and this made a significant difference to the working lives of staff. Woodhill staff knew that there was a marked contrast between Woodhill, its regime, physical layout, facilities and management team, and that of most other local prisons at that time. In addition to this sense of pride, they continually received the message from management that they had been carefully selected, with a high proportion coming directly from the training school. One of the main reasons cited for Woodhill's achievements was the quality of the staff:

> I mean, we've got a higher than average percentage of good quality prison officers who are committed to delivering a post-Woolf prison; they are coming fresh from college and have no preconceived ideas about these . . . that are coming in off the streets to make their life a misery in prison. (Specialist)

Many of the staff at Woodhill were committed, enthusiastic, proud and hard working. At the same time, many felt under considerable pressure. We found some discrepancy between the views of staff and management, and there were signs of low morale among some of the staff despite the establishment's many natural advantages. In some ways, our own exposure to life for staff at Wolds, made us feel that staff at Woodhill were relatively well off, however 'driven' the regime. Their own comparisons were not with these radically low staffing levels but with the Prison Service's own history of overtime, relative over-staffing, deteriorating regime provision and (in one or two cases) the 'pre-Fresh-Start-when-there-was-still-a-Chief-Officer-to-look-after-staff' era, now long gone. However, the new environment of competition, job insecurity, new open regimes and stringent attention to budgets, did pose a problem to some of the staff (see below). The question of how to encourage staff to reflect the ambitious aspirations of management and, perhaps first, how to recruit, select and train the 'right' staff, emerged as an important issue from our interviews and discussion with staff and senior management. By November 1994, 58 staff members had left Woodhill on transfers to other establishments (the vast majority for 'geographical' reasons). Thirty staff had resigned and five had retired (some on medical grounds).

Many staff (especially senior staff) had come to Woodhill with high expectations. The fact that it was a new and uniquely designed prison had attracted them in the first place but, as at many of the new local prisons, a major concern at Woodhill was the relatively high proportion (over half) of young and inexperienced staff. There were feelings that some of the units suffered from having too high a proportion of new and young staff, who tended to 'let prisoners get the upper hand' and, occasionally, it was felt by some senior staff that staffing levels were rather too low to allow adequate supervision of new staff by more experienced officers. There was a higher proportion of uniformed female staff at Woodhill than at many public sector establishments then – 58 out of 397 (15 per cent) – but very similar to Wolds (16 per cent). It was felt by many (but not all) of the staff, and by most of the prisoners, that the presence of women officers was a positive feature of modern prison life.

Staffing Levels

As noted above, staff perceptions of the adequacy or otherwise of their staffing levels was determined in part by their expectations. Compared to Wolds, we perceived staffing levels at Woodhill to be relatively generous! However, few of the staff at Woodhill (28 per cent) were happy with their staffing levels:

> If we had another two staff we could ease off the throttle a bit. For a local prison to deliver the regime we are delivering with the amount of education, the amount of time out-of-cell, our escort commitment . . . OK, peaks and troughs make extra demands on us, but to commit ourselves to achieve a full searching programme is unheard of in local prisons. (Senior manager)

Like Wolds staff, those at Woodhill felt that 'we haven't got enough leeway', particularly 'if something were to happen'. Although each unit accommodated 60 prisoners, many of them were elsewhere during the day (for example, in education, work or other activities), so the question of how many staff were actually necessary to the 'safe and efficient running of the unit' was not straightforward. Some of the managers felt that Woodhill had been treated fairly generously in receiving the staff they had requested:

> What we did, we identified the work and then we created our profiles from this document and they said, if that's the amount of staff you want . . . and we practically got exactly what we asked for, so we have no complaints in that area. (Senior manager)

An unexpectedly high number of bedwatches, sick absences, leave, sudden influxes of prisoners and other features of prison life did cut into staff availability, with some departments being hit harder than others. Some of the staff felt concerned for their safety – 45 per cent (compared with 71 per cent at Wolds) reported that there were not enough staff on the units to ensure safety and efficiency – but many did not (or did not like to admit this), despite feeling that staffing levels were too low:

> Do I feel there are enough staff on the units to ensure safety? No I don't. Let's take the cleaning officer first. His job is to get the cleaners out to

work and get them moving and working. There are periods of time when he has to leave the wing with a cleaner to go on the outside area to clean up. This leaves the wing down to an SO and one. The one that is left behind is the movements officer, who could be at the gate downstairs covering movements, leaving just the SO on the wing, although technically speaking he is outside the gate, so he is not actually left on the unit as such. (Principal Officer)

The experience (and gender) mix of staff had been a concern 'in the early days' as officers occasionally found themselves with no experienced officers on a unit during some shifts. At these times, uncertainty about how to handle difficult situations became an important issue, and on occasion, staff felt 'unsure [as to] who is actually running Woodhill' (Principal Officer):

> I mean when we have had bad incidents I think they've responded superbly well and for a fairly junior staff – there's never been an occasion, I don't think, where the response from them hasn't been above and beyond, sometimes well beyond their years. One or two things happened quite early on that were quite tricky and left people very white faced, were dealt with very well. . . . I think we've got some of the best quality young officers that I've ever come across. (Principal Officer)

Staff were less concerned about safety than about order, which was harder to maintain with few staff visible on the units. The relationship between the 'temperature' on the units and the staffing levels was sometimes important – as we observed at Wolds. This relationship can be illustrated by an incident which occurred during the second phase of our fieldwork at Woodhill. An occasion arose when prisoners were locked up early one lunch-time without prior warning. They were angry about this and began to threaten to refuse to return to their cells. There was one staff member on the unit when this resistance occurred, and his attention was being fairly fully taken up by a prisoner requesting something else. At this time, there was no permanent Senior Officer (SO) available for the wing, and so new faces were appearing each day. This had been noted by staff and prisoners, both of whom complained about the lack of continuity. The atmosphere on the unit began to get rowdy, and two prisoners began to demand of the one officer on the unit that they speak to the SO, shouting to other prisoners not to lock up at 11.00 – an hour earlier than usual. The officer discovered that he was on his own on the unit ('Oh, bugger,' he said) and rang through to another office to ask for a Senior Officer. Within 10 minutes, two SOs and the acting SO for the unit appeared (there were comments from the officer about the 'influence of researchers' on this very satisfactory response!) and once the increased staff presence on the unit was noted by prisoners, they quietened down. The officer who had been alone was much more relaxed in the way he handled prisoners, and the tension which had begun to build up dissipated.

What this incident illustrated for us (and there were many others like it) was not only the significance of staff presence, but also of staff confidence on the units, and the way in which events could take a sudden turn for the worse, or better, for a variety of reasons. Staff numbers were a relevant (but perhaps not the most relevant) factor. Prisoners did point out to us that they were often not sure exactly how many officers were on the unit at any time, and that they tended to assume that there was normally more than one. If only one officer was visible, it was always possible that another officer was around, but out of sight (for example, in a cell or an office). When the unit was, even briefly, down to one officer (or exceptionally, no officers at all), this was under certain circumstances a signal to prisoners that advantage could be taken of the situation. Most of the time this did not occur, or it was not noticed that staff were alone. Some of the female officers preferred not to be left alone on the units, but others were no more concerned (some rather less) than some of the male officers. The kind of game playing and deliberate 'running rings around' staff which we observed at Wolds was not present to quite the same degree at Woodhill.

As at the other new local prisons studied in our research, the very high proportion of newly trained officers at Woodhill had significant advantages and disadvantages in terms of establishment functioning and morale. Many new entrant staff had not got the posting they had requested and were therefore unsettled, a long way from home (or could not sell their houses and move), and put in requests for transfer as soon as this was 'acceptable' (normally after completing their probation year). Many of the staff, new and experienced, were 'from the North' and could not envisage a life in Milton Keynes. The advantages of high numbers of new entrant staff were that management could 'mould' them according to their own philosophy, they were enthusiastic and they had undergone a much improved training course before taking up their posts. A key advantage of the staff recruitment process at Wolds was that most of the staff were local and inevitably, it will be some time before local recruitment in the public sector solves the problem of staff being in the 'wrong part of the country'.

Regime Delivery: Using Time in the Public Sector

One of the similarities between Wolds and Woodhill was the commitment expressed by the management teams in each establishment to delivering a high-quality regime for prisoners, and treating them with dignity and respect. Woodhill was less inclined to 'normalize' (or 'liberalize') the prison experience, and remained firmly committed to security, order and discipline as its baseline, with constructive activity carefully structured into the day. It was – on the surface – a much more ordered prison. It was also committed to very generous 'unlock' hours, providing at least a 12-hour day for the vast majority of its prisoners. This meant that as a prison, Woodhill faced the same challenge as Wolds: how to occupy usefully prisoners who were not (all) obliged to work, in an establishment which had been built without workshops. Considerable energy and effort was expended on this task by members of Woodhill's senior management team.

Prisoners were complimentary about most aspects of the Woodhill regime, feeling that 'I shouldn't think anyone would want to "kick off" here, the regime is very humane and personal' (Prisoner). Prisoners were given a voice in many regime matters, through participation in meetings and committees. In some respects, the house units at Woodhill were quite similar architecturally to those at Wolds. Instead of 50 prisoners per living unit there were 60, on three storeys instead of two, and the design was triangular instead of square. However, the units had a similar 'feel' to them because of their relatively small size and because of their radical departure from typical prison landings. There were normally three officers (a Senior Officer and two officers) detailed to each unit during most of the day, in contrast to the one supervising officer characteristic of 'direct supervision' at Wolds. One (or sometimes two) of these officers might leave the unit for short periods, but the presence of more than one uniformed staff member for most of the day was the main contrast between Wolds and Woodhill. Although staff at Woodhill felt relatively 'thinly spread', the prison was relatively generously staffed compared to Wolds and there was a marked difference for staff between the lone supervision of 50 prisoners and working in the company of colleagues.

Woodhill had a policy of keeping prisoners out of their cells as much as possible. Morning unlock was at 07.30 and evening lock-up was at 21.00. Prisoners were locked in their cells between 12.00 and 13.15 to carry out a roll check and allow staff to go for lunch (in traditional Prison Service fashion), in contrast to Wolds where staff remained on the living units and ate with prisoners. One officer remained on the unit which was in 'patrol state' (with just one officer on duty) during this time. Prisoners were also locked up between 17.15 and 17.30 for a further roll check, just before their evening meal. On Wednesdays there was an early lock up (11.00) before lunch, to allow the staff to have an 'activity hour'. There was a strict no-smoking policy at Woodhill, breach of which carried a £4 fine.

Prisoners could smoke in their cells and on the exercise yards, but not on the landings, in association areas or in the TV rooms. They could not smoke in visits.

Prisoners were encouraged to get up early. More than half were up before 08.00. More prisoners at Woodhill than at Wolds described the provision of activities as 'good' (41 per cent at Woodhill, compared with 27 per cent at Wolds). Two-thirds of the prisoners interviewed at Woodhill worked (as did 70 per cent at Wolds) but both establishments were struggling to tackle the same 'new' problem of occupying remand prisoners who were out of their cells for most of the day. When Woodhill opened, there were no workshops and the problem of providing activities for prisoners was continually raised at management meetings. At the time of our fieldwork, more than a year after the prison opened, there was a total of only 200 activity places (on works, farms, education, domestic work (cleaners), painting and decorating, bricks, orderlies jobs and community placements) available to the 550 prisoners at Woodhill.

There were 12 hours of 'unlock' per day during the week and 11.75 hours at weekends. The management group was working hard to achieve 12.5 hours per day, and a special staff meeting was held to invite staff to suggest ways in which this might be done. The pay scheme was intended to provide incentives for prisoners to get involved in work or other activities. The basic unemployment rate was £2.50, providing inmates were willing to work and had completed a labour application form. (For over 65s the rate was £3.25). Attendance at education classes attracted an allowance of £4 per week. Less than 10 per cent of the prisoners interviewed remained on their units all day. Most left the unit at some stage to take up visits, go to education, work or to use the gym.

Sixty-two per cent of the staff felt that the range of activities available to prisoners at Woodhill was 'good' or 'quite good' (compared with 45 per cent at Wolds). There was a feeling, however, among 38 per cent of those interviewed (compared with 55 per cent at Wolds) that the provision of work and other activities at Woodhill was too low. Furthermore, as at Wolds, it was difficult motivating prisoners to use what facilities did exist (see below). Some prisoners ended up on the unit all day, playing table tennis and snooker, talking, hanging around, watching TV and videos and feeling bored. Staff had to 'work hard to actually get them out of their wing settings' (Principal Officer). However, whereas nearly half the staff at Wolds felt that prisoners did not use the facilities on offer very much, only 10 per cent of the staff at Woodhill felt that this was the case.

Education was popular in Woodhill and the gym was very well used. The PE Instructors (PEIs) put on a very full programme for prisoners which included weekends and most evenings. The approach taken to inmate activities was proactive, with departments doing 'roadshow' appearances on wings to entice prisoners over. In addition, two-thirds of the prisoners we interviewed at Woodhill worked. Most felt that this 'helped them pass the time'. Some were more 'constructively occupied' than others:

> What did I do yesterday? I got up at seven, washed, dressed, cleaned my cell, had breakfast at eight; done my chores, spent some time talking to you, banged up for dinner. Socialized, showered, went in the TV room, till tea-time. After tea, I phoned my wife – I do that every night. In the evening, I played backgammon, sometimes with an officer, sometimes with an inmate. Locked up at nine o'clock. It's alright to be locked up then or the day gets too boring. (Prisoner)

Almost two-thirds of the prisoners we interviewed at Woodhill said that they were frequently or often bored (compared with only one-third at Wolds). They found the evenings, weekends, dinner hours and days when 'there's nothing on the television' particularly boring, but more than a quarter reported feeling bored 'all the time'.

Staff suggested various ways of reducing the levels of boredom at Woodhill, such as emptying particular wings during the day and freeing up staff to supervise prisoners doing other things besides association, and the management team were looking at the introduction of real wages for real work schemes. Some of the staff felt that the hours out-of-cell were too long, however, given the limited work and other activities available to prisoners, and insufficient constructive activity was seen as potentially dangerous, leading to bullying, arguments, tension and increased drug use, which was reminiscent of the situation at Wolds. As remand prisoners, most of those we spoke to were not obliged to work, but they were given the opportunity to do so. If work was not available, they received £2.50 'unemployment pay'. If they chose not to work, they did not receive any pay. This new problem of encouraging remand prisoners who were unlocked for most of the day into activities was continually addressed at meetings:

> It's about motivation. It strikes me now looking back on it, particularly now that we've got half of the prison full of remand prisoners who don't have to work, you either have to have work that is intrinsically satisfying and therefore they do it because they enjoy doing it or you have to have work that is well paid and that is your motive for doing it, because you get lots of money, or, quirkily enough, I think you have to have work that has some kind of charitable basis in it because it seems to me that prisoners do sign up to that notion for short periods of time because of the feeling they get from doing that. (Governor grade)

Incentives

> Part of the problem here, particularly at Woodhill, is that we do have a problem in getting prisoners to engage in the regime. That's shown quite easily by the fact that we've got quite a lot of education places left unfilled. (Psychologist)

Just as in the private sector, prisoners in the new local prison regimes had to be 'seduced' into using their newly available time out-of-cell constructively. The post-Woolf era of compacts, prisoner participation in regimes and a required minimum time out-of-cell per day was having a dramatic effect on public-sector regimes despite the lack of an explicit contract between the Prison Service and establishments to this effect. Pay and non-pay incentives were offered at Woodhill (for a fuller discussion, see Lomas, 1995) as a way of motivating prisoners to engage constructively in activities. Compacts were being introduced and an 'enhanced privileges scheme', as well as inter-wing competitions, were offered as ways of encouraging prisoners towards 'good behaviour and willing co-operation' (cp. Prison Service Business and Corporate Plans, HM Prison Service, 1994a, 1994b). The enhanced privileges scheme was seen as an important element of Woodhill's regime and it was hoped that it would be useful in encouraging positive relationships and in developing positive attitudes amongst the prisoner population (HMP Woodhill, 1994b).

The incentives scheme applied to sentenced and remand prisoners alike. The aim was to reward good behaviour by identifying incentives for prisoners who showed exemplary behaviour or a positive contribution to Woodhill – 'merely keeping out of trouble or maintaining a low profile will not necessarily be sufficient to attract enhanced privileges' (Governor's Order 35/93). The six incentives available through the scheme were in-cell television, enhanced cell facilities (mugs, a rug/mat, bedspread, personal towels, sheets, etc.), privileged incoming telephone calls, extra or enhanced visits, enhanced canteen facilities and a personal fitness programme. An Enhanced Privileges Board (consisting of the Head of Residential, Head of Inmate Activities and a group manager) met monthly to consider applications from prisoners. Applications were accompanied by a brief wing report and a recommendation from the group manager. Staff were encouraged to nominate or encourage prisoners they felt were making a positive contribution. As a result, all prisoners seemed to be achieving outstanding reports from staff on their units.

Woodhill also offered enhanced family visits as a reward for prisoners who made 'a positive contribution to the life of the prison'. This was defined as, having not been on governors' reports for six weeks, having gained employment, having taken an orderly job, having participated in any local charity or fund-raising event, having become a member of one of Woodhill's staff/inmate committees. These visits, which were supervised, took place in the small group room of the Chaplaincy between 10.00 and 16.00. Prisoners who were awarded such visits were allowed to invite immediate family members who could bring food and non-alcoholic drinks. Feedback solicited by the establishment about the success of the scheme suggested a great deal of enthusiasm from prisoners and their families. Apart from the security restrictions, which were disliked by prisoners (mainly the close surveillance by cameras), the visits facilities at Woodhill were praised.

Prisoners' Experience

In general, prisoners acknowledged the advantages of being in a prison like Woodhill and valued its facilities. As at Wolds, most of the prisoners we spoke to had experience of other local prisons, such as Bedford and Pentonville, with which there was a huge contrast – both in the physical conditions and the provision of activities and services. The geographical layout and relatively small size of the individual units made the prison seem more relaxed than other prisons, and this was also welcomed. However, this was contrasted with the 'slow dawning' that Woodhill was highly security conscious, in a way that many prisoners found oppressive. Some prisoners felt that this contrast – between apparent liberality and actual tight security – was 'all mind games'.

Woodhill had adopted a very high-profile and proactive approach to security matters. There were several category 'A' and 'E' list prisoners in the establishment and there had been two attempted but no successful escapes from Woodhill. Prisoners felt that Woodhill was 'run like a Cat "A" nick'; that staff were very strict on searching, controlling the degree of physical contact during visits and the granting of home leave. They were also 'paranoid' about high-security risk prisoners and (according to one prisoner's account) had '30 men in stripes at one stage' (categorized as escape risks and having to wear trousers with yellow stripes for quick identification). One of the concrete sculptures of sheep (which 'grazed' on the grass inside the prison) was given yellow striped trousers (by a PEI, we were reliably informed!) for a time, because it had been seen in areas of the prison it was not supposed to be. One prisoner complained that although he was pleased that they got longer than average for visits, he had been told in front of his wife 'not to be so friendly' to her during a visit and he had felt 'gutted' about this and very angry (stories of 'liberal' visits policies at Wolds were being reported in the press at this time). Woodhill's 'tight' approach to security matters did result in its remand population being held in more secure conditions than might have been required.

There were also complaints from prisoners that the long hours out-of-cell were not easy to fill and that not enough thought had gone into providing meaningful activities and work for prisoners, who often stayed at Woodhill for quite long periods, despite being on remand. The concrete sheep, which were frequently mentioned to us, symbolized for prisoners the conflicting messages prisoners perceived from management:

> It's a piss-take. Why didn't they buy five lambs and let some guy have the benefit of looking after them at least? Why did they do that? (Prisoner)

'In a normal prison' (a refrain we heard often from prisoners) 'you know where you stand – here, you don't; no-one knows what's going on' (Prisoner). Staff were not always sure of the rules and prisoners – unusually – did not know them either, so there was no way in which new prisoners could be 'eased in' by staff or by other prisoners. This was, in many ways, remarkably similar to the messages we had received from both staff and prisoners at Wolds. Prisoners compared their experiences with those at 'traditional' locals and found the new ethos quite a shock. Everyone was mystified by the lack of 'traditional' rules, boundaries and customs, and by the apparent uncertainty about procedures.

Many of the more senior officers at Woodhill, who had worked in traditional prisons and so had something with which to compare their experiences, also found the apparent 'new liberalism' very difficult. Officers from the training school found the regime more manageable, but both groups of staff complained about their uncertainty about where the boundaries were and where they should be drawn. Prisoners on the units wanted to 'know where they stood' and felt most acutely the effects of having a high proportion of new entrant staff, whilst experienced staff were being asked to do the job in a different way. Many of the prisoners we interviewed admitted feeling surprised, when they arrived at Woodhill, at the number of hours spent out of cells, at the fact that they could wear their own clothes, the cleanliness of the prison, their access to showers, its integral sanitation, single cells and the general facilities. In fact, their initial reactions were very similar to those of prisoners on arrival at Wolds.

Maintaining Order

There was a slightly unstructured feel to life on many of the house units at Woodhill, rather like at Wolds, simply because prisoners were expected to organize their own activities, present themselves for work, and so on. In view of the relatively low visibility of staff on the units, and as part of the ethos of the establishment, responsibility for maintaining discipline was placed as much upon prisoners as upon staff. Some prisoners felt that the officers relied too heavily on prisoners to maintain discipline:

> Discipline is a joke, there is absolutely no discipline here. It causes friction in the mornings, because the officers rely on prisoners to shut people up for playing music on the radio too loud at 11p.m. Eventually, one of us gets fed up at them, then this causes friction when you're unlocked in the morning for whoever had to tell them off. This causes animosity between prisoners. It's too free and easy. (Prisoner)

Because of this situation, many of the older prisoners tried to find ways of avoiding too much contact with younger prisoners on the wings. For example, the prison newspaper was run by a small and industrious team of 'over 30s' who gathered each day in an office at the back of the library, 'for peace and quiet'. All of them described life on the units as 'a bit of a headache' and felt that prisoner power was destructive and disruptive for prisoners like themselves. Older prisoners (the minority) preferred quiet, predictable routines, and fairly strict control. They resented having to push their way into a dinner queue, for example, and so preferred the staff to 'keep on top of' order on the units in order to make their lives in prison more tolerable. Some were critical of the discrepancies between 'what is said' and 'what is done' and of the superficiality of some of the statements and achievements of Woodhill – done 'for show' and not for 'real results'. They did feel, however, that the Governor was trying to 'run a tight ship at his end' and that he was 'probably the fairest Governor I have ever come across' (Prisoner).

Staff also complained that prisoners had a great deal of power at Woodhill, because of the small numbers of officers physically present on the units. This made the enforcement of rules and regulations more difficult, particularly if prisoners complained about their enforcement. Although almost half of the staff felt that discipline was well or very well maintained on the units (48 per cent compared with only 21 per cent at Wolds), some commented that 'it's not what we're used to' (Officer). The challenge to staff authority made by prisoners throughout much of the prison's first year apparently reached dangerous stages at times and it seemed that a heavy price was being paid for the liberal, open regime, and that drawing boundaries and maintaining order were more difficult tasks to accomplish. There were also some inconsistencies between units as to the enforcement of rules; for example, prisoners were not supposed to have access to 'leisure' facilities such as the pool tables and televisions until all the wing cleaning had been carried out, but some unit staff were more likely to enforce this than others. There were also periodic difficulties on particular units when strong groups of prisoners formed, including 'power struggles' between different groups of prisoners from different areas of the country.

Maintaining order and control whilst securing good and close relationships between staff and prisoners was difficult and staff were frequently tested. For example, a series of false alarms occurred during our fieldwork period, particularly over the weekends, with five occurring during one weekend and seven on another. This resulted in staff being late finishing their shifts and a feeling that prisoners were 'giving us the runabout'. The Governor sent out a notice informing prisoners that any further false alarms would result in the units being locked up after tea-time the next day, so that searching could be carried out and staff could leave early. This response was effective – the alarms ceased and staff were pleased to be supported in this way.

Staff felt that they were expected to 'talk prisoners round' rather than rely on adjudications to secure compliance and the whole question of managing a relatively 'free' population in a fairly liberal manner, whilst securing good order and avoiding violence, was a constant challenge (exactly the same management issues that Wolds staff had wrestled with throughout their first year and into their second). Behaviour had to be 'channelled' – staff did not like working on units when they became undisciplined and many prisoners were unhappy about such phases too. Some prisoners were quick to pick up and take advantage of any apparent weakness among staff and the atmosphere could change very quickly from humour to tension and back again. The remand units were more likely than the units for convicted prisoners to become part of this cycle, although the unit with the most consistent 'worst reputation' for trouble was the Young Prisoner (YP) unit.

The question of unacceptable behaviour by prisoners on the units was one of the issues raised by prisoner representatives at Regimes Committee Meetings. Staff on the unit were not tackling this behaviour and this made life on the units harder for the majority. Because of this, one 'model prisoner' had lost his temper, assaulted one of the 'trouble-makers', and 'been nicked for it'. Prisoners felt that staff were 'too lazy to do the paperwork' and so turned a blind eye. That these issues were discussed constructively with prisoners was one of the aspects of the Woodhill regime prisoners valued highly. However, resolving the question of unit discipline and, in particular, the dependence of staff on key influential prisoners in controlling other disruptive prisoners was not straightforward. This strategy was sometimes effective but occasionally risky for the prisoner concerned and staff often expressed the need for clearer guidance from management on maintaining discipline. Some prisoners reported that one of the main methods used to maintain discipline was 'the enhancements', or the extra privileges – 'a lot of people are chasing for that'. Like the prisoners at Wolds, they also said: 'We maintain our own discipline, too'. It was not unusual to see chairs stacked neatly on tables and carpets being hoovered quietly in the mornings.

The view of senior management was that the threshold 'quality of life' at Woodhill was good, that prisoners were treated well and that they were given considerable responsibility since the regime was 'reward-driven' rather than 'sanctions-driven'. However, those who abused this 'trust' were dealt with swiftly and firmly. Prisoners on the whole recognized this and accepted it as 'fair'. However, some complained both that discipline on the units was too lax and that adjudications were too firm:

> There is a high level of reports in here, sometimes nine or ten a day. I think that's because we're operating a local prison system, well, local prison rules in a training environment and sometimes the two are not compatible. They clash a bit, because things like, we have to get them out of bed and get them to court but he wants a shower because the shower is open and we can't. . . . We do have a level of reports made, higher than Birmingham for instance; Birmingham may have three or four a day. (Senior manager)

Assaults and Bullying

The number of assaults on both staff and prisoners at Woodhill was a matter of concern to the senior management team and to staff. In 1993/4 there were 17.7 assaults per 100 of the population at Woodhill (compared with 12.5 at Wolds, which was the average for all public-sector local prisons). One of the factors influencing the high level of assaults may have been the long hours spent out-of-cell. A second factor may have been the presence of the Control Review Committee (CRC) units for disruptive prisoners, where some of the assaults had occurred. A study carried out by the psychology department found that high levels of assaults were concentrated in two of the house-blocks (one remand and one young offender unit); that the majority of assaults in the main prison (excluding the CRC units) took place at the weekends when the availability of activities were less and the prison tended to be more full; and that the majority of the prisoners who assaulted staff (66 per cent) were aged 25 or under. An average of 6.2 assaults were committed each month in the main prison (of which 41 per cent were against prisoners and 59 per cent were against staff), most of these occurring on the landings and during association, although some staff were assaulted in cells and at the servery.

There were slightly different views about the nature and extent of the bullying problem at Woodhill. Forty-five per cent of the staff felt that bullying went on, and a further 38 per cent felt that some did, or that bullying occurred 'on some units' (compared with Wolds, where as many as 81per cent of staff felt that bullying went on and a further 19 per cent said some bullying went on). However, it was felt that the problem was no worse at Woodhill than at any other prison. Many of the staff (and prisoners) felt that there was very little anyone could do to reduce or control it, although a small number felt that less time out-of-cells might reduce it. Most of the bullying was thought to be concentrated on the YP wing and most of those who did report that bullying occurred said that it tended to happen to particular types of prisoner: sex offenders, police informants and debtors. The main reasons for bullying were said to be 'power', 'the nature of the population', 'greed' and 'drugs'.

Prisoners did have an investment in holding on to what they saw as the most positive aspects of the regime (the freedom, the number of hours out-of-cell and the opportunity to exercise a certain amount of choice and responsibility), and so most tried to minimize the level of bullying on their units. There was an 'anti-bullying campaign' being encouraged by management, to increase staff awareness and intervention and to encourage prisoners to refuse to comply with threats or illicit activities. One or two of the prisoners commented that there was less bullying and violence in a prison like Woodhill because 'you live in the open here, you get to know each other, you accept people more and get used to them' (Prisoner).

The Use of Drugs

Eighty-five per cent of the prisoners we interviewed said that drugs were used in Woodhill – slightly lower than the proportion at Wolds (95 per cent) – and that drugs were 'easy' to get. The types of drugs available was a difficult topic to persuade prisoners to talk about openly and honestly during interviews, although some did, and 40 per cent of the prisoners at Woodhill said that heroin was available (compared with 54 per cent at Wolds). Staff were aware of the use of drugs, and were constantly seeking effective ways of minimizing their availability in the prison. Fewer of the staff said there was a 'drugs problem' at Woodhill (69 per cent compared with 91 per cent at Wolds). It was difficult to establish whether the drugs problem was more or less serious than at other local prisons, however, as perceptions varied and the evidence was hard to find:

> A good search will cough up maybe as much as 80 good finds so far in 12 months, but I don't think that means we've got a terrible drugs problem, it means we've got an excellent searching programme. Ten per cent of the people coming through visits are strip searched and sometimes we actually go down there and search every single one. (Senior manager)

The drugs problem was felt to be significant not just in itself but because of the associated violence, bullying, taxing, coercion and theft. Prevention efforts tended to focus on the security aspects of drug prevention and included a thorough searching programme which was carefully monitored, liaison with police specialists, the reporting of incidents, and closed-circuit TV surveillance in visits. Some of the staff wanted to see urine testing, a drug-free unit and the use of sniffer dogs introduced. Staff were also checked at regular intervals – their baggage would be checked and they would be given rub-downs searches. Most of the staff did not want to see closed visits and recognized that this was the threshold at which their security efforts reached 'a dead end'. Provision aimed at helping those who wished to reduce their dependence on drugs included twice weekly visits by outside drugs counselling agencies and the provision of drug awareness courses.

Prisoners did not think there was any greater access to, or use of, drugs in Woodhill than at any other establishment (21 per cent thought there were less, 33 per cent the same and 13 per cent thought there were more), but they did know that cannabis was regularly available and some reported that 'heroin is generally available if you want it. Charlie [cocaine] and pills are too, but they're disgusting'. Prisoners thought drugs came in through visits and prisoners 'coming in from other jails' and 77 per cent thought staff were probably aware of the use of drugs, but that 'it's not so easy to catch, is it?'. Some toleration of marijuana was assumed: 'The staff don't like coming to work when there's no puff. It keeps the lid on the jail' (Prisoner). Prisoners used drugs 'to make their time easier' and 'for the same reasons they use drugs on the out': 'because they're addicted'; for 'escapism'; 'because of boredom and loneliness'. Drugs were exchanged for 'phone cards, or even shared, unlike in many other prisons where they were sold for three to four times the profit available on the streets. Those who had used the counselling services generally thought they were good. Those who had not, felt 'they can't help no-one'. Many felt that more help with drug-related problems should be offered to those who wanted it. Prisoners 'policed' the drugs problem themselves, some deciding that they wanted their unit to be 'clean' and not tolerating hard drug use by other prisoners.

Staff–Prisoner Relationships

One of the distinctive features of the regime at Wolds was the nature of staff–prisoner relationships. As we have described in the previous chapter, the informality and closeness of these relationships did create problems of their own, particularly in the context of a remand prison. Nevertheless, the quality of relationships between staff and prisoners was undoubtedly one of the real successes of the Wolds regime. At Woodhill, the same emphasis was placed by management upon the value of the staff–prisoner relationship and its centrality to the regime. Interestingly, however, fewer prisoners saw these relationships as mostly or very good (52 per cent at Woodhill, compared with 64 per cent at Wolds). Whereas only 5 per cent of prisoners at Wolds described their relationships with staff as 'difficult', 18 per cent did so at Woodhill. These differences are not huge, but they illustrate an important point of principle: that something about the selection, training, management and self-concept of Wolds staff, and their lack of a background of experience in the Prison Service, did indeed facilitate the establishment of very good relationships with prisoners.

Explaining these differences is difficult, although prisoners brought to their relationships with staff at Woodhill 'historical' perceptions about prison officers which may have influenced their judgement. Other explanations include the view expressed by proponents of private-sector involvement in prisons: that the public sector has within it some negative or intransigent staff; or the counter view, held by its opponents, that the private-sector staff are still learning and will inevitably lose some of their enthusiasm to respect, trust and relate to prisoners. Confirmation that good staff–prisoner relationships are by no means simply a matter of private-sector employees ('good') versus public-sector employees ('bad') was indicated by one of our visits to a second privately managed prison, where prisoners were highly critical of staff and their behaviour and were extolling the virtues of Prisoner Officers' Association/public-sector staff by comparison.

However, relationships between prisoners and staff at Woodhill were generally very good. Many of the staff agreed that the best way of maintaining discipline was through good relationships with prisoners based on respect, honesty, consistency and fairness. This could only be achieved through talking, listening and interacting. A high level of good communication led to co-operation, information, support and trust. Many of the staff also thought that clear boundaries were important and commented that prisoners prefer staff to be reasonably firm. Flexibility and support were also identified as significant factors in the maintenance of discipline:

I know that on my wing if the staff I have on are the ones who are too disciplinary or who 'go by the book' then I know it's going to be a bad shift. You need to be flexible. The same goes for higher up management. I know how my day is going to be just looking at my detail. (Senior Officer)

Staff–prisoner relationships were also described as mostly (45 per cent) or very good (35 per cent) by staff at Woodhill – very similar proportions to staff at Wolds (52 per cent and 39 per cent, respectively). Staff were very proud of their positive relationships with prisoners and felt that this was a significant feature of their establishment. Prisoners reflected this in their comments:

Ninety per cent of the officers in here are good officers. They are fair. If you ask them to do something, they usually do it. They treat you right. (Prisoner)

Good communication, involving prisoners in the running of the wings, providing plenty of activities and high staff involvement were all seen as ways of securing 'right relationships' between staff and prisoners. Talking and listening were essential – giving prisoners time. Prisoners appreciated the use of first names, and noticed when staff remembered their names. They commented that staff were 'more helpful than I expected'. Contrasts were drawn with previous experiences in some other establishments, where prisoners had accumulated grievances and become cynical. Staff were described as 'easy going', and 'certainly never violent' at Woodhill.

Prisoners thought that staff suffered far more from boredom than they did, and often called in at their cell door to badger them into games of chess or pool during the evenings. Thirty-two per cent felt that staff were 'not fair' in the application of the rules (no prisoners said this at Wolds). One-third reported having experienced difficulties with staff. However, 59 per cent of the prisoners reported that staff at Woodhill were better than staff at other prisons they had been to. Some prisoners at Woodhill felt that uniforms were not consistent with the Woodhill philosophy and atmosphere, which was not authoritarian. They would have preferred staff in 'something like a sweat shirt, jogging pants and trainers'. A 'good officer' was one who 'didn't have favourites', who was 'approachable', 'impartial', had 'time for you' and was 'genuinely interested'. A good officer 'respects you – as a human being'. Most prisoners reported fairly open relationships with staff, a small group saying that they talked to unit officers regularly and often went to them for help. They reported 'having a laugh' with officers and some reported sharing information fairly readily: 'They tend to be people here – human; you can have conversations with them' (Prisoner). Prisoners did feel on the whole that staff spent much of their time 'mingling' and that they did often rely on good relationships to deal with trouble on the units and maintain order. Many of the prisoners welcomed the fact that staff were young and new, although some complained that they spent all their time in the office and drinking tea.

Almost half of the prisoners were happy with the numbers of staff on the units, although 28 per cent felt there were 'too few' (compared with as many as 51 per cent at Wolds) and a further 8 per cent (14 per cent at Wolds) felt that there were too few in the event of trouble or incidents occurring. Prisoners saw staff as uncertain as to their role, which seemed to be changing from day to day; some were disillusioned and others were highly talented, but there was little staff continuity on the units: 'You can see between 15 and 20 staff on a wing in a week – you don't even know their names' (Prisoner).

Prisoners sensed that staff found their own lack of knowledge about procedures frustrating, and the uncertain boundaries difficult to negotiate. Again, more similarities than differences were found between prisoners' perceptions of Wolds and Woodhill: 'All the staff laugh at Group 4, but these officers know nothing. The regime is great, but it's frustrating' (Prisoner).

To summarize, as at Wolds, most of the prisoners thought Woodhill was better than a typical local prison: 'For the head – it's better for the head – locking up people is no good' (Prisoner). Many commented that 'the novelty wears off' fairly quickly and that 'there is not enough to do here'. They complained that the prison did not have 'a prison atmosphere' and that there was a confusing mixture of freedom and control which they could not adjust to: 'You're out more, but you get nicked for staying in bed!' The closer relationships with staff also had an impact:

> People are paranoid about other people. It's confusing by associating with the staff. Some of them are back-stabbers. If they ask you about your family and that and then you get put on report, it's all too much. I prefer clear lines. (Prisoner)

Fifty-one per cent of prisoners interviewed felt that Woodhill was better than other prisons they had been in, and a further 23 per cent thought it was better in some ways (the corresponding figures for Wolds were 88 per cent and 3 per cent respectively). A small proportion (23 per cent) felt that staff were the main positive feature, but the staff–prisoner relationship was not perfect and was praised more uniformly at Wolds. Forty-four per cent of Woodhill prisoners interviewed identified 'the facilities' as a key feature of the prison which they liked; 26 per cent mentioned 'the atmosphere'; 41 per cent mentioned the hours out-of-cell; and 10 per cent of the prisoners interviewed mentioned all of these things. From our observations, it seemed well managed and a significant improvement on 'typical local prisons' at that time. It also seemed to be safer and more ordered than in the early days at Wolds. But there were new problems associated with the greater freedom of, and better consultation with, prisoners at both establishments. These 'problems of a new era' were expressed to us most powerfully by the staff.

Morale and the Competitive Environment

Generally, morale was described in slightly more favourable terms by staff at Woodhill than by staff at Wolds, with 18 per cent saying that it was good or very good at Woodhill (compared with only 5 per cent at Wolds), but with 57 per cent at Wolds describing morale as poor or very poor, compared with 48 per cent at Woodhill. Most of the staff on the units identified a 'good team spirit' and they compared Woodhill favourably with other new establishments rumoured to be having greater problems. However, 52 per cent of the staff felt that morale was on the decline, as a result of even greater cuts to the budget, accumulating time-off-in-lieu (TOIL), increasing pressures to 'perform' well on Key Performance Indicators and the threat of market-testing. But they had not experienced the 'low' expected by staff as a result of their experiences at other new establishments – usually at around 12–18 months into the life of a new prison:

> My impression is that staff morale has remained quite good throughout. There is a high degree of commitment from staff – particularly in the residential units – they are as good a bet as any, where prisoners are there all day every day – same prisoners, same jobs, same surroundings. . . . We had a battle there early on, because staff were not confronting prisoners with things like cleanliness, procedures and so on . . . they were almost colluding with them. We worked our way through that and my impression is that staff confidence is 'quite good'. (Senior manager)

Morale was very high in the early months, but as several of the staff pointed out, some of this 'buoyancy' was associated with the newness, excitement and opportunity represented by the opening of any new prison. The vast majority of staff reported some feelings of anxiety in their work (93 per cent compared with 96 per cent at Wolds), which they related to high levels of contact with prisoners, uncertainty and management issues. There was an important and frequently expressed sense of anxiety relating to market-testing and contracting-out among members of staff – often older, but also younger staff at the beginning of their careers. Many felt that the security and the benefits of working in the Prison Service were being threatened by competition and market-testing, and they could no longer assume that their jobs were safe. Staff were concerned at the already high use of auxiliaries, who were paid much less than officers and who cost less to recruit and train (a situation which was closely monitored by the Prison Officers' Association, with whom the use of auxiliaries had been negotiated and agreed), and had fears (largely exaggerated) about staff pay and conditions in the private sector. Several of the staff felt that senior management were not sufficiently aware of the strain under which uniformed officers were working, or that if they were aware, they were not making sufficient efforts to support and encourage the staff in what was seen as a time of considerable pressure and uncertainty.

There were also occasional complaints from older staff with many years' service that new shift patterns meant that staff did not see so much of each other. The perceived 'team spirit', associated by them with old Victorian prison landings and long hours of overtime, was no longer built into the job. Staff tended not to feel such a sense of 'ownership' about a particular wing or unit, since they were required to do shifts in different areas of the prison. This meant working with different groups of staff and with different prisoners, who also disliked frequent changes of staff on their units. There was a high number of officers with transfer requests in, which had a negative impact on morale.

There were occasions when we witnessed less than professional attitudes among some staff, thereby confirming reports by prisoners that some staff on some of the units had a 'bad attitude'. We frequently heard staff talking about the domestic and financial problems of officers who were having to work in parts of the country where they did not have their homes, reflecting low morale, resentment and a lack of interest in their work which was also noticed and commented on by prisoners. Sometimes prisoners knew enough about the officers' domestic circumstances to see that there were reasons for instances of off-hand behaviour but more usually, they simply assumed that the officers concerned were indifferent. Occasionally, staff who were normally very keen and responsive adopted the 'low motivation' and unresponsive attitude of the 'disaffected' group present on the unit at the time.

Many acknowledged that their perceived problems and dissatisfactions were not local but national problems of 'direction', 'pressure' and 'increasing expectations'. The contradictory pressures of meeting 'performance measures' and the need to run the prison carefully occasionally irritated staff:

> Prisoners are complaining about having to be locked up for the whole morning tomorrow for a staff meeting to take place. The meeting is about whether they should extend prisoners time out-of-cell by 15 minutes. We're locking them up for hours to discuss whether they should be out

longer when they can't even find enough to occupy the time they're out at the moment. (Officer)

There was a feeling expressed by some staff that 'everything is pro-inmate' and that more should be expected of prisoners in return. Many of the staff felt that morale could be improved by an increase in staffing levels, a settling-in period, local recruitment and better training. Staff particularly felt the need for training where they were being asked to 'tighten up'. Many of the problems they experienced were put down to the opening of a new establishment, which presented them with 'unique' difficulties which only experience would resolve.

The rate of sick leave at Woodhill was slightly higher than the national average (3.68 per cent of effective time), at 4.76 per cent. Sick leave was carefully monitored by the senior management group and staff on long-term sick leave were encouraged to return to work as soon as they could. Officers were conscious of the attention paid to sick leave – indeed, they received 'warnings' if they exceeded the average and those whose sick leave was above average were mon-itored for three months, whatever the cause of their absence. This sensitivity was magnified for the high numbers of staff still in their probationary year because of the unfavourable reports they were likely to receive if they did not keep their absence to an absolute minimum, and a system was being introduced to assess whether other significant trends in staff sick leave were identifiable (for example, particular shifts or weekends). On the units, staff had a mixed attitude towards the establishment's sick policy ('This nick hates sick'). One or two of the younger staff felt that whilst they were doing their probationary year, they could not take time off for any reason, but once they were through this, they would take sick for things they would not 'get away with' in their current position.

Financial Management

There is a popular assumption and common fear among public-sector employees and opponents of privatization that private prisons will economize to the detriment of the regime offered. It was therefore interesting to observe the considerable emphasis on financial matters at public-sector Woodhill. Indeed, in many ways, it was more similar to what might have been expected of a contracted-out prison, with its stringent attention to budgets and financial planning, than to a typical pre-1990s local prison, before the introduction of agency status, strategic planning and the threat of market-testing. At Woodhill, the budget was negotiated between the Governor and the Area Manager, in consultation with Headquarters, and financial matters were the responsibility of the Head of Finance, who played a crucial role in the senior management team and held considerable power and influence in the establishment. Fifty-six per cent of the staff felt that financial matters were 'very important' in the running of Woodhill (compared with only 36 per cent at Wolds). A further 26 per cent felt that they were 'very important, but should be less so' (compared with 21 per cent at Wolds).

There was considerable recognition that the threat of market-testing had concentrated the minds of all those who had responsibility for financial matters to reduce unit costs and improve overall efficiency at Woodhill and the traditional resistance to change and adherence to custom was unable to survive in this climate. Senior managers knew that poor performance might lead to market-testing, whereas good performance would be more likely to ensure their survival. Although staff recognized that financial management had to improve, and that this was realistic and important, there were, however, some reservations:

> How far are they going to go before they say, hang on a minute, we've stretched this piece of elastic too far, it's going to break? (Principal Officer)

> I've never known so much emphasis on finance. Its something again that I think we are being expected to learn without much guidance, training, and we perhaps don't have . . . a feel of it yet. (Principal Officer)

Devolution was seen by management as increasing Principal Officer interest and ability in spending matters and as introducing an element of healthy competition across the units. House units had therefore been given their own budgets for public utilities and domestic items, and were encouraged to be as economical as possible. Thus, a careful eye was kept on electricity use, telephone bills, photocopying, expense claims, prisoners' pay and all other aspects of expenditure. The sense of competition between the house units spurred many staff to monitor their own use of resources very effectively and although it was not necessarily effective in securing good relations between the different units, it did result in serious questions being asked about all aspects of expenditure, which would not have been asked without this kind of monitoring. It also led to improved practices and responsibility:

> Certainly POs adapted very quickly to this exercise. . . . The other big thing I found is that up to March of '93, I was going to morning meetings and probably at least once a fortnight a PO would stand up and say how short they were of something like washing powder or detergent liquid and we never gave them enough. Since they had a budget, there hasn't been one complaint. We've actually had a lesson to learn as well because one of the things when you actually give people a budget is that you have to let them decide what to spend the budget on, and this was a lesson not just

for myself but for the staff. . . . It was important that they actually had that feeling of being in control, that it was their money and they could spend it as they wished. (Senior manager)

The senior management team were proud of the progress they had made in this direction:

I think we've gone further down that road than many places that many of the staff who came here have been used to before – devolving budgets to Principal Officers, they have a budget to run their wings with – I can honestly say that none of them ever had that before they came to Woodhill – and being responsible for doing that and at the end of the year recognizing that if they've overspent, they're going to have a problem. (Governor grade)

Financial considerations were seen as 'very dominant' by most of the staff in the day-to-day running of the establishment. Many felt this was appropriate, but others thought higher priorities were being overlooked in efforts to control expenditure, and staff at all levels lacked experience and training in aspects of financial management, since 'good housekeeping' was not seen as one of the Prison Service's traditional skills.

Pressures on Staff

Among the main problems and concerns raised by staff were the volume of work ('going home at half past eight at night instead of five o'clock') and, most recently, the problem of overcrowding and the faster turnover of prisoners. At the time when our fieldwork ended (April 1994), Woodhill was in an overcrowding situation, whereby prisoners were constantly being received and discharged in an effort to keep numbers below the CNA (Certified Normal Accommodation). This created enormous amounts of additional work for the Observation, Classification and Allocation (OCA) unit and for the staff with responsibility for population management at Woodhill. The need to transfer prisoners also created disciplinary and other problems, as many prisoners did not want to leave. Some had to go from the Segregation Unit under Control and Restraint:

Internally, the problems for us are the increase in the number of people being committed to us by the courts, so that eventually, over the past couple of weeks, as I said in the meeting, we're a bit like a canoe that's got lots of holes in it and we're bailing out as quickly as we can and we've achieved some equilibrium, but I think that's maybe going to be a threat to us in the longer term. (Senior manager)

There had been some feeling from staff that the promises made to them – for example in respect of training – had not been delivered, and yet they were giving everything to the job and were continually expected to give more. The pressure was unrelenting. One or two of the staff commented that the Woodhill regime was over-ambitious, and that they were being asked to deliver a training (or even dispersal) prison regime in a local prison but with fewer staff: 'Main problems? Getting the staff numbers down and achieving the same results' (Officer).

Some felt that the job was changing and that the notion of 'a career in the Prison Service' was being eroded by short-term contracts, the threat of competition and the removal of the traditional 'perks' of the job. The effect of this on staff, where it was felt, was demotivating and demoralizing, and when staff were unhappy, the treatment of prisoners tended to suffer. Despite these problems, most of the staff felt that their expectations of working in Woodhill had been fulfilled: 'It has far outweighed anything I expected it to be. I had no idea you could do things like this in a local prison' (Senior manager).

The achievements and strategic plans of the Woodhill management team, discussed with senior management towards the end of our fieldwork period, were unrecognizable compared to most public-sector local prisons of the 1980s and before. We were constantly aware of the similarities between the innovative, business-like and dynamic way in which Woodhill was being managed, and what we had seen in the private sector, at Wolds. Management worked hard on presenting a 'positive self-image' which provided a sense of focus and leadership with which staff identified:

> The major thing for me is that Woodhill has proved that 'you can do it', 'if you want to do it, you can do it'. What we've proved is that with the right motivation, the right resources, a good degree of forward looking, planning, and a good degree of wanting to do it, you can do it. (Senior manager)

What we were unable ultimately to judge was the all-important question of whether Woodhill would have been such an impressive establishment without the threat of market-testing and the incentive provided by the apparent initial successes of Group 4 in the management of Wolds. Other unanswered questions included how to address the particular needs of remand prisoners, whose circumstances may not have been met by the Woodhill regime, and how to maintain the initial momentum once the particularly powerful blend of personalities, present at Woodhill at the time of our research, began to move on.

'Good Practice' in Prisons – Private or Public Monopoly?

Our detailed comparison between the privately managed Wolds Remand Prison and the publicly managed Woodhill Prison reveals no simple balance sheet of good/bad practice or high/low-quality provision according to the private/public distinction. The realities of prison management and regime delivery are far more complex than proponents on either side of the debate may wish to acknowledge. The complexity of this picture receives further support from evidence from the four other prisons in our study, comprising the second contracted-out prison in the UK, Blakenhurst (for sentenced prisoners, opened a year later than Wolds, in May 1993), and three new public-sector local/remand prisons, namely Belmarsh, Bullingdon, and Highdown (opened between April 1991 and September 1992).

Drawing on all this evidence, we shall now attempt to summarize the main conclusions that emerged from the comparative element of our research, in terms of three central objectives underlying the introduction of contracted-out prisons: 1 to encourage innovation in management; 2 the constructive use of increased time out-of-cell; and 3 the maintenance of high standards of provision for prisoners.

Managing to Innovate

One of the primary official aims and justifications put forward by the government for the introduction of market-testing and the contracting-out of the management of prisons in the UK was that it would encourage greater innovation in regime delivery in a Prison Service that had become rather stagnant and slow to react to the constantly changing penal and political environments. The aims and objectives of Wolds Remand Prison have been outlined above (see Chapter 4), and focused around the central concept of 'direct supervision'. It seems likely that the radical new philosophy proposed by Group 4, and the innovative regime that flowed from it – based on principles such as the presumption of innocence, normalization and control by relationships – were major factors in the success of their bid for the Wolds contract. For a variety of reasons, including particularly the contrast between the prisoners' criminal sophistication and previous penal experience, and the relative lack of experience of 95 per cent of the staff at Wolds, there were some compromises with the original ideals of the notion of direct supervision and the 'normalization' of the prison regime. Nevertheless, it can be claimed with some justification that the regime that emerged was still quite innovative and successful, especially considering the relatively low staffing levels that obtained at Wolds.

It would appear that one of the main factors that contributed towards the successful innovation at Wolds was the personal role of the first Director, who recruited an initial team of senior managers who shared his goals and enthusiasm, and were able to communicate these to the newly recruited staff. A distinctive 'Wolds ethos' of treating prisoners with respect was established from the outset, and although this received some initial set-backs in the form of occasional displays of non-co-operation and a few individual incidents of indiscipline in the first year, staff–prisoner relationships at Wolds nevertheless remained generally very positive throughout the period of our research.

Perhaps one of the most significant lessons to emerge from our comparative analysis of Wolds, Woodhill, and the four other recently opened local prisons was that there was evidence of similar or greater innovation by prison management in some of the public-sector prisons. The aims, objectives and achievements of Woodhill have been described at some length in this chapter; and the prison subsequently received an unqualified and rare accolade from HM Chief Inspector of Prisons, following an inspection in 1993:

> Woodhill is a credit to those involved in its management. The reasons why this prison has opened successfully and quickly established a first-class regime should be analysed and the lessons applied to other establishments. (HM Chief Inspector of Prisons, 1994: para 7.11)

Among the contributory factors and characteristics of the highly successful Woodhill regime was a detailed mission statement of its purposes, values and commitment, implemented by a Governor and senior management team imbued with the commitment and drive to deliver a 'high-quality service', and able to communicate their enthusiasm and dedication to the staff group as a whole. In fact, and perhaps not very surprisingly, the features we identified at Woodhill as conducive to successful innovation in the opening of that new local prison were very similar to those we found at Wolds. However, Woodhill was a far larger and more complex prison, performing a number of very different functions, and it had been able to recruit a core of experienced staff at middle-management level for the residential units, in a way that was not possible for Wolds.

Other examples of successful innovation and 'good practice' were found in several of the prisons we visited, confirming that there is no necessary relationship between innovation in regime delivery and contracted-out status of management, but not of course ruling out the possibility that the latter may act as a powerful spur to encouraging innovation in the public sector. Thus, in addition to the innovative achievements of Woodhill management, we were also particularly impressed by what we saw and learned about Highdown Prison from prisoners and staff. A unique feature of this prison was the way in which remand prisoners were generally fully integrated with convicted/sentenced prisoners throughout the prison. Although Highdown had no truly distinctive philosophy of its own equivalent to 'direct supervision' at Wolds, nor such fully elaborated documentation on its aims and objectives as at Woodhill, the Governor had drawn up a statement of 'The Principles of Population Management in Prisons and their application at Highdown', setting out eight key principles of the regime, including full recognition of prisoners' rights, treating them with respect and justice – as well as 'value for money'.

Once again, the features that were associated with and, in our view, largely responsible for the high quality of the regime and aspirations at Highdown included a Governor and experienced senior managers who were fully committed to delivering both the letter and the spirit of their mission statement and operational principles. Their particular style of management impressed us – as it did most of the prisoners and staff with whom we talked – combining certain traditional features (such as the Governor regularly 'walking the job') with a determination to deliver up to 12 hours time out-of-cell, with opportunities to take advantage of a good range of work and educational facilities. In a similar way to all the prisons in our research, Highdown opened with as many as three-quarters of its staff being new entrants, resulting in some initial uncertainties and lack of confidence, but at the same time enabling the positive principles and good practices of the management team to influence the way they viewed their job and treated prisoners from the outset.

There can be no doubt, therefore, that innovation in regime delivery plus high-quality, committed and effective senior management are to be found as much in new public-sector prisons as in those where the management has been contracted-out to private companies.

Constructive Use of Time Out-of-cell

A particular feature of Wolds, and the other contracted-out prisons, was the very detailed regime-delivery specifications written into their operating contracts. In particular, Group 4 was required to provide 15 hours out-of-cell for all prisoners at Wolds, of whom the large majority were unconvicted remands who could not therefore be required to work or otherwise engage in purposeful activity. This was the 'contractual challenge' taken up by Group 4, as the successful bidder for the first contracted-out prison in the country, housing a particularly volatile category of prisoner for whom the provision of time out-of-cell and purposeful activities elsewhere in the public-sector prisons at that time was probably lower than for any other prisoners. There were no direct precedents at that time for this level of regime specification for untried prisoners anywhere in the UK prison system.

However, it was significant that at around the same time as the first tender documents for Wolds were being drawn up by the Remands Contracts Unit, and the first contracts signed, the Prison Service was putting the final touches to its *Model Regime for Local Prisons and Remand Centres* (HM Prison Service,1992b). Although the specifications set out in the Model Regime document did not have the same binding authority as the contracts for Wolds and subsequent contracted-out prisons, all the new public-sector prisons in our study were aware of what they would be expected to deliver, for example in terms of time out-of-cell, purposeful activities for all prisoners, etc. In addition, the perceived threat of market-testing served as a powerful incentive to management and staff to equal or exceed the targets of regime delivery written into the Wolds contract, with the 'high cost'/'low performance' prisons feeling particularly vulnerable.

As a result of these various pressures, three of the public-sector prisons (Belmarsh, Bullingdon and Highdown) provided 10 to 11 hours out-of-cell for all prisoners at the time of our study, Woodhill provided 12 hours, compared with Blakenhurst's 13 hours and Wolds' 14.5 hours out-of-cell. However, the question of whether simply maximizing prisoners' time out-of-cell is an unqualified benefit for a prison depends on a rather complex and interrelated set of factors, including the provision and take-up of activities, the level of boredom experienced by prisoners, the successful maintenance of order and the prevention of abuse by prisoners of so much free association time.

The task of usefully occupying the time of prisoners (whether sentenced, convicted or untried) who are unlocked for over 10 hours a day during the week, and only slightly less at weekends, was probably the most difficult challenge faced not only by Wolds but by all the other prisons we studied. Evidence of various kinds, both qualitative and quantitative, was collected showing the relative success of the different prisons in addressing this central problem. Any direct comparison between Wolds and the other prisons on this set of factors is not strictly equitable, in view of the fact that (at the time of our research) Wolds held no sentenced prisoners. In contrast, the proportion of remand prisoners at the other prisons varied from around 10 per cent at Woodhill, and 35–40 per cent at Bullingdon, Highdown and Blakenhurst, to approximately 60 per cent at Belmarsh.

Prisoners and staff at all the prisons we studied said there were quite high levels of boredom among prisoners, unlocked for long hours every day, with variable take-up of the activities on offer. As indicated above, one-third of prisoners interviewed at Wolds said that they often or frequently felt bored, compared with almost two-thirds who admitted to this level of boredom at Woodhill. Over one-quarter (26 per cent) of Woodhill prisoners said they felt bored all the time, compared with only 14 per cent at Wolds.

It seems, therefore, that no clear conclusions can be reached or straightforward comparisons made between Wolds and the other prisons in terms of the implications for management or the use made by prisoners of the long time out-of-cell, required by contract or local targets. All prisons were striving to find ways of increasing the availability of workshop places (handicapped sometimes by no workshops having been built when the prison opened) and of devising meaningful incentives to encourage prisoners to take up whatever opportunities for purposeful activities were on offer. New incentive or compact schemes had been introduced at both Wolds and Woodhill during the course of our research, and have subsequently been developed further both at Wolds and very many public-sector prisons in 1995–6 (see HM Prison Service, 1995; Liebling and Bosworth, 1995; Liebling et al., 1997).

The extent to which the extended hours out-of-cell for all prisoners, particularly when combined with sometimes quite low levels of purposeful activities, contributed to problems of the maintenance of order and discipline in the prisons must remain a largely open question, although it is clear that some prisoners found this difficult to cope with. The news media quickly seized upon allegations of the widespread availability of drugs at Wolds in the early months after it opened, but prisoners and staff at all the prisons we studied admitted that drugs were available to a similar extent in almost every establishment whether in the public or in the private sector.

Prisoners' Perspectives and 'Customer Satisfaction'

Apart from believing that contracting-out the management of local and remand prisons would introduce significantly more innovation into regime delivery, the government also expected that staff–prisoner relationships would be improved by virtue of the fact that the vast majority of staff in private-sector prisons would not be 'tainted' by the past history or stereotypes of HM Prison Service. However, an element of this situation that was almost certainly underestimated was the effect on staff–prisoner relationships of the generally far greater prison experience and criminal sophistication of the majority of the prisoners (including those on remand), compared with the almost totally inexperienced (in prison terms) staff recruited by private companies to work in the first contracted-out prisons.

As we have shown, prisoners at Wolds rated Group 4 staff rather more highly than prison officers in the public sector. The main reasons for these good staff–prisoner relationships were that staff were seen to treat prisoners with respect; they talked to them and mixed with them rather more than at Woodhill. Significantly more prisoners found officers helpful at Wolds (70 per cent compared with 41 per cent at Woodhill), especially with regard to practical matters, and more than twice the proportion of prisoners at Wolds felt that officers treated them fairly according to the rules than at Woodhill (84 per cent compared with 41 per cent).

The admissions procedures at Wolds made a particularly positive impact upon prisoners – and also received special praise from HM Chief Inspector of Prisons in his Annual Report for 1993/4. Staff at Wolds treated new prisoners humanely and with respect on admission – although, in this particular aspect, prisoners at Woodhill were almost equally impressed by their initial treatment by reception staff.

Confirmation that good staff–prisoner relationships are not simply a matter of private-sector employees ('good') versus public-sector employees/Prison Officers' Association ('bad') was indicated by our experience of talking to prisoners at the other contracted-out prison in our study. The group of prisoners whom we met during our short visit were very critical of the inconsistency and the apparently 'petty bureaucratic decision-making' and behaviour of the staff, and were therefore – somewhat uncharacteristically in our experience – extolling the virtues of 'POA staff', thereby graphically warning against any simple generalizations about the nature of staff–prisoner relationships in private-sector versus public-sector prisons.

All the prisons in our research provided prisoners with markedly superior conditions and facilities to those which they had experienced elsewhere in the prison system. At one level, therefore, there was really very little point in asking prisoners how conditions in Wolds, or Belmarsh, for instance, compared with conditions in other prisons where they had been remanded – as these other prisons would usually have been old Victorian locals, such as Leeds, Hull, Pentonville or Brixton, which clearly could not be expected to compete on the same terms.

Interestingly, however, when prisoners at Wolds were asked how conditions there compared with other prisons in which they had been, their responses were generally more favourable than those of prisoners at Woodhill when asked the same questions. Almost three-fifths (58 per cent) of prisoners at Wolds said it was better than other prisons on remand, compared with just over two-fifths (41 per cent) at Woodhill. Similarly, 54 per cent of prisoners at Wolds said it was better than other prisons in which they had served sentences, compared with 36 per cent at Woodhill. Almost three-quarters (72 per cent) said living conditions were good at Wolds, compared with just under three-fifths (59 per cent) at Woodhill. The food at Wolds was rated far higher than at Woodhill, where almost two-thirds (64 per cent) of the prisoners thought it was bad, compared with only 5 per cent of prisoners at Wolds – where staff had the same food!

Prisoners' overall judgement on whether Wolds was better than the other (public-sector) prisons in which they had been was unequivocal: only 1 out of 43 prisoners interviewed said it was not – whereas 7 out of 39 prisoners interviewed at Woodhill said that it was not better than other prisons. When asked to give reasons why they felt it was a better prison, over half (56 per cent) of Wolds prisoners said it was because of the staff (compared with 23 per cent at Woodhill), over half said it had a better atmosphere (compared with 26 per cent at Woodhill), and over half (56 per cent) of Wolds prisoners said it was because of the better facilities (compared with 44 per cent at Woodhill). It came as little surprise, therefore, that as an overall measure of 'customer satisfaction' 58 per cent of prisoners at Wolds were in favour of 'private prisons', with almost half saying that all prisons should be contracted-out!

Conclusions: Wolds in Context

Having reviewed the findings of our evaluation of Wolds Remand Prison in the broader context of the experience of five other new public-sector and private-sector local prisons, the overall 'balance sheet' allows few simple conclusions about the advantages or disadvantages of private-sector compared to public-sector prison management.

The achievements of Group 4 at Wolds cannot be denied. An innovative regime was introduced for remand prisoners, unlocked for around 14 hours a day, in living conditions and with facilities that were among the best to be found anywhere in the public or private sectors at that time. Although there were some subsequent modifications to the original aspirations of the Wolds' philosophy, nevertheless most prisoners recognized the quality of what was offered at Wolds and rated staff there rather more highly than those in the public sector.

Whilst fully acknowledging what has been achieved at Wolds – initially in the face of considerable hostility from many different quarters – it must be repeated that similar and, some might argue, better achievements are to be found in some new public-sector local prisons, showing that the private sector has no exclusive claim on innovation or ability to deliver high-quality regimes to prisoners.

There is, therefore, little evidence that Wolds' achievements were directly or exclusively related to its contracted-out status.

Prisoners' perceptions of the 'quality of life' at Wolds were generally very favourable, especially with regard to staff–prisoner relationships and the way they were treated by staff. However, there is evidence, both anecdotal and officially recorded, that, particularly in the first 12 months after opening, the level of bullying and assaults by prisoners on other prisoners was considerably higher than that experienced by new prisons in the public sector, which allowed similar (although not quite as long) time out-of-cell. Similarly, evidence on the availability of drugs – linked both to the open visits arrangements and the degree of free association on the units – whilst not demonstrably very much greater than in some of the other prisons we studied, raises question about whether an appropriate balance between supervision, order and prisoner freedom was achieved at that time. Although Wolds has so far experienced no major breakdown of order, there are still some issues surrounding discipline and control in contracted-out prisons that need careful monitoring – related to regime factors, staffing levels and staff training/experience.

The actual and potential cost in relation to staff probably caused us the greatest concern with regard to the operation of Wolds. Group 4 recruited over 95 per cent of its staff from people with no experience of prisons or prisoners. This was a much higher proportion of new and inexperienced staff than at any of the new public-sector prisons surveyed, with a particular 'experience gap' at the level of middle managers on residential units. The fact that Wolds staff achieved what they did despite this lack of previous prison experience perhaps, at one level, adds further credit to their achievements. At another level, however, it shows that contracted-out prisons tend to be at a distinct disadvantage in staff recruitment terms, compared to their counterparts in the public sector, and that the responsibilities of training, supporting and developing staff to work in the private sector may be too difficult for them to fulfil successfully within their current operating constraints. Thus, from the staff perspective, the achievements of Wolds and other private-sector prisons may be at the cost of higher levels of stress and greater job insecurity for many of those recruited to work in them.

6

Legitimacy and Consent: Ethical Issues and Contracting-out

In the often heated debate about contracting-out, perhaps the most frequent attacks levelled by its opponents are against the failure of contracted-out prisons to achieve the kind of savings which they were supposed to offer, and the perceived immorality of introducing both the dynamics and the ethics of the market place into punishment. The first criticism, which is primarily instrumental, is open to close empirical scrutiny and although the evidence currently available is inconclusive, and there is frequent disagreement about the costing parameters which should be used in any attempt to clarify the issue, the dimensions of the debate are nonetheless relatively transparent.

The second criticism – that 'punishment for profit' is morally offensive – is, however, often taken to be axiomatic. This assertion is therefore too often presented as a proposition which is obvious to, and unproblematic for, all 'right-minded' people, without any attempt to consider more carefully the moral and ethical issues raised or the way in which these are defined and constituted. The research on which this book is based, however, points to the need for a more careful consideration of these issues. Why do staff at Wolds have few moral qualms about working in a contracted-out prison? Is it solely because of self-interest? Why do prisoners have so few objections to being supervised by staff wearing Group 4 uniforms and insignia, as opposed to those of HM Prison Service? Or are their views, by virtue of their status as prisoners (albeit remand prisoners who are not in custody for the purpose of punishment), somehow less valid than other citizens, less worthy of consideration? These questions raise important issues which must be explored if we are to move beyond taken-for-granted assumptions and high rhetoric to a fuller understanding of this complex but key dimension of the contracting-out debate.

In order to set the scene for an exploratory discussion of some of the issues relating to the ethics and legitimacy of contracting-out prisons, we shall start by briefly reviewing some of the empirical findings of our research which provide important benchmarks for this discussion, drawing primarily upon the experience and views of prisoners at Wolds.

Privatization, Legitimacy and Prisoners' Experience

A fairly clear picture emerged from our research (see Chapters 4 and 5), showing that the majority of prisoners in Wolds rated the prison highly, even in comparison with prisoners' experience of the very high standards of new public-sector prisons such as Woodhill – not only in terms of its physical conditions, time out-of-cell, facilities on offer, visiting arrangements and so on, but perhaps especially with regard to staff–prisoner relationships. When asked the direct question 'Do you think Wolds is better than a state prison?' almost four out of five prisoners (79 per cent) answered in the affirmative. Similarly, almost six out of ten prisoners at Wolds (58 per cent) were unreservedly in favour of prisons being run by private companies, compared with less than one in five (18 per cent) of Woodhill prisoners. Furthermore, half of the prisoners interviewed at Wolds thought that it would be better to have all prisons contracted-out to the private sector, thus serving as persuasive testimony that, whatever ethical or principled reservations they might have, their experience at Wolds left most of them with few fundamental doubts about the practical benefits to prisoners arising from this first privately managed prison. To repeat what we have said earlier, it was the conditions in which they had to live and the way in which they were treated that concerned prisoners rather than who was running the prison.

Among the key aspects of prisoners' experience at Wolds (as indeed at any prison) likely to influence their overall perceptions and judgement of the 'legitimacy' of a prison being managed by a private company – and, therefore, the extent to which they are likely to accord their qualified consent to what is inherently and inevitably a coercive experience – we would identify the quality of staff–prisoner relationships, fairness in the application of rules, and the successful maintenance of order. On virtually all of these criteria, our observations and interviews at Wolds confirmed the well-grounded nature of prisoners' favourable attitudes towards Wolds – particularly bearing in mind that 84 per cent of those interviewed had been in prison before (including 30 per cent five or more times). Over 70 per cent of prisoners found staff at Wolds helpful, with almost three-quarters (74 per cent) saying that they thought Wolds staff were better than at other (public-sector) prisons, especially in the way most of them treated prisoners as people, rather than as numbers (or 'animals'), and afforded them respect.

Closely related to (and undoubtedly affecting) their general views about Group 4 staff at Wolds, over 8 out of 10 prisoners interviewed (84 per cent) said that Unit Supervisors treated prisoners fairly when applying the prison rules (compared with only 4 out of 10 prisoners at Woodhill, who felt that prison officers there applied the rules fairly). Partly as a result of this, when asked what they thought of the disciplinary system at Wolds, 38 per cent of those who answered this question said they thought it was fair (24 per cent thought it unfair), compared with only 20 per cent of prisoners at Woodhill, who thought the disciplinary system there was fair and 32 per cent who thought it was unfair.

At an even more practical level, a key issue for prisoners and staff at any prison is the extent to which order is maintained – whether by virtue of restricted opportunities for disorder (such as fewer hours unlocked), the quality of staff–prisoner relationships, or the formal (and informal) disciplinary systems in operation. Despite the attraction of 'disorder', or lack of control, to those prisoners who might wish to take advantage of the situation to abuse and exert power over the more vulnerable prisoners, the majority of prisoners prefer an 'ordered' environment in which to serve out their sentence or time on remand, rather than the dangerousness and unpredictability of a prison that is under the control of a minority of fellow prisoners. If it were to be their experience that privately managed prisons are more liable to be 'out of control', then this would be a major factor leading prisoners to challenge the legitimacy and/or withdraw their 'consent' from those prisons. In fact, from the evidence of our research, the levels of perceived safety in Wolds (for both prisoners and staff) were quite comparable with those experienced in Woodhill: 60 per cent of prisoners felt safe at Wolds, as did 54 per cent at Woodhill. However, 9 of the 43 prisoners interviewed at Wolds had been assaulted there, compared to only 3 of the 39 prisoners at Woodhill. Similarly, although 68 per cent of staff interviewed at Wolds felt at least some concern for their personal safety at work, so did 76 per cent of staff at Woodhill.

Eighty per cent of staff at Wolds admitted that there was bullying among prisoners, whereas only 45 per cent of Woodhill staff said that it occurred there. Although the availability of drugs in any prison is a rather more indirect measure of 'disorder' than the rate of assaults upon prisoners and staff, it certainly indicates something about the degree of effective surveillance – both on the units and, especially, during visits – and thereby the general extent to which prisoners exert some control over the conditions of their custody. Unfortunately, there are no precise data on which to base accurate estimates of the availability of illegal drugs in any prison. Eighty-one per cent of prisoners interviewed at Wolds said that drugs were available in the prison, and 65 per cent said they were easy to obtain. At Woodhill also, 87 per cent said drugs were available, with 51 per cent saying that they were easy to obtain. Seventy per cent of staff at Wolds said they thought that drugs were a problem there (without, of course, having any knowledge or experience of the extent of drugs in other prisons), whereas, only 35 per cent of staff at Woodhill said that drugs were a particular problem there.

It does seem, therefore, that from the prisoners' perspective of life at Wolds Remand Prison, there were few grounds for them to challenge or indeed wish to challenge the 'legitimacy', on a practical day-to-day level, of how they were being treated or by whom the prison was managed. However, most of the arguments about the ethics and legitimacy of contracting-out the management of prisons are not usually conducted at this rather mundane level, but at higher, more sophisticated levels of discourse. It is to some of these arguments that we shall now turn our attention, in the hope, *inter alia*, of being able to relate the various levels of argument to one another, and at the same time trying to draw out some of the implications of this more philosophical debate for interpreting the experience of prisoners and regime delivery at privatized prisons.

Moving the Goal Posts?

How we define what constitutes moral probity and ethical acceptability, and for whom, are clearly of central importance in terms of making a moral judgement about the rights and wrongs of contracting-out. This is not any easy task, however, for as we have argued elsewhere, 'any attempt to reach firm conclusions about such issues solely on the basis of empirical research such as this is fraught with difficulties' (Bottomley et al., 1997: 49). As Lacey argues:

> It is all too easy to allow definition to serve a covert normative function, to represent just those practices which we want to justify. To the extent that we do so, we risk treating the justifiability of the described practices as a fixed intuition, not subject to substantial modification in a process of reflective equilibrium. (Lacey, 1988: 4)

This process is evident on both sides of what appears to be an almost unbridgeable divide between the proponents and the opponents of contracting-out. In general, those who favour it appear unwilling to move beyond a narrow ideological and economic justification based on the perceived merits of the introduction of market forces into public-sector organizations, whilst opponents seem equally unwilling to question the assumption that prisons are so central to the apparatus of the state that their administration must remain unequivocally and directly in the hands of the state.

As we have argued in previous chapters, however, both positions have historically been accorded legitimacy in Britain at different times and neither reflects a self-evident and self-sustaining philosophy which therefore requires no defence against change. Indeed, it is stating the obvious to point out that the debate itself is a product of the pressures for change and understanding these must therefore be an important part of any attempt to determine the parameters of the moral debate.

A number of these pressures, which have been operating at a more general political, economic and social level, have already been considered in Chapter 3. In addition to and as a result of these, however, there have been some important changes, none of which is unique to the UK (see Chapter 1), which have made it possible for some to question the *status quo* concerning the role of the state and whether the goal posts are currently in the best or the only position. In a valuable analysis of these, Bottoms (1995) has argued that changes in penal policy and sentencing in different countries can be understood in terms of three main conceptual developments – just deserts/human rights, managerialism, and 'the community' – which he locates in the context of theories concerning the development of modernity.

As part of this general process, he argues that one of the particular consequences of the development of the just deserts/human rights perspective is that:

> In prisons, too, in many jurisdictions the prisoner is now regarded, to a much greater extent than thirty or forty years ago, as a person with rights . . . this increasingly influential conception of prisoners, and of defendants facing sentence, as *people with rights*, of course incorporates, as a dominant conceptual influence, the liberal individualism of the eighteenth century Enlightenment. (Bottoms, 1995: 8–9; original emphasis)[1]

It is also clear, according to Bottoms, that 'managerialism has a consumerist dimension' (1995: 18), reflected in the Citizens Charter and related developments. The growth of managerialism, which was to effect such far-reaching changes in public-sector organizations in the UK, therefore arguably also helped to create an environment in which the drive to improve conditions for remand prisoners in particular became increasingly credible. Thus, somewhat ironically perhaps, the libertarian perspectives of Thatcherism contributed to a process of change which appears to be inimical to the emphasis on punishment, control and the curtailment of the rights of offenders, and on increasing security and austerity in prisons, which has been evident in recent Conservative penal policy and reflects a view that when people offend, thereby breaching the social contract, they forgo the rights of citizenship.

In addition, in considering the growth of managerialism, and drawing on Simon's (1988) analysis of the spread of actuarial practices as part of this, Bottoms argues that 'the actuarial tendency of managerialism does tend to produce a predilection – often an unthinking one – in favour of instrumentalism' (1995: 20) and thereby to weaken moral or other arguments. Thus:

> . . . once one has adopted a version of consumerist managerialism in which 'efficient and effective service delivery' is a key concept, then it seems a morally neutral question to ask whether such service delivery would be more efficiently and effectively achieved by private contractors or by public bodies. (Bottoms, 1995: 44, note 24)

In a complementary analysis, Feeley and Simon argue that what they call the 'new penology'[2] 'is neither about punishing nor rehabilitating individuals, it is about identifying and *managing* unruly groups' (Feeley and Simon, 1992: 455; emphasis added).

In such a context, therefore, it has become possible to undermine or negate the prevailing moral consensus about the role of the state in managing prisons by giving increasing weight both to issues of cost-effectiveness and the management of prisoners. Given that the remand population is regarded as potentially the most volatile group in the prison system and that, as Windlesham and others have argued, they should also be regarded as a special category, this aspect of managerialism and the 'new penology' has buttressed the just deserts/ human rights arguments about remand conditions in particular, but also about prison conditions more generally.

Power and Legitimacy

The issue of prison conditions has therefore become one of increasing significance in terms of the functioning of the prison system, not only because of the changing context outlined above but also, particularly since the riots at Strangeways and other prisons in April 1990, for operational reasons. Apart from the many valuable detailed recommendations contained in the Woolf Report (Woolf, 1991), its explicit focus on the contribution to the riots of prisoners' grievances and their sense of injustice about the conditions of their confinement, and the implicit emphasis on the importance of legitimacy in the operation of the prison system, has opened up an important theoretical perspective and discourse concerning power and legitimacy in prisons, which is central to understanding the moral and ethical dimensions of the debate about the contracting-out of prisons. As Carrabine argues, 'if the prison violates certain standards then the legitimacy of the institution and the penal system are called into question' (Carrabine, 1995: 8).

The concept of legitimacy – where power is acquired and exercised according to justifiable rules and with evidence of consent – has recently been the subject of renewed interest from both political philosophers, such as Beetham (1991), and criminologists (see, for example, Sparks, 1994; Sparks and Bottoms, 1995). As Beetham argues, however, different groups define legitimacy differently – thus, for example, although to the lawyer 'legal validity is a recognisable element in legitimacy' (Beetham, 1991: 4), it cannot by any means exhaust it; to the philosopher 'legitimacy entails the *moral justifiability* of power relations' (1991: 5; original emphasis); and to those social scientists following Weber, power relations are legitimate 'when those involved in them, subordinate as well as dominant, believe them to be so' (1991: 6).

Importantly, Beetham takes the social scientific analysis of legitimacy further by insisting that the exercise of power must also accord to people's values and beliefs in order to be accorded legitimation and that 'a given power relationship is not legitimate because people believe in its legitimacy, but because it can be *justified in terms of* their beliefs' (Beetham, 1991: 11; original emphasis). Moreover, he argues, 'what is important for legitimacy is evidence of consent through *actions* which are understood as demonstrating consent *within the conventions of the particular society*' (1991: 12; second emphasis added), within which he includes actions such as 'concluding an agreement or entering into a contract with a superior party' (1991: 12). Conversely, he argues that actions 'ranging from non-cooperation and passive resistance to open disobedience and militant opposition on the part of those qualified to give consent will in different measure erode legitimacy, and the larger the numbers involved, the greater this erosion will be' (1991: 19). Thus, whilst legal validity and moral justifiability are important elements in the exercise and legitimation of power, they are necessary but not sufficient conditions for the exercise of power to be accorded legitimacy.

Within the context both of the changing goal posts of the moral debate outlined above, and of the empirical data with which we seek to illuminate this, it is important to note Beetham's argument that the social scientist assesses power arrangements:

> . . . not against independent or universal criteria of the right or the good, but against those that pertain within the society in question . . . [not] against ideal conditions or ideal criteria for consent, but in relation to the

conventions of a particular society. Legitimacy for social scientists is always legitimacy-in-context'. (Beetham, 1991: 13–14)

The legitimacy of power, according to Beetham's analysis, is therefore multi-dimensional and requires three conditions (see Figure 6.1), all of which contribute to legitimacy, to be met – power is legitimate to the extent that there is *conformity to established rules*, which are *justified on the basis of shared beliefs, and to which express consent, demonstrated by actions, is given by the subordinate*. The existence of these conditions 'provide the subordinate with moral grounds for compliance or cooperation with the powerful' (Beetham, 1991: 16) and conversely, their non-existence the moral grounds for non-compliance. Similarly, power can be rendered non-legitimate by the converse of these in terms of illegitimacy (breach of rules), legitimacy deficit (discrepancy between rules and supporting beliefs), and delegitimation (actions demonstrating withdrawal of consent).

These distinctions help to identify an important disjunction in the perspectives which are brought to bear on this debate. In considering the question of the moral probity of contracting-out the management of prisons, it seems clear that implicit in the reactions of many of its opponents is a question about its legitimacy. What, in particular, is being challenged is: first, the extent to which established rules are being followed in seeking to contract-out what is regarded as an inalienable function of the state; and secondly, the extent to which there are shared beliefs which justify these rules. To the proponents, of course, and the Conservative Party in particular, the rules concerning managerialism and the discipline of market forces are, indeed, based on shared beliefs and the innovation is therefore both morally and instrumentally fully justified, and therefore legitimate. Such a

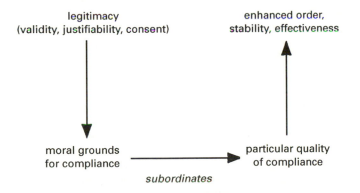

Figure 6.1   *Characteristics of a power system or relationship (Beetham, 1991: 34)*

gulf in perspectives is, indeed, wide and relegates any definitive judgement about the moral issues at this level of society to a relativistic impasse.

However, whereas this analysis focuses upon societies at a macro level, the context with which we are more concerned, and that of our research, is that of the prison, whilst our task is to try to understand at a micro level the legitimacy-in-context of the 'society of captives'. In terms of this level of analysis, it is arguable that the issue of legitimacy might be somewhat easier to determine.

The existence of the three conditions identified by Beetham as prerequisites for the accordance of legitimacy to a power relationship provides those who are subordinate within that relationship with the moral grounds for co-operation and obedience. His analysis goes further, however, and in terms which are particularly apt for understanding 'the society of captives'. As he argues:

> . . . normative grounds or reasons are not the only reasons people have for obedience . . . power relations are almost always constituted by a framework of incentives and sanctions, implicit if not always explicit, which align the behaviour of the subordinate to the wishes of the powerful. . . . Obedience is therefore to be explained by a complex of reasons, moral as well as prudential, normative as well as self-interested, that legitimate power provides for those who are subject to it. . . . People relate to the powerful as moral agents as well as self-interested actors; they are cooperative and obedient on grounds of legitimacy as well as for reasons of prudence and advantage. (Beetham, 1991: 26–7)

Thus, to analyse and to begin to understand the construction and operation of legitimacy in prisons, and the relationship between legitimacy and conformity, requires not only an understanding of the extent to which the basic conditions for the legitimation of power relations exist, but also of a complex set of subsidiary but contingent factors.

Of equal, if not greater importance in analysing and understanding the moral and ethical dimensions of contracting-out are their significance for and potential impact upon contractors. If it is valid to argue that the greater the degree of legitimacy, the greater the enhancement of the order, stability and effectiveness of a system of power, 'then we should expect that the powerful will seek to secure and maintain the legitimacy of their power, in view of its advantages to them' (Beetham, 1991: 34). Thus, as Logan argues:

> Commercial prisons will be strongly motivated to treat inmates with fairness and justice. To the extent that they are treated this way, inmates will be more inclined to legitimate their keepers' authority and to co-operate with them. . . . Legitimation constitutes one of the most effective methods of cutting the cost of power in all forms of social organization; prisons are no exception. Since legitimation is generally granted in

exchange for the fair exercise of power, a profit-seeking prison has a vested interest in being seen by inmates as just and impartial in the application of rules. . . . Thus, economic self-interest can motivate good governance as well as good management. At the least, there is no inherent incompatibility between the making of profit and the pursuit of justice. (Logan, 1987: 2)

Importantly, however, the maximization of legitimacy requires more than mere ideological manipulation since, as Beetham has argued, legitimacy depends on more than just beliefs *per se*: 'an essential feature of legitimacy [is] that it sets limits to the behaviour of the powerful as well as imposing obligations on the subordinate' (Beetham, 1991: 36) since it not only circumscribes these obligations, it also contributes to the definition of what can legitimately be demanded by the powerful and the processes by which such demands can be made.

The more fundamental importance of legitimacy as a constraint on the powerful, however, is that it requires them 'to respect the basic principles that underpin the rules or the system of power, and to protect them from challenge' (Beetham, 1991: 36). In other words, if the prison system becomes so unjust and inhumane that it begins to be defined as non-legitimate in terms of illegitimacy, legitimacy deficit, and delegitimation, then the legitimacy of imprisonment itself is challenged and, thereby, it might be argued, the legitimacy of the authority of the state. This is precisely the issue identified implicitly by the Woolf Report (Morgan, 1992; Sparks, 1994) and it is, of course, quite clearly one which applies whether prisons are managed by the public or private sectors.

The above analysis is particularly instructive when considering the relationship between legitimacy, prison regimes, and public- versus private-sector management. For example, a prison regime might be legitimate in that it derives from the rules which validate the system. However, Beetham argues that 'the power arrangements . . . [the rules] define, can only be justified by moral considerations which go beyond them' (Beetham, 1991: 57). Thus the reintroduction of chain gangs, leg-shackles, rock-breaking, etc., and generally harsher regimes in some US prisons may be legitimate according to the rules, but the question of whether they can be regarded as legitimate in terms of their ability to satisfy moral considerations (leading them to suffer from a legitimacy deficit), and how long they can be sustained before being delegitimated by a major failure of coercion to elicit prisoners' co-operation, identifies serious reservations about their overall legitimacy.

Thus the negative features involved in power relations, such as exclusion, restriction and compulsion, must be justified by moral considerations 'if the powerful are to enjoy moral authority as opposed to merely *de facto* power, or validity under a given system of law' (Beetham, 1991: 57) and if such regimes are to be legitimated. It is an irony that such morally questionable regimes are being reintroduced in public-sector prisons in the USA and that similar if, as yet, less extreme pressures for tougher regimes are being witnessed in the UK,[3] since public-sector prisons are commonly endowed by the opponents of contracting-out with moral superiority and put forward as the only legitimate means of providing imprisonment because they are under state and not private control. This irony is given added poignancy by a critical account of private prisons in the USA by Donahue which concludes by referring to 'The worst fears of the opponents of private corrections – widespread deprivation of constitutional rights; systematically worsened conditions; even a return to the chain gang' (Donahue, 1988: 24).

It is clear, however, that the erosion or absence of legitimacy does not necessarily lead to a breakdown of power or the cessation of obedience, since this can be sustained to some extent by incentives and sanctions. However, as Beetham argues, coercion has to be much more extensive and omnipresent and this is costly to maintain. Thus, it is arguable that a relative absence of legitimacy in prison regimes can only be concealed through higher levels of coercive power, which requires more staff and tougher regimes. It is equally clear that under such circumstances, the threat of force can 'collapse very rapidly if coercion is insufficient or *people believe that those in power have lost the will to use it*' (Beetham, 1991: 28; emphasis added).

Such a process is well illustrated by Morgan (1992), who comments of the prison disturbances in April 1990 that because of the injustices of much prison life, prisoners became alienated, embittered and disaffected. In consequence, disorder arose making both staff and prisoners feel insecure, as a result of which staff adopted defensive tactics – they became 'excessively reliant on "control and restraint" physical control measures and have resorted to what the Prison Officers' Association has honestly described as the "alternative" disciplinary system' (Morgan, 1992: 233). In addition, the significance of the lack of a swift and authoritative response from prison staff because of the failure in communications with Headquarters staff during the early stages of the Strangeways riot, noted in the Woolf Report, also provides graphic confirmation of this argument. Beliefs are therefore also a key factor in understanding why co-operation might cease and control break down in systems where coercion is an element in the sanctions available to ensure obedience. This theoretical understanding of legitimacy therefore helps in part to explain and understand why prisons with regimes which run on the basis of enhancing co-operation by maximizing legitimacy can be run with lower staffing levels.

Power, Legitimacy and Morality

A number of issues become clearer as a result of this analysis. First, it is difficult, if not impossible, to justify any absolute moral position in relation to the contracting-out of prisons, at least on the basis of a consideration of the legitimacy of such developments. At a macro level, it is clear that both the proponents and opponents of such developments believe in the legitimacy of their respective positions and can justify these in terms of their beliefs, whilst at a micro level, legitimacy is a product of particular sets of power relations and how these are organized and perceived in particular contexts, rather than being a product of general systems, structures and principles of organization.

Secondly, it is clear that the legitimacy of any given set of power relations is relative, not absolute, and that there are degrees of legitimacy. Indeed, we can postulate that, based on the three conditions specified by Beetham, there is a continuum running along each dimension from non-legitimate to legitimate which would allow the description, analysis, and ultimately perhaps the classification of different sets of power relations according to their degree of legitimacy. Such a continuum (see Figure 6.2) would have particular value from a social science perspective in exploring legitimacy in the context of individual prison regimes at a micro level, regardless of whether these were state-run or contracted-out.

This general view is apparently shared by Sparks and Bottoms who, drawing on the work of Beetham, argue that although there is an 'inherent legitimacy deficit' (Sparks and Bottoms, 1995: 54) in *all* prisons by their very nature, 'the *variety* of existing and possible prison regimes, and prisoners' differential responses to them' (1995:

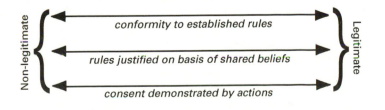

Figure 6.2 *A continuum of legitimacy*

54) is crucial in terms of minimizing this deficit. As they go on to argue:

> . . . a defensible and legitimated prison regime demands a dialogue in which prisoners' voices (as to what is 'justified in terms of their beliefs') are registered and have a chance of being responded to. Moreover . . . legitimacy, thus understood, demands reference to standards that can be defended externally in moral and political argument . . . [and] the recognition of prisoners in terms both of their citizenship and their ordinary humanity. . . . Where this can be achieved, prisoners are to that extent more likely to acknowledge the legitimacy of the regime. (Sparks and Bottoms, 1995: 59)

It is clear, therefore, that at the heart of this analysis lies a crucial moral dilemma concerning how the nature and status of prisoners are defined in terms of their humanity, their civil status as citizens, and therefore their power to accord legitimacy to prison regimes. As Beetham argues, 'Where the subordinates are not conceived as having any interests of their own meriting attention . . . there can be no moral community between them, and no legitimacy to the relationship' (Beetham, 1991: 59). The greater the desire to exclude and punish prisoners and the more coercive that prison regimes become, the greater the denial of prisoners as members of a moral community and the less the legitimacy of their relationship with the prison authorities. Thus the very moral authority and therefore the legitimacy of imprisonment is laid increasingly open to challenge. Conversely, the more prisoners are regarded as retaining some civil status to which certain constitutional and other rights are attached, and the more they are conceived of as having interests which do merit attention and which give them membership, albeit circumscribed, of the moral community, then the greater the legitimacy of the relationship between prisoners and prison staff.

Within this general proposition, the question of how much weight should be attached to the particular status of remand prisoners is of crucial importance. As we have argued elsewhere, 'The ethical significance of this question, and all that it signifies about concepts of citizenship and the rights associated with this, should not be obscured by the debate about contracting out' (Bottomley et al., 1997: 51). The criminal justice system must surely decide which way it faces on this issue. On the one hand, the law clearly regards unconvicted prisoners remanded in custody as innocent until proven guilty and according to this principle allows them, in theory, to enjoy a different status and conditions from convicted prisoners which are governed by different rules (for a useful discussion, see Morgan, 1994, and Windlesham 1993). This special status was embodied in the original policy of

Wolds to provide a regime which allowed prisoners to pursue a lifestyle as close as possible to their normal lifestyle.

On the other hand, however, this perspective conflicts with the pervasive (some might say corrosive) influence of other powerful dynamics within prisons and the prison system. Among experienced staff, remand prisoners are in practice regarded as 'cons' who need to be treated with all the circumspection of any convicted prisoner. Unlike the judicial system, the operation of prisons cannot be blind to a prisoner's previous criminal history until a court has determined the question of guilt in relation to a specific charge. Thus, the special status of the remand prisoner is easily overlooked and/or undermined, a process which has contributed to the steady degradation of the conditions in which they have been held in the UK, described by Windlesham (1993) and many others (see Chapter 3).

Equally insidious is the kind of moralistic judgement reflected in Judge Tumim's criticism of the 'corrupting lethargy' of the regime for remand prisoners at Wolds. As a consequence of this, considerable efforts have been made to introduce a more 'active' regime. However, as we have already argued:

> important ethical issues arise from this in terms of the justification for 'encouraging' remand prisoners to participate in activities which may not be part of their normal lifestyle and the question of at what point does reasonable 'encouragement' become unreasonably coercive must be addressed, as must the question of the extent to which the mixing of remand and convicted prisoners and offering them the same regime is justifiable. In short, is remand status something to which only lip-service is or should be paid, or is it something of greater substance which, as a matter of principle, should be reflected meaningfully in the way in which remand prisoners are treated? (Bottomley et al., 1997: 51)

General Considerations

A leading American academic proponent of private prisons, Charles Logan, has considered the moral case concerning private prisons in some detail, albeit that his standpoint may be inferred from the fact that his analysis was published by the Adam Smith Institute. He argues, *inter alia*, that:

> While the state may *delegate* to a private agent its authority and responsibility for administering penalties, it cannot *relinquish* them. Thus, what is now under serious consideration in Britain is not a corporate takeover of the legislative and judicial functions of the state, but the subcontracting of some of the managerial and administrative aspects of the executive function. (Logan, 1987: 1; original emphasis)

In addition, he goes on to argue that the central point is that, whatever the reasons for placing the power to punish in the hands of the state, it does not originate with the state, it must be transferred. It therefore follows that the power and authority of the state to imprison, as with all its powers and authority, are derived from the consent to be governed. These may therefore, he suggests, with similar consent, be delegated further. This is because:

> The state does not *own* the right to punish. It merely *administers* it in trust, for the people and under the rule of law. There is no reason why subsidiary trustees cannot be designated, *as long as they, too, are ultimately accountable to the people and subject to the same provisions of law that direct the state*. (Logan, 1987: 1; last emphasis added)

Logan is not alone in this view. In similar vein Vagg, in a generally sceptical review of contracting-out in Britain, also argues that 'in so far as governments contract companies to run prisons, the ultimate responsibility for regimes and good governance remains with the contract issuer, since poor performance should result in termination of the contract' (Vagg, 1994: 293). Donahue, in an equally sceptical review of the development of private prisons in America, broadly concurs with this view, arguing that:

> If comprehensive contracts could easily be written, performance perfectly monitored, and promises costlessly enforced, then private prisons would provide exactly the conditions of incarceration the community desires. There are few objections to private involvement in corrections that cannot be answered by calls for careful contracting and rigorous performance evaluation. If contracts will be perfectly enforced, the potential efficiency gains need not be very great to grant privatization a measure of appeal. (Donahue, 1988: 20)

There is a cogent argument therefore that where such powers are further delegated to contractors by the consent of the people, there is no necessary diminution of the state's responsibility.

We must consider, however, whether such consent can be said to have been given, either to the original transfer of power or to its further delegation, or whether it can only be inferred. The problem with such constitutional analyses is that they imply a specific act of transfer or consent, whereas in terms of the evolution of the state, we are dealing with the gradual concentration, acquisition or assumption of power by the institutions that came to constitute the state rather than a specific transfer. Similarly, with regard to the further delegation of the powers and authority to imprison which contracting-out represents, given the nature of parliamentary democracy and the particular history of these developments in the UK, it is certainly arguable that such consent has never been explicitly given, even by Parliament in view of the way the powers conferred by the Criminal Justice Act 1991 were (ab)used by the then Home Secretary (see Chapter 3, and Windlesham, 1993: 424–7).

Addressing another dimension of the moral debate – concerns about the use of force – Logan goes on to argue that:

> In a system characterized by rule of law, state agencies and private agencies alike are bound by law. For actors within either type of agency, it is the law, not the civil status of the actor, that determines whether any particular exercise of force is legitimate. (Logan, 1987: 1)

Apart from this general accountability in law there are, in the UK, additional safeguards which further narrow the gap between the public and the private sectors. For example, private-sector employees require Home Office certification before they can work as prisoner custody officers, as well as working under the same rules which apply in public-sector prisons. At the level of civil liability, it is also worth noting that private contractors do not enjoy the protection of Crown immunity which is enjoyed by public-sector prisons and which removes them from the scope of certain regulatory mechanisms such as health and safety legislation and protects them from actions in the civil courts for breaches of these.

Conversely, there do not appear to be any historical or constitutional grounds for arguing that contracting-out the management of prisons in the UK is breaching any principle by virtue of which the management of prisons can be said to inhere in the functions of the state. As Beetham has argued, 'Social order and personal security depend upon a coercive framework; the effective *organisation* of coercion to this end is the basis of the state's rationale and hence of its legitimacy' (Beetham, 1991: 138; emphasis added). Thus for Beetham, it is the organization rather than the management or provision of coercion which is the key element of the state's role in relation to the coercive framework.

Similarly, in her detailed analysis of the relationship between punishment and the power of the state, Lacey argues that for punishment to be legal, it must be inflicted by 'a *state-constituted* institution' (1988: 11; emphasis added), which is clearly not the same as a state-*run* institution. Moreover, it is clear that none of the legitimate and complex functions of punishment identified by Lacey, either particular or general, is undermined in principle, nor arguably in practice, by contracting-out. Indeed, in so far as contracted-out institutions offer superior conditions, sentences served in such prisons might be regarded as having greater legitimacy by prisoners, and certainly by some sections of the general population. As Lacey argues, according to what she terms 'the principle of residual autonomy', 'no punishment must be so severe as to reflect a complete absence of respect for or denial of the offender's autonomy – or indeed for her [*sic*] welfare' (Lacey, 1988: 195). By extension therefore, and other things being equal, the greater the degree of autonomy preserved by a given punishment, the fewer its moral limitations and thus the greater its legitimacy.

More specifically, one of the most frequent forms of criticism of contracting-out is based on a repudiation of the profit motive as a basis for running a prison, linked with either implicit or explicit questioning of the motives of those involved. Logan argues that as a matter of logic (if not necessarily of empirical validity), 'the motivation of those who apply a punishment is not relevant either to the justice or the effectiveness of the punishment' (Logan, 1987: 2) and that if punishment is considered to be a moral enterprise, this is a consideration which applies much more to the legislature and the judiciary. He also expresses the view that:

> Of various possible motivations for serving as an agent of punishment, the profit motive is among [t]he most benign. . . . The history of imprisonment . . . is a road paved with many good intentions that produced bad results. The lesson drawn from this history by criminologists of all ideological persuasions is that criminal justice policies and practices must be judged by their consequences, not by their motives. (Logan, 1987: 3)

This view notwithstanding, we have argued elsewhere that those working with offenders in prisons have 'a wide range of motivations, and neither self-interest nor moral probity is unique to either position' (Bottomley et al., 1997: 50). What is clear, however, is that many of those we came across working in contracted-out prisons were genuinely committed to achieving real improvements in the conditions in which prisoners are held, to giving prisoners greater autonomy and a real voice, whilst also being equally sensitive to the need to avoid any abuse of power.

What is equally clear is that financial considerations are becoming increasingly important in the running of all prisons, and whilst it might be argued that there is an important distinction between the pursuit of profit and the pursuit of economy, any difference in the impact of the cash nexus in terms of regime management is much more difficult to discern. Whilst we have argued above that a case can be made that lower staffing levels might be conducive to achieving greater legitimacy in prison regimes, it is also clear that there are substantial pressures in the prison system as a whole, both in the public and private sectors, to reduce staffing levels in order to achieve efficiency savings and thereby to reduce costs. It is equally clear that as a result, there can be adverse consequences for staff, prisoners, prison managers and prison security. This raises a moral and ethical dimension revolving around the impact of financial considerations which is a product of the general political and economic context of all prisons rather than being unique to the private sector.

Notes

1 Morgan (1992), in a slightly weaker form of this argument, developed from administrative law, refers to prisoners being entitled legitimately to have certain expectations, a position also taken by Woolf LJ.

2 It should be noted in passing that DiIulio (1991) seems to hold a somewhat different and narrower understanding of the 'new penology', at least as it applies to prisons.

3 See, for example, the 'A1 Restricted Regime' at Swaleside Prison in Kent which might, as Grewcock argues, 'give a green light to victimisation and harassment' (1995: 22) in the prison system more generally.

7

Privatizing Prisons: Current Issues and Future Prospects

In the previous chapters, we have described in some detail our evaluation of the first privately managed prison in the UK and comparisons with public-sector prisons. Our data, and the issues we have focused upon in the subsequent discussion, are based on fieldwork which was completed in April 1994. Since then, of course, much has happened in relation to the penal system, the extension of privatization and at Wolds prison itself, all of which has fundamentally altered the context of the debate about private-sector involvement in the penal system. As we argued in Chapter 6, the external context in which prisons exist is as important as the internal context when it comes to defining the terms of the debate and understanding the complex issues which are raised by any study of prisons. Before drawing together the themes and issues raised by our research therefore, it is essential that we should outline the main changes.

Privatization Continues: From Experiment to Political Reality

Although Wolds was contracted-out supposedly on an 'experimental' basis (see Chapter 3), by the time our research had come to an end, the notion that it had been an experiment, the results of which would be awaited before further prisons were contracted-out, had long since been abandoned. This was partly due to a renewal of the pressures in the penal system (see below) but also to the continuing political commitment to privatization as a means of reducing public spending.

The clearest reflection of this commitment was in the Private Finance Initiative (PFI) which was launched in November 1992 to encourage all government departments to explore actively the scope for the use of private finance. As a result of this continued emphasis on private-sector involvement, from November 1992, a number of prison-related services were market-tested: the Directorate of Works; Headquarters Training; the Prison Dog Service; the Prison Service

College facilities management; the Prison Service information technology group; fleet management; superannuation administration; canteens (prisoners' shops); warehouse and distribution; court escort services; and prison education services. Indeed, the first contracts for the provision of education in prisons, made possible by the changes introduced in the Further and Higher Education Act 1992, came into effect in April 1993. Strangeways Prison in Manchester was also market-tested, the contract being awarded in-house in July 1993.

In addition, although up until 1988 the construction of all new prisons had been managed and funded by the Property Services Agency (PSA), subsequently the Prison Service had not been tied to the agency and it had been meeting the cost of new prisons from the Prisons budget. In December 1992, however, the PSA Projects Division, which was responsible for the management of prison building projects, was sold to Tarmac Construction Ltd and, trading as Tarmac Black and Veatch (TBV) Consult, it has continued to provide this project management service for all remaining new prisons in the existing programme, although new contracts are now being let on a design, construct, manage and finance (DCMF) basis as a result of the PFI.

Also reflecting this new ethos was the appointment of Derek Lewis (previously Chief Executive and Chairman of the Board of Management of Granada Group Plc) as Director General of the Prison Service with effect from 6 January 1993. Shortly afterwards, in April 1993, Blakenhurst, run by UKDS, took its first prisoners, followed by the third privately managed prison – Doncaster, contracted-out to Premier Prisons – in June 1994. Following this, on 29 July 1994, Group 4 was announced as the preferred contractor for Buckley Hall Prison in Rochdale, Lancashire (with the value of the five-year contract being £33 million) and in August, Derek Lewis announced a list of 20 existing prisons from which one or two would be selected for market-testing. The resulting confidence of private contractors in the continued growth of private-sector involvement in the penal system became evident when, on 1 September 1994, *The Guardian* reported that 'Group 4 executives believe that it will run at least four British prisons by the next general election and have put forward proposals to design and build a new prison'.

The following day, the Home Secretary announced that the management of a further nine prisons would be offered to the private sector, in addition to the three already in operation, bringing the total to about 10 per cent of the prison estate in England and Wales. About three of these were expected to be prisons currently managed by the Prison Service, which would therefore involve further market-testing. The aim, according to the Home Secretary, was to create 'a climate in which existing practices are questioned and new ideas and approaches tried. If these objectives are achieved, the private sector must be large enough to provide sustained competition and involve several private-sector companies – a genuinely mixed economy.' At the same time, Derek Lewis claimed that:

> . . . the private sector has demonstrated the ability to deliver more effective regimes at lower costs. And I am sure more benefits will follow, particularly as we integrate the supervision of privately managed prisons more closely with the management of the public sector. (NACRO, 1993: 3)

In December 1994, Buckley Hall Prison in Lancashire opened under the management of Group 4 and the initial Directorship of Walter McGowan, who had been transferred from Wolds where he had been succeeded by David McDonnell, one of the original management team. By the time Buckley Hall opened, the required building work had been carried out by Mowlem Management, a subsidiary of the John Mowlem company which is part of UKDS and jointly runs Blakenhurst, and which also jointly built Wolds.

These rapid developments took place in spite of concerns in some quarters about difficulties at Blakenhurst and Doncaster prisons. Some of these had resulted in the issue of default notices by the Home Office in both prisons, although the only occasion so far, of which we are aware, on which financial penalties have been imposed as a result of these was a fine of £41,000 imposed on UKDS for a loss of control of Blakenhurst during a riot in February 1994 (Nathan, 1995c: 16). Continuing problems experienced by Premier Prisons at Doncaster also resulted in a second senior prison Governor being seconded to monitor the contract, whilst the company also brought in a number of additional managers and a Wackenhut corporate task force to review the prison's operation. A major contribution to the problems being experienced at Doncaster was the rapidity with which the prison was taking in prisoners (Nathan, 1994b), although this was something to which Premier Prisons had agreed. Significantly, Blakenhurst had also had to fill more rapidly than had been expected because of the rising prison population (see below).

As part of the continuing review of public spending, in July 1994 a report by the National Audit Office (NAO) on the cost of building new prisons was published (National Audit Office, 1994a). It revealed that since 1980, when the Prison Service had embarked on a major prison building and modernization programme, 21 new prisons had been built and 11,000 places provided at a cost of some £1.2 billion. Refurbishment work and redevelopment has produced an extra 7,500 places at existing prisons and an increase in 24-hour access to sanitation from 46 per cent to 90 per cent by 1994. The report also revealed cost-overruns of nearly £80 million in the building or refurbishing of these prisons by private contractors, which included £200,000 for Wolds and £24.4 million for Woodhill. The report concluded that these were a consequence of a range of problems caused by the overload of Prison Service staff resulting from the pace of the government's programme. It also noted, however, that the average time to build a prison had fallen from seven to four years.

A further report from the NAO (National Audit Office, 1994b) revealed that before the Wolds contract was drawn up, the Remands Contracts Unit, as it then was, had examined contracts for running private prisons in other countries – Junee Correctional Centre, NSW; Borrallon CC, Queensland; and New Mexico Corrections Department, USA (para. 2.1). It also made it clear that the contract specifications for Wolds had been designed with the clear intention of stimulating change in the penal system more generally, since:

> The standard of facilities and access to activities specified for Wolds were higher than the standard regime then operating in Prison Service remand prisons. The Wolds specification was intended as *a statement of what could be achieved in a modern, uncrowded establishment in the light of developments in working practice.* (National Audit Office, 1994b: para. 2.4; emphasis added)

The report also made public information about financial and other aspects of the contracting-out process and helped to dispel some of the criticisms about secrecy and non-disclosure of commercially sensitive information made by opponents. The report contained information about current custodial staffing levels at Wolds and revealed that Group 4 had bid £21.5 million over five years for the contract and that it had received £1,605,000 start-up costs and £1,921,000 phase-in costs from the government as part of the contract, in addition to £4,419,000 annual operating costs.[1]

The NAO report concluded, however, that 'It is perhaps too early to say whether Wolds is providing value for money compared to prisons run by the Prison Service' (National Audit Office, 1994b: para. 3.41), an issue which they hoped would be clearer when the results of our research were published. However, a subsequent report from the Public Accounts Committee (House of Commons, 1995) revealed that Group 4 was in fact being paid £5.9 million a year to run Wolds instead of the £4.4 million estimated when they were awarded the contract and quoted by the NAO, a discrepancy accounted for by the fact that the original tender excluded the cost of the provision of maintenance and gas, water and electricity which were not known at the time the contract was let. These costs were paid by the Home Office during the first year of the contract, after which they were included in the main contract.

As part of its scrutiny of the process by which Wolds was contracted-out, the Public Accounts Committee expressed concern 'that a full explanation was not available as to why the contract was awarded to Group 4 when its bid was higher than one of the other short-listed firms, even though both bids were substantially less than the Prison Service bench mark' (para. 21). The Committee also 'took particular interest in the fact that one of the eight members of the panel (Mr Erickson) had left the Prison Service nine months after the contract was placed and had then joined Group 4' (para. 23). They also recommended 'that the research [by the Universities of Hull and Cambridge] should be made publicly available and that the Prison Service should apply any general lessons learned from the private sector operation of Wolds and other prisons to the management of establishments in the public sector' (House of Commons, 1995: para. 40).

The greater openness about such issues and the concerns implied by these reports did not, however, lead to any direct response from the government. It was announced in October 1994 that a DCMF (design, construct, manage and finance) prison was to be built in Scotland following the Criminal Justice and Public Order Act 1994 which extended the statutory scope for privatization to Scotland. Plans for another new DCMF prison for 800 category B prisoners to be built in Salford, to relieve overcrowding at Strangeways were also announced (and were confirmed by the Prison Service the following year on 29 June 1995). In November 1994, Michael Howard went on to announce the provision of 4,000 new prison places by 1997/98, of which 1,200 were to be provided by the first two privately financed (DCMF) prisons, two more of which were planned by 1998/99, whilst the Prison Service's Strategic Estate Plan 1994/95 referred to the possibility of further contracts being awarded for DCMF prisons in the Midlands and the South East.

The Private Finance Initiative had been launched in November 1992 to encourage all government departments to explore actively the scope for the use of private finance but it had only recently been decided that the Treasury would no longer agree to new public expenditure unless the use of private finance had first been considered (Nathan, 1995c: 11). On 31 March 1995, the Home Office invited tenders for the first two of the proposed DCMF secure training centres for 12 to 14 year olds. Those invited included Group 4, Premier Prisons, UKDS and a number of major construction firms. At the same time, Nathan also reported that:

> On 1 May 1995 the Prison Service appointed consultants Coopers and Lybrand to find out how far privatisation could be extended under the

guise of the Private Finance Initiative (PFI). The Prison Service's prioritised capital expenditure programme from 1995/6 to the year 2000 is £546.6 m. . . . Coopers and Lybrand noted that 'virtually all PFI projects would lead to Prison Service jobs being replaced by private sector contractors,' and that contracting-out has 'already demonstrated that all aspects of prisons can be run by private sector companies'. (Nathan, 1995c: 11)

On 1 June 1995, the Prison Service announced that Group 4/ Tarmac were the preferred contractors for the new DCMF prison at Fazakerley in Liverpool for 600 category B prisoners, whilst Securicor/Seifert/WS Atkins, with Costain and Skanska won a similar contract for Bridgend in Wales for a prison to hold 800 category B prisoners. Both prisons, which were agreed at a cost of £50 million each and planned to open in late 1997, are intended to be multifunctional in order to accommodate women and young offenders. The contracts, which are for 25 years, will be paid on the basis of making available the specified number of prisoner places and by achieving specified performance targets, rather than on the basis of payment for the number of prisoners accommodated which was preferred by the Prison Service but rejected by the contractors. The first payment will be made when the first places become available. Details of these contracts or the performance criteria have not been made public, although it is known that the private sector will arrange finance to meet the capital costs and the contract payments will meet operating and maintenance costs, repay the finance plus interest *and* provide a return on their investment (NACRO, 1995). At the same time, it was announced that invitations to tender were about to be issued for a further three court escorting areas, which would bring seven out of the eight areas under private management. Contracts were expected to be fully operational by January 1997.

On 14 July 1995, the government claimed in Parliament that privately run prisons were some 15–25 per cent cheaper than public-sector prisons, with savings to the taxpayer £5–10 million a year on the four privately managed prisons (Wolds, Blakenhurst, Doncaster and Buckley Hall) then operating. Subsequently, details of the wide range of private finance contracts negotiated under the PFI (a total of well over 1,000 projects throughout the public sector) were released on 29 November 1995 (*The Independent*, 30.11.95). As part of the government's determination to see the initiative succeed, Treasury guidance made it clear that no more than three or four bidders should be invited to tender for projects, a restriction intended to streamline the process and to reduce the bidding costs for the private sector but one which also seems likely to reduce the scope for competition.

Michael Jack, Financial Secretary to the Treasury, argued that the initiative would reduce the government's capital spending by some £2 billion and that 'the public sector no longer simply signs a contract to buy a prison . . . it pays to have specific services at guaranteed levels of performance over 20 or 30 years' (*The Independent*, 30.11.95) and at the end of the contract, the assets transfer to the public sector. In the meantime, however, and offsetting the modest reduction in capital costs, it was also reported that the schemes would commit the government to billions of pounds expenditure in future years in order to meet the revenue costs associated with buying these services (a proportion of which will consist of the financial return to the contractors for their investment) and although these remain unclear, the Treasury was reported to have roughly estimated the running costs of the average project to be between two and four times the capital cost (*The Independent*, 30.11.95).

Pressure in the Penal System

The continued expansion of private-sector involvement, both in the penal system and in other parts of the public sector, was clearly a key element of the government's political and ideological agenda. However, as with the circumstances which first led to its introduction (see Chapter 3), pressures and events in the penal system also played an important part.

The Criminal Justice Act 1991 had come fully into effect in October 1992, bringing with it a clear emphasis on just deserts, proportionality, the use of community penalties for less serious offenders, and therefore on the work of the probation service. Of particular importance among the measures it introduced, both practically and symbolically, was the unit fine system, the intention of which was to ensure that fines imposed by courts took full account of offenders' means, not least because to do so would, it was anticipated, result in fewer people being sent to prison in default of payment. The effect of the Act was reflected almost immediately in a fall in the prison population (see Figure 7.1).

Within months, however, there were growing concerns among sentencers about the restrictions imposed by the Act and particularly about the reduced weight which could be given to previous convictions, which many sentencers felt resulted in unrealistically lenient sentences being imposed. Consequently, in March 1993, following increasingly vocal opposition and one or two *causes célèbres*, the government decided to abolish the means-related unit fine system. The Criminal Justice Act, 1993, which came into effect on 16

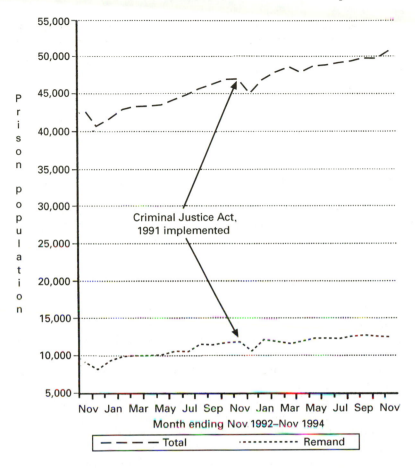

Figure 7.1 *Prison population after the Criminal Justice Act, 1991 (Cavadino, 1995: 3)*

August, reversed the key 'liberal' reforms of the 1991 Act which had restricted the use of custody and, on 20 September 1993, new sentencing guidelines were issued to magistrates. This reversal set the scene for a surge in punitive rhetoric, a clear shift of direction in penal policy and a rapid growth in the prison population.

This was presaged in a leak in August which revealed that the Home Secretary, Michael Howard, had ordered a review to design a 'more austere' regime for prisoners, requiring them to spend more time working and less time on what it was argued most people would regard as leisure activities. The flames of this new, tough reforming zeal were also undoubtedly fanned by the fact that on 7 September

1993, there had been a serious disturbance at Wymott Prison. It was against this background that on 6 October, Michael Howard outlined his 27-point plan for getting tough on criminals to the Conservative Party conference in Blackpool, in which he set a clear political agenda by declaring 'Let us be clear. Prison works', by announcing the building of six new prisons, and by promising a new era of austerity in prison regimes. Later that month, five private prison contractors were asked by Home Office officials to include an overcrowding quota in their tendering for private prisons (the contract for Doncaster Prison had included an option to overcrowd beyond its Certified Normal Accommodation (CNA) of 771 should the need arise).

As a consequence of these various pressures, in the first 11 months of 1993, the prison population rose dramatically so that the average remand population reached 10,700, close to its previous historical peak in 1988, whilst by November, police cells were being used again because of overcrowding in prisons. In October 1993, Derek Lewis, the new Director General of the Prison Service, estimated that from there having been a surplus of places in the prison system in 1993/4, there would be a deficit by 2000/1, with 55,700 prisoners in the system with a CNA of 53,800 (an increase in the estimated CNA of over 3,500 from that given in November 1992 by the then prisons minister, Peter Lloyd), in spite of the fact that over 20 new prisons had opened since 1983.

By the following year, the average remand population had increased to 12,400, 4,200 more than in 1993 and the biggest annual increase since 1970. Estimates of the prison population by the year 2000 were also revised upwards by 5,000 to 56,600 (Home Office, 1994) and by 16 March 1995, the prison population had reached its highest ever level. Thus between November 1992 and November 1994, the population rose by 7,501, an increase of 17 per cent, whilst the number of remand prisoners rose by 37 per cent (see Figure 7.1), a figure which was estimated to increase to 15,400 by 2002 (Home Office, 1995).

The new 'prison works' rhetoric was backed by a substantial increase in spending on prisons, with a total of £620.3 million being assigned to prison building for 1994–7. By late 1993, in addition to the new private prisons he had already decided should be built at Bridgend and Fazakerley, the Home Secretary had announced that a further four new prisons would be built (as well as a number of secure training centres for young offenders), with the private sector being responsible for their finance, design, building and operation. In January 1994, it was also announced in Parliament that there were plans to increase the number of prison places available at existing establishments by some 2,000 through the building of additional houseblocks, at an estimated cost of £117 million.

By 1995, however, other tensions were becoming apparent in the penal system. On 21 September 1995, the Prison Service announced a project to consider the feasibility of building one or two maximum security prisons, following the Whitemoor and Parkhurst escapes (see below). As a result of the Learmont Report into the Parkhurst escape (Learmont, 1995), Derek Lewis was forced by the Home Secretary to resign on 16 October amidst acrimonious accusations of excessive Home Office intervention in the running of the Prison Service Agency. Michael Howard also seemed increasingly intolerant of criticism and the contract of Her Majesty's Chief Inspector of Prisons, Judge Stephen Tumim, who had recently been highly critical of the Learmont Report (*The Independent*, 20.10.95), was not renewed amidst allegations that the Home Secretary found his outspoken and critical stance on prison conditions unacceptable. Indeed, when he retired on 1 November, Judge Tumim commented that the Home Secretary no longer seemed to want independent advice.

This observation was given added weight by Michael Howard's reported criticism (*The Independent*, 22.10.95) of Sir Peter Woodhead, the Prisons Ombudsman (a post established in the aftermath of the Strangeways riot in 1990 and the Woolf Report), for upholding too many prisoners' complaints (51 per cent in the first 6 months). In the event, 18 per cent of the recommendations made (which are not binding) were wholly or partly rejected by the Prison Service. As the report observes, 'This compares poorly to other Ombudsmen. . . . The difficulty in obtaining timely information from the Prison Service and the relatively high rate of rejection of the Ombudsman's recommendations are of particular concern' (Woodhead, 1995: 17–19). It was also reported that in future, the Ombudsman's reports would have to go through the Home Office and may be censored before being presented to Parliament (*The Independent*, 22.10.95).

Additional pressures had also been generated by the attempted escape from the special security unit at Whitemoor on 9 September 1994 and the escape from Parkhurst on 3 January 1995. The report of Sir John Woodcock into the Whitemoor incident, which had been published on 19 December (Woodcock, 1994), was highly critical of the many poor practices which had been allowed to develop, thereby compromising security, and further condemnation of security and the functioning of the Prison Service as a whole came from the report of General Sir John Learmont (Learmont, 1995) into the Parkhurst escape. Consequently, more stringent and very costly security measures were instituted at all dispersal prisons, whilst the Prison Service Business Plan for 1995/96 had already indicated that improving performance on security and implementing the Woodcock proposals were to be given priority. Similarly, new rules on temporary release were introduced on 25 April 1995, resulting in a 40 per cent reduction in the number of prisoners released temporarily, and revised disciplinary powers for Governors were also introduced (on 25 April 1995) at the same time.

The cost of implementing the recommendations of the Woodcock and Learmont Reports and the resulting emphasis on security also came at a time when prison budgets were being cut by up to 5 per cent and the prison population was continuing to grow, having reached a record level of 52,521 (*The Independent*, 29.11.95). As a consequence, there was increased doubling up of prisoners in single cells, more prisoners were spending longer periods locked up, whilst plans were introduced to cut back work, education and offender treatment programmes run by probation officers in prisons (*The Independent*, 28.11.95 and 29.11.95).

In addition to the pressures caused by this massive expansion of the prison population and the need to establish more 'active' and 'austere' regimes, the Prison Service was also having to cope with other innovations such as the introduction the previous year of prisoner compact schemes similar to those first introduced at Wolds. By May 1994, 20 prisons were operating prisoners' compacts and a further 14 were operating experimental schemes (NACRO, 1994a: 30) and by 30 June 1994, 61 establishments were operating them (NACRO, 1994b: 27). In addition, the Prison Service was also striving to increase the amount of time prisoners were able to spend out of their cells and by March 1994, 27 per cent of prisoners were being held in establishments where prisoners were unlocked for 12 hours or more (Howard League, 1994), whilst by May 1994, this figure had increased to 32 per cent (*Criminal Justice Digest*, No. 82, October 1994: 27).

Whilst the Prison Service was committed to increasing this even further, it was also having to cope with the demands of a national framework of incentives and earned privileges for good behaviour and hard work, the first phase of which had been introduced on an experimental basis in over 30 prisons in July 1995, with the expectation that all prisons would introduce schemes by December. This led to resistance from some prisoners which became evident in the disturbance in Full Sutton Prison in November 1995. It was against this background of turmoil that changes had also been taking place at Wolds.

Changes at Wolds

In the light of these pressures in the penal system and of the recommendation of Her Majesty's Chief Inspector of Prisons, following his inspection of Wolds in May 1993, that Wolds should become more closely integrated with the rest of the Prison Service, Wolds has inevitably changed since the fieldwork for the research came to an end in April 1994. One of the most significant changes followed an agreement, reached in July 1993 between the Home Office and Group 4, that sentenced prisoners would be introduced into Wolds with the aim of making it more stable. As the Board of Visitors commented in their third annual report:

> During the year there have been periods when, due to pressures within the Prison Service nationally, there has been an overcrowd of 15% so that the population reached 368. Some of these extra prisoners have had to be housed three to a cell. The latter part of the year has seen a gradual shift in the population as the prison has changed from a purely remand function to that of a local and category B training prison. When the transformation is complete, it is envisaged that the population will consist of half remand and half sentenced prisoners. (Board of Visitors, 1995: 1)

It is clear from this that the role of Wolds in providing high-quality and uncrowded conditions solely for remand prisoners had already begun to be eroded.

In terms of improving the stability of the prison, the introduction of sentenced prisoners seems to have had the desired effect. In terms of order and control, 1994 saw continued improvement when compared to 1993 – a 40 per cent fall in the number of adjudications (from 1,246 to 746), a 25 per cent fall in the number of prisoners segregated under Prison Rule 43 for reasons of good order and discipline (from 106 to 75), a 74 per cent fall in the number of occasions on which prescribed Control and Restraint procedures were used (from 116 to 30), and a 62 per cent fall in the number of occasions on which the special unfurnished cell in the segregation unit was used (from 21 to 8) (Board of Visitors, 1995: 4–5).

The Board of Visitors also noted an improvement in the atmosphere and control within Wolds. As they point out, 'The possibility of remaining at Wolds after sentence has had a positive effect on some prisoners who have been prepared to modify their behaviour on remand in the hope that their request to remain after sentence would be regarded sympathetically' (Board of Visitors, 1995: 2). It is worthwhile observing in passing that the acquisition of an observation, classification and allocation (OCA) role, which Wolds now fulfils when determining where prisoners should serve their sentences, has given Wolds' staff and management an additional and significant, but low-visibility, source of power and control over prisoners, one which is not so readily open to monitoring and is therefore, in principle, more susceptible to abuse.

The changes in the external environment provided by penal policy which have affected public-sector prisons have, however, also had an affect on Wolds, now that it is more closely integrated with the system as a whole, and 'The gradual introduction of a more structured and disciplined regime, with privileges having to be earned, has caused resentment among some prisoners who were familiar with the less demanding pattern of life laid down in the original terms of the contract' (Board of Visitors, 1995: 2). In addition, the times of visits have been changed so that these now take place in the afternoon and evening, instead of the morning and afternoon. Although this change was welcomed by prisoners and families, 'Visits which are longer and more frequent than the minimum required by the Contract now have to be earned by the fulfilment of the responsibilities to which prisoners subscribe in their individual compacts with the prison' (Board of Visitors, 1995: 3), and the induction process has also been revised, making prisoners much more aware of what is expected of them and what they can expect in return.

Further changes resulted from the need to provide a more active regime for all prisoners and employment for those under sentence. Buildings which originally housed the prison maintenance department have been converted into workshops for prisoners, the large central yard has been fenced off to create smaller areas which allow structured movement and separate exercise periods for prisoners from different units, whilst A and B units have been adapted and refurbished to equip them for their new role accommodating sentenced prisoners. Although there are now more employment opportunities, however, the Board of Visitors comments that progress in this respect has been slower than would have been wished 'due in part to the delay in the necessary amendments to the Contract being agreed' (Board of Visitors, 1995: 4). Moreover, the arrangements for the provision of education, initially contracted to Humberside Further and Continuing Education Department, were found by Wolds' management to be less than satisfactory. Consequently, in December 1994 Manchester College was sub-contracted to provide education services to sentenced prisoners on A unit, together with classes on E unit and the Health Care Centre, and in April 1995, when the original education contract expired, they took over all responsibility for education provision.

In the midst of these many changes, there was a second change of Director, as well as other changes in senior and middle-management teams, as a consequence of Group 4 winning the contract for Buckley Hall. An advantage of this, as the Board of Visitors observes, is that

'Such moves have had the positive result of allowing the promoti
to management posts of staff who have demonstrated their ability ar
capacity for greater responsibility' (Board of Visitors, 1995: 1). They
also comment positively that 'With more involvement by the Area
Manager and Directors of HM Prison Service, the earlier sense of
isolation has lessened and staff are proud to be part of HM Prison
Service Agency' (Board of Visitors, 1995: 7).

It is clear, therefore, that Wolds has been affected considerably by
the changes which have occurred in the penal system which reflects
its closer integration with the Prison Service. Ironically, however,
although closer integration might arguably reassure opponents of
privatization to some extent, another effect of this has also been to
increase the similarities in conditions between the two sectors. As the
Board of Visitors observed, 'There are indications that the earlier
pioneering role assigned to Wolds is gradually being eroded, and
worthwhile initiatives are being curtailed in the interests of uni-
formity' (Board of Visitors, 1995: 6).

Caveats, Key Issues and Conclusions

Caveats – Some Methodological Considerations

Perhaps the most difficult task of all for researchers is to distil the
essence of years of work and to summarize the manifold subtleties
and complexities of their data in a way which does justice to both
their research and those on whom it focused, whilst also communicating these accurately to a diverse and critical audience. Where such
work involves the evaluation of a controversial and major – arguably
the major – innovation in a country's penal policy, the political
context of such research gives an added dimension to this task
because of the use which all interested parties, whether for or against
such developments, will seek to make of the 'results' of such
research. There is, as a consequence, pressure on researchers to
provide simple 'answers' to what are inordinately complex questions
– pressure to conclude that the 'experiment' has or has not worked,
that 'privatization' has or has not been a success.

The need for such simple answers by politicians, civil servants,
private contractors and the penal reform lobby, not to mention the
public (whether in the guise of taxpayer, a member of the electorate,
or an interested humanitarian) is easily explained and understood.
What is sometimes less easy to explain is that there *are* no simple and
yet truthful answers which encompass the myriad of complex practical, moral and theoretical questions raised by an initiative such as
the contracting-out of Wolds, not least because the data are open to

various interpretations. In consequence, different commentators will inevitably either draw different and selective conclusions from such research and seek to dismiss other interpretations which do not fit with their agenda, or dismiss the research as inconclusive or flawed and therefore of little or no value. However, the reality for those engaged in the study and evaluation of such issues is that complex questions seldom yield simple answers and that this simple truth is one to which they must cleave. As Donahue has argued, 'theoretical descriptions are satisfyingly crisp; empirical comparisons are messy, tentative, and hedged about with conditions' (Donahue, 1989: 57).

Although perhaps of less interest to those who primarily seek to make use of research findings, methodological issues are nonetheless an important part of the reason why there can be no simple answers. One important factor which presented us with methodological problems was the process of continuous change during the period of the research, not only within the prisons, but also in their external environment (outlined in Chapter 4 and in earlier sections of this chapter), which affected all of the prisons studied but Wolds in particular. Under such circumstances, evaluating the results of the Wolds' 'experiment' and comparing its achievements with those of the other prisons included in the study has therefore posed significant problems. It is seldom the case in social scientific research that environmental conditions can be held stable for experimental purposes. However, the wide-ranging changes outlined above make it impossible to argue that what we were evaluating by the end of the research period was the same as when we started, as well as making it difficult to attribute direct causal significance to a wide range of factors or to discern, with any accuracy, the impact of such changes on interviews and other data collection which took place throughout the research period.

Perhaps one of the clearest illustrations of this problem is the significant shift towards requiring the provision of more active regimes for all prisoners, the unprecedented growth in the prison population and the decision to admit sentenced prisoners to Wolds. When Wolds was designed and built, there was no expectation that prisoners would be expected to be encouraged to work or that it would cater for sentenced prisoners who could be required to work. As a result, no provision for workshops was made. The fact that Wolds was subsequently criticized by Her Majesty's Chief Inspector of Prisons for the amount of boredom and lethargy among prisoners, was required to accept levels of overcrowding which had never been anticipated, and was required to accept sentenced prisoners, all served fundamentally to change the ethos which had moulded the unique nature of the prison when it first opened.

Quite apart from pressures such as these in the penal system and the resulting changes to the ethos and regime of Wolds, the study also highlighted the significance of another important factor which raised methodological issues – the fact that prisoners are not passive recipients but extremely active and influential participants. It is apparent that whatever the ambitions and regime of a new prison, whether it be under public- or private-sector management, the way it develops will be shaped as much by prisoners as by staff or management. Thus, the attribution of cause and effect when making comparisons and evaluating an initiative such as this is no easy task.

A further difficulty in comparative prisons research is that the direct comparison of prisons is almost impossible because no two prisons are alike in virtually any respect, and, consequently, it is very difficult to identify criteria by which they can be evaluated, even in terms of relatively objective indicators such as cost (see Chapter 2). Therefore, to expect research to produce clear and simple comparisons of qualitative dimensions, no matter how desirable a research objective this might be, is even more unrealistic. When one adds to this the fact that prisoners, staff and management all make their own contribution to the creation of those indicators by which we define quality in prisons (whether in terms of simple indicators such as standards of cleanliness, or more complex and abstract issues such as the quality of management, staff–prisoner relationships, or perceptions of justice), and that the mixture of these and the resulting human chemistry will vary from prison to prison no matter how similar they may be in other respects, the difficulties of giving clear, simple answers to questions about qualitative comparisons become obvious.

In putting any conclusions from this research into context, the impact of the Hawthorne effect must also be borne in mind. Wolds was an 'experiment' and although the government did not wait for the results of this before deciding whether or not to increase private-sector involvement in the penal system, there is no doubt that prisons participating in this research, and Wolds in particular, were influenced by the fact that the study was taking place and that 'privatization' was under the spotlight. The pressures generated by being the first prison to be involved in such an experiment were evident at Wolds (see Chapter 4), whilst competition with the private sector and the pressures of market-testing were clearly evident in Woodhill's reaction to the research (see Chapter 5). For both of the main prisons involved in this study, the awareness of these factors framed their actions and reactions to issues both small and large, and this therefore provides an important part of the context in which the research was conducted and our conclusions must be understood. To seek to define the extent to which their relative performances might have been otherwise had this context been different, whilst an important and highly relevant question, is, however, not possible to answer.

Key Issues

Public vs private.   Having entered these caveats, however, a number of key issues have emerged from our research. Perhaps the most important of these is the fact that the private/public dichotomy is false in some respects and misleading and/or unhelpful in others and that other factors are more important when it comes to successful, innovative and efficient prison management. As we argued in Chapter 5, it is apparent that the introduction of contracted-out prisons and market-testing has been a highly significant factor in public-sector prisons and was consciously used by senior management at Woodhill as part of their efforts to change working practices and staff attitudes, and to improve the regime and the cost-effectiveness of the prison. However, we cannot judge conclusively the extent to which recent changes in public-sector prisons have their origins in the introduction of competition as opposed to being a response to other pressures and managerialist trends in the penal system more generally.

Thus, whilst it was clear that Woodhill had more in common with Wolds in terms of its management ethos and style than it did with more traditional public-sector prisons, it opened in the post-Woolf era, as part of a Prison Service with agency status, with a new Director General, a new corporate strategy, a new approach to business planning, and a commitment to greater devolution of financial and management responsibility to prison governors. When Woodhill opened, therefore, it was in a Prison Service environment which expected innovation and demanded more effective use of resources, so its managers and staff were more performance- and output-oriented from the start. Under such circumstances, whilst there is little doubt that the introduction of private-sector competition and the threat of market-testing acted as a significant spur to further change, to attribute the many achievements of Woodhill solely to this would be to tell only part of the story.

Opening new prisons: challenges and opportunities.   Another part of the story that has become much clearer is that many of the issues we encountered were a reflection of the problems and processes of opening a new prison, rather than whether the prison was publicly or privately managed. As we have just argued in relation to Woodhill, the context in which a prison opens is very important, since it is this which provides the benchmarks for its operation and suggests the goals to which its senior managers might aspire. In the wake of the searching review offered by the Woolf Report, all prisons were given a vision of how they should be run. In a new prison, with new managers, new staff, a commitment to succeed and a clear view of what success might look like in the light of the Woolf Report, the potential to achieve change is clearly much greater, whether that prison is in the public or private sector, than in an established prison which has already achieved a state of organizational equilibrium, or even inertia.

New prisons also have an inbuilt advantage over older prisons, simply in terms of having the benefits of the latest developments in design and thus being able to offer considerably superior physical conditions to prisoners. More importantly, however, is the fact that prisons are considerably more than just bricks and mortar. They are complex and dynamic social organizations and the larger the prison, the more complex its structures and its dynamics. In established prisons, to challenge the *status quo* and to achieve fundamental change requires existing patterns of behaviour, attitudes and expectations to change and this, in turn, requires that the existing ethos and equilibrium of the prison be disturbed, a process which inevitably encounters resistance, both passive and active, from both staff and prisoners.

In a new prison there is, by definition, no existing ethos or equilibrium. In terms of innovation, this gives a new prison some clear advantages. The disadvantages under such circumstances, however, are that the tasks of developing such an ethos and of putting this into effect, of building a new and effective staff team, of coping with the highs and lows of staff morale which is more volatile during the process of developing these, are extremely demanding. In such a context, it is difficult to over-emphasize the significance of the senior management team whose enthusiasm, commitment, vision and competence are crucially important in shaping the regimes of new prisons, whether publicly or privately managed, or to deny the fact that some senior management teams will be less able to deal with these challenges than others.

To these ingredients must be added the crucially important role of prisoners in shaping the social organization of a new prison. As we have argued above, prisoners are not passive and it is apparent that the ambitions and regime of a new prison, no matter how innovative, will be shaped in part by prisoners and their experience of other prisons. It is clear that at least some of the problems and subsequent regime modifications at Wolds were necessitated because prisoners brought with them their own expectations and their own inflexibilities. It is also clear that at both Wolds and Woodhill, the inexperience of staff created considerable opportunities and scope for prisoners to influence the day-to-day running of the living units.

It is clear, therefore, that part of the challenge of opening a new prison is to manage the induction of an entirely new population of prisoners in such a way that the desired ethos and *modus vivendi* is established as quickly and effectively as possible, so that order and control can be established via shared 'ownership' by staff and prisoners. Once this has been achieved and there is a degree of equilibrium in the prison, there will be sufficient continuity and stability provided by staff and prisoners to make the introduction of new prisoners as part of the normal turnover of the prison population manageable under normal circumstances. It may be no coincidence, therefore, that when Blakenhurst and Doncaster opened, they were required to build up to full capacity much more rapidly than Wolds and that, as outlined above, they have experienced considerably more problems than Wolds.

Systemic pressures.   Part of the reason for the rapid intake of prisoners at Blakenhurst and Doncaster was the sudden surge of growth in the prison population as a consequence of the shifting emphasis of penal policy. Under such circumstances, as the prison population increases, the need to make best use of available prison spaces will inevitably override other considerations and although Wolds was initially contractually shielded from such pressures, this protection has now been compromised. Such pressures in the penal system are therefore also crucial factors in influencing the 'success' of any new prison.

However, systemic pressures are not restricted to managing the number of available prison places. Thus, for example, financial imperatives and the development of key performance indicators (KPIs) in the prison system as a means of monitoring financial efficiency and other outputs (including regime improvements) are of growing importance and therefore having an increasing impact on the management of prisons. As we argued in Chapter 3, these are an integral part of current public policy, the growth of managerialism and the new penology, and they have had the effect, *inter alia*, of introducing competition and a 'market' ethos into the entire prison system. The efforts of Directors of private-sector prisons to meet contract specifications and agreed outputs are now mirrored by the efforts of Governors of public-sector prisons to meet their KPIs.

Significantly, the risks associated with such demands are therefore also now present in both sectors. Part of the concern of the opponents of privatization has been that the imperative to maximize profits would encourage private contractors to find ways of purporting to achieve specified targets and outputs when in reality they had failed to do so. As a result of these systemic developments, however, such pressures are now present in all prisons. The need to reduce the number of assaults and to increase the proportion of time prisoners spend on constructive activities, for example, will inevitably lead to pressures for a reconsideration of the criteria by which such issues are defined in order to be seen to be meeting the required targets.

Conclusions

Successful innovation. It is clear, in the changed context of a Prison Service with agency status, greater devolution of financial and operational accountability to prison Governors, and market-testing, that innovative management is neither unique to privately managed prisons, nor a unique product of privatization, a point underlined by the fact that virtually all senior managers in the private sector are ex-Prison Service Governors. Donahue argues that his analysis of the evidence confirms two powerful principles:

> First, the profit-seeking firm is *potentially* a far superior institution for efficient production. Second, that productive potential can be tapped only under certain circumstances. *Public versus private* matters, but *competitive versus noncompetitive* usually matters more. (Donahue, 1989: 78; original emphasis)

He reaches this conclusion, which supports the arguments put forward by the proponents of privatization prior to its introduction in the UK, because 'Organizations (including public ones) that must match the pace set by ambitious rivals are virtually always more effective than organizations (including private ones) that are secure against challenge' (Donahue, 1989: 218).

Our research is not able to shed much light on the first of these principles, but it does tend to support the second – that it is the new competitive ethos rather than the introduction of privatization *per se* which has encouraged and enabled managers to innovate. What is also clear from our research is that whilst the drive, energy, commitment and vision of senior managers is crucial to designing innovative regimes, the importance of middle managers in effectively implementing and sustaining such regimes in new prisons should not be underestimated.

Whilst, as we have argued above, new prisons have considerable advantages in terms of the recency of their design and fabrication, it is also clear that this is not sufficient to overcome the inherent limitations of design and building when these are not matched to regime requirements, or when the latter change. Wolds, although new and of recent design, was not entirely suited to the model of direct supervision used by Group 4, a fact which arguably limited the effectiveness of their intended approach to prison management. More generally, neither Wolds nor Woodhill (a prison of equally or even more innovative design) were designed to provide work for prisoners on the scale which was subsequently required with the new emphasis on active regimes, an issue which has required further work in both prisons. Such fundamental policy changes pose problems for all prisons, no matter how new, if the innovations required cannot be effectively accommodated within the physical limitations of their design. Under circumstances such as these, compromise solutions must be found which will therefore seldom be as effective as intended.

Private prisons – public accountability.   Such constraints are echoed in the effect of the mechanisms designed to ensure the accountability of private contractors. It is clear that the contract for Wolds has provided a higher level of controls and accountability than that which has traditionally existed in relation to public-sector prisons. However, it has also created a degree of inflexibility. On several occasions, Group 4 experienced considerable delays in implementing regime changes at Wolds, especially if these necessitated changes to the fabric of the prison, whilst the necessary renegotiation of the contract took place. Against this relative lack of flexibility must be set the advantages given by such contractual arrangements in terms of the detailed specification of regime requirements and performance targets. As Donahue has argued:

> The more precisely a task can be *specified* in advance, and its performance *evaluated* after the fact, the more certainly contractors can be made to *compete*; the more readily disappointing contractors can be *replaced* (or otherwise penalised); and the more narrowly government cares about *ends* to the exclusion of *means*, the stronger becomes the case for employing profit-seekers rather than civil servants. The fundamental distinction, however, is between competitive, output-based relationships and non-competitive, input-based relationships rather than between profit-seekers and civil servants *per se*. (Donahue, 1989: 97–8; original emphasis)

In public-sector prisons in the UK, however, it is clear that there is an increasing tendency to specify and evaluate prisons' performance, albeit the basis for this is not contractual, through the introduction of innovations such as the *Model Regime* and the use of output-oriented KPIs. Such devices reduce the significance of Donahue's distinction between profit-seekers and civil servants but underline the importance of output-based relationships. There may be just cause for concern, however, if Donahue's analysis is accepted, that such developments in both the public and private sectors might signify a greater concern about ends than means. At present, our research suggests that those involved in delivering regimes continue to be concerned about means, whilst concerns about ends are arguably more evident at more senior levels of the organizational and political hierarchy. The need for vigilance in this respect should be noted, however, for as we have argued above, the pressures created by management mechanisms such as these also generate pressures to undermine systems for ensuring accountability, a possibility which gives cause for proper concern.

There is no evidence from our research, however, that these systems have yet begun to be undermined or that the fears held by some about possible abuses of prisoners' rights by private contractors have been justified. The role of the Controller appears to have worked reasonably well and the safeguards provided by mechanisms such as the Boards of Visitors and of Her Majesty's Chief Inspector of Prisons continue to play an important role. Indeed, paranoid press reports notwithstanding, Wolds has, in some respects, been more open than many public-sector prisons and the continuing need for the provision and involvement of community-based services for prisoners, together with the lack of Crown immunity and the interest of other public watchdogs, such as the National Audit Office and the Public Accounts Committee of the House of Commons, all offer some considerable reassurance.

It is equally true that the public sector is not immune from concerns about abuses yet they have, for many years, received much less attention than contracted-out prisons such as Wolds. However, the current level of interest and concern might reasonably be expected to be eroded over time and under such circumstances, the independence and effectiveness of the Controller and the retention of disciplinary powers by the Controller are of crucial importance. Similarly, the role of Boards of Visitors and of Her Majesty's Chief Inspector of Prisons as independent and effective watchdogs must be protected.

Prisoners as consumers. One of the main overall conclusions which can be drawn from our study is that Wolds provided a much-improved environment for prisoners than that which prevailed in other local prisons in the region at that time. As we outlined in Chapters 4 and 5, the quality of staff and the fact that they generally treated prisoners fairly, with respect and humanity were the most important dimensions in this perception. Prisoners at Woodhill also compared that prison favourably with other local prisons in that region, and relationships with staff were again an important factor, but these did not seem to be of quite the same high standard as at Wolds. This suggests that whilst improvements can be made in staff–prisoner relationships in public-sector prisons, the ethos imparted to Wolds staff during training may have been an important dimension in creating such high-quality relationships, although it must also be pointed out that as standards improve in the public-sector prisons, prisoners' perceptions of the superiority of Wolds might begin to change.

More importantly, however, as we have argued in Chapter 6, a crucial dimension in determining the quality of prison regimes lies in the legitimacy accorded to them by prisoners. Quality of staff–prisoner relationships are undoubtedly an important part of this, as are attempts to normalize the prison environment, and incentives and compacts also have an important part to play in ensuring that order is maintained in prisons. Of overriding importance to prisoners, however, as was made clear in the Woolf Report, is the issue of ensuring that they are treated fairly and consistently (albeit with flexibility) by staff. It is when prisoners become conscious of injustice and inconsistencies in the way they are treated that they begin to question the legitimacy of a given regime and that the risk of loss of control is at its greatest (Sparks and Bottoms, 1995).

Inexperienced staff.   In spite of concerns expressed by some opponents of privately managed prisons, it is also clear that the recruitment of inexperienced staff is not necessarily a major problem in opening a new prison. However, it is clear that lessons can be learned from the experience at Wolds, especially about the ease with which those with previous experience of working in prisons can overlook the lack of routine knowledge and understanding of those without such experience, and the importance of the provision of adequate support and supervision of main grade staff by an experienced, competent and properly resourced tier of middle management which is still not generally available to private-sector recruiters.

It is also clear, however, that although staffing levels are important, the simple ratio of staff to prisoners reveals little about the significance of staffing levels. Wolds generally ran well with a ratio of 1:50 – the main problem was that there were insufficient numbers of staff to cope with externals (for example, hospital bed-watches), sick leave and other operational contingencies, particularly during the early months of the prison's operation, which made the implementation of changes more difficult and left staff feeling exposed in the event of an incident arising because of a lack of adequate back-up.

Such pressures raise a number of personnel issues, although again, not all of these are unique to private-sector prisons and some, such as the relative lack of a career structure, may be specific to this particular stage in the history of private-sector involvement in prison management in the UK. Equally, some are more peculiar to public-sector prisons. Thus, as became apparent at Woodhill, a major problem for many of the high proportion of newly qualified prison officers in public-sector prisons is that of being posted away from home and wishing to return to their home area at the earliest opportunity, adding an element of staffing instability which can complicate the process of establishing a new prison. Whilst such issues may also be specific to a particular stage in the history of Prison Service recruitment, and are likely to diminish with the spread of local recruitment, there is no doubt of the pressures created for many new officers in public-sector prisons by such arrangements.

The privatization debate – empirical research and moral dilemmas. Perhaps the most contentious set of issues raised by the contracting-out of Wolds are those which lie in the moral domain and here, in particular, our conclusions cannot be unqualified or unequivocal. As Donahue has argued:

> Debates over the competence of governmental organizations frequently become confused with debates over the proper boundaries of collective activity. The issues, while undeniably related . . . are separable. It is no offence against logic to believe that bureaucracy is inherently inefficient, and at the same time to believe that expediency or justice call for an expansive common realm. (Donahue, 1989: 221)

This reflects the reality of the position of many UK opponents of privately managed prisons who recognize the deficiencies of the Prison Service but nonetheless feel that in the interests of justice, prisons should remain in the public sector. However, the distinction between justice, as an abstract concept, as opposed to legitimacy, as a dynamic concept, which helps to organize our understanding of social life and institutions such as prisons around notions of *perceived* justice, remains problematic for the opponents of privatization who must address the fact that prisoners at Wolds have accorded it a high degree of legitimacy. Moreover, as Donahue points out:

> ideologically fervent commentators of every political stripe too often neglect . . . [the fact] that no set of studies can prove any *universal* assertion about either public or private institutions. . . . The best that any empirical survey can hope for is to find some suggestive tendency in the way the evidence falls. (Donahue, 1989: 57)

Unfortunately, however, as we argued in Chapter 6, judgements on moral issues such as the rights and wrongs of contracting-out the management of prisons to the private sector are not readily open to empirical evaluation. The evidence of our research suggests that many of the practical concerns of the opponents of such developments are not necessarily warranted. It also suggests that prisoners who, it might be argued, should be the ultimate arbiters of the morality of such developments, make their judgements according to different criteria from those employed by most of those who oppose privatization.

What has become clear, however, is that there remains a deep and unresolved ambivalence about the treatment of unconvicted remand prisoners. In law, they are regarded as innocent and at Wolds the aim was therefore to provide as normal a regime as possible. In practice, however, the prison system regards them mainly as experienced prisoners (in many cases, rightly so) and the emphasis of regimes and attitudes is therefore to treat them the same as other prisoners, leading to the virtually complete integration of sentenced and remand prisoners at prisons such as Highdown and Belmarsh.

This ambiguity touches on some very real moral and ethical issues, as well as key operational concerns about control and security. The more remand and convicted prisoners are mixed (even if this is intended to improve the conditions under which they are held), the more their special status is blurred; the more remand prisoners are 'encouraged' to participate in the currently favoured active regimes and the greater the remand population, the greater the number of people whose rights and humanity might be infringed or abused. This, also, is not unique to either the public or the private sector, but is a function of the use of imprisonment for remand purposes. The absence of remand-only prisons, now that Wolds has changed its function, should only serve to heighten our concern about such issues, regardless of whether overall standards are improving or not.

More than this, however, is the fundamental ambivalence that is evident about how *any* prisoner should be treated. Whilst regime improvements are sought and there is a recognition of the need to treat prisoners humanely, there remains a profound ambivalence for many politicians and members of the public towards such improvements, which are too readily defined as luxuries, and calls for more austere regimes meet with choruses of approval. The continued use of political rhetoric which enhances the public's fear of crime and the punitive obsession, together with the highly debatable belief that 'prison works', even for petty offenders, is resulting in a huge expansion of the prison population. This represents, in our view, a far more fundamental moral challenge, a positive response to which will simultaneously address other concerns about the influence of the emerging commercial-corrections complex. As Donahue concludes:

> Delegating tasks to profit-seekers can make public action *less* awkward – more efficient, more accountable, more firmly under the citizenry's control – when contracts can be clearly written and fairly enforced, and when suppliers' efforts to affect decisions can be contained. It would be wrong and wasteful to deny the considerable potential of privatization in these cases. But it would be reckless to claim that private delivery is any sweeping remedy for the fundamental complexity of the public realm. (Donahue, 1989: 223)

Epilogue

The research on which this book is based, although lasting over two years, was essentially contemporaneous and short-term, and our conclusions must be seen in the context of a major innovation (no longer an experiment) in penal policy which has therefore attracted much public and political concern and debate. A similar study in the future may raise concerns about privately managed prisons which we have not identified, particularly as they become familiar and accepted within the system and especially if the current climate in penal policy continues in its present direction. Procedures for ensuring accountability may become a matter of routine and cease to function effectively, and the mechanisms for ensuring regular and critical scrutiny of the operations of private contractors may fall into desuetude as public concerns and the political agenda change. Under such circumstances the safeguard of being able to terminate a contract in the event of non-compliance may be more apparent than real.

As with the question of legitimacy, therefore, we must ultimately be concerned with context – the context in which the privatization of Britain's prisons is occurring, and the context in which it might exist in years to come. At present, the evidence suggests that in spite of the success of Wolds in general terms, there is little *inherent* advantage in privately managed prisons and that much can be achieved in well-managed prisons in the public sector. Our evidence also suggests, however, that there are no major practical objections to a small proportion of prisons being managed by private contractors, subject to proper safeguards and mechanisms for accountability, and that they may have a contribution to make to the work of the Prison Service.

However, were this context to change fundamentally, such conclusions would need to be revisited. A major shift of the presently envisaged balance between public and private prisons would raise new concerns and revitalize old ones. Evidence of influence being brought to bear on penal policy and sentencing practices by private contractors would also be an intolerable development and we should be alert to the risk that the debate about privatization, important though it undoubtedly is, might divert attention from the need to address more fundamental penal policy issues, such as sentencing and punitiveness. Less dramatic, but in some ways more worrying, is a scenario in which the prison population is continuing to rise; there is the development of more punitive prison regimes; there is greater power over prisoners being given to private contractors managing prisons; there is reduced accountability and a reluctance to use sanctions to enforce contract compliance; and in which the political leadership is characterized by an unquestioning belief in its own moral and ideological rectitude, a disregard for the rights of prisoners, and a lack of accountability to parliament or the electorate. Under circumstances such as these, whatever the cost benefits of private-sector involvement in the penal system might eventually be determined to be, the conclusions reached about the propriety of privately managed prisons will almost certainly be different.

Note

1 Other information, obtained by the Prison Reform Trust from the USA (NACRO, 1994a: 11) and not published in the UK, revealed that UKDS had received £3.3 million from the government in start-up costs to manage Blakenhurst, plus £4.5 million phase-in costs, in addition to the annual operating cost of £9.88 million, bringing the first year's costs for Blakenhurst to £17.7 million.

References

Aughey, A. and Norton, P. (1984) 'A settled polity: the Conservative view of law and order', in P. Norton (ed.), *Law and Order and British Politics*. Aldershot: Gower. pp. 137–48.

Baldry, E. (1994) 'USA prison privateers: neo-colonists in a southern land', in P. Moyle (ed.), *Private Prisons and Police: Recent Australian Trends*. Leichhardt, NSW: Pluto Press Australia. pp. 125–38.

Beetham, D. (1991) *The Legitimation of Power*. London: Macmillan.

Belton, D. (1992) 'Private sector involvement in corrections' (Prison Officers' Association of Australasia). Paper presented at New Zealand Conference on Private Sector and Community Involvement in the Criminal Justice System, Wellington, New Zealand.

Beyens, K. and Snacken, S. (1994) 'Privatization of prisons: an international overview and the debate'. Paper presented at the 'Prisons 2000' Conference, University of Leicester, 8–10 April.

Biles, D. and MacDonald, D. (1992) *Deaths in Custody in Australia 1980–1989: The Research Papers of the Criminology Unit of the Royal Commission into Aboriginal Deaths in Custody*. Canberra: Australian Institute of Criminology.

Biles, D. and Vernon, J. (eds) (1994) *Private Sector and Community Involvement in the Criminal Justice System*. Canberra: Australian Institute of Criminology.

Board of Visitors (1993) *Wolds Remand Prison: Annual Report to the Secretary of State for the Home Department*. Board of Visitors, HMP Wolds.

Board of Visitors (1995) *Annual Report to the Secretary of State for the Home Department, Year Ending 31st December, 1994*. Board of Visitors, HMP Wolds.

Borna, S. (1986) 'Free enterprise goes to prison', *British Journal of Criminology*, 26: 321–34.

Bottomley, K., James, A., Clare, E. and Liebling, A. (1997) *Monitoring and Evaluation of Wolds Remand Prison and Comparison with Public-Sector Prisons, in Particular H.M.P. Woodhill*. London: Home Office Publications Unit.

Bottoms, A. (1995) 'The philosophy and politics of punishment and sentencing', in C. Clarkson and R. Morgan (eds), *The Politics of Sentencing Reform*. Oxford: Clarendon Press. pp. 17–49.

Brake, M. and Hale, C. (1992) *Public Order and Private Lives: The Politics of Law and Order*. London: Routledge.

Brakel, S. (1988) 'Prison management, private enterprise style. The inmate's evaluation', *New England Journal of Criminal and Civil Confinement*, 14: 175–244.

Brown, A. (1994) 'Economic and qualitative aspects of prison privatisation in Queensland', in P. Moyle (ed.), *Private Prisons and Police: Recent Australian Trends*. Leichhardt, NSW: Pluto Press Australia. pp. 194–218.

Butler, E., Pirie, M. and Young, P. (1985) *The Omega File*. London: Adam Smith Institute. (Part III, Justice Policy, 230–65)

Carrabine, E. (1995) 'The state of power: taking the "New–Old Penology" seriously in understanding prison riots'. Paper presented to the British Criminology Conference, Loughborough, 18–23 July.

Casale, S. and Plotnikoff, J. (1990) *Regimes for Remand Prisoners*. London: Prison Reform Trust.

Cavadino, P. (1995) 'Recent trends in the use of imprisonment', *Prison Service Journal*, September, 101: 2–4.

Chan, J. (1992) 'The privatisation of punishment: a review of the key issues', *Australian Journal of Social Issues*, 27: 223–47.

Chan, J. (1994) 'The privatisation of punishment: a review of the key issues', in P. Moyle (ed.), *Private Prisons and Police: Recent Australian Trends*. Leichhardt, NSW: Pluto Press Australia. pp. 37–62.

Christie, N. (1994) *Crime Control as Industry: Towards GULAGS, Western Style* (2nd enlarged edn). London: Routledge.

Clark, R.B. (1992) 'HMP Woodhill: new generation of prison design for Milton Keynes'. Unpublished paper.

Cody, W. and Bennet, A. (1987) 'The privatization of correctional institutions: the Tennessee experience', *Vanderbilt Law Review*, 40: 829–49.

Deloitte, Haskins and Sells (1989) *Report on the Practicality of Private Sector Involvement in the Remand System for the Home Office*. London: Deloitte, Haskins and Sells.

DiIulio, J. (1990) 'The duty to govern: a critical perspective on the private management of prisons and jails', in D. McDonald (ed.), *Private Prisons and the Public Interest*. New Brunswick: Rutgers University Press. pp. 155–78.

DiIulio, J. (1991) 'Understanding prisons: The New–Old Penology', *Law and Social Inquiry*, 16: 65–99.

Donahue, J. (1988) *Prisons for Profit: Public Justice and Interests*. Washington, DC: Economic Policy Institute.

Donahue, J. (1989) *The Privatization Decision: Public Ends, Private Means*. New York: Basic Books.

Dunmore, J. (1996) *Review of Comparative Costs and Performance of Privately and Publicly Operated Prisons*. Prison Service Research Report No. 2. Economics Unit, Research and Statistics Department. London: Home Office.

Durham, A. (1989) 'Origins of interest in the privatisation of punishment: the nineteenth and twentieth century American experience', *Criminology*, 27:107–39.

Elliott, N. (1988) *Making Prison Work*. London: Adam Smith Institute.

Erickson, C. (1992) *A Report on the Development and Principles of Direct Supervision in American Prisons*. Unpublished paper.

Feeley, M. and Simon, J. (1992) 'The new penology: notes on the emerging strategy of corrections and its implications', *Criminology*, 30: 449–74.

Gallo, E. (1995) 'The penal system in France: from correctionalism to managerialism', in V. Ruggiero, M. Ryan and J. Sim (eds), *Western European Penal Systems: A Critical Anatomy*. London: Sage. pp. 71–92

Gamble, A. (1994) *The Free Economy and the Strong State: the Politics of Thatcherism* (2nd edn). London: Macmillan.

Grewcock, M. (1995) 'A seg by any other name?', *Criminal Justice*, 13 (4): 22.

Hall, G. (1995) 'Corrections' in K. Hazelhurst (ed.), *Crime and Justice: An Australian Textbook in Criminology*. Sydney: Law Book Company.

Harding, R. (1992a) *Private Prisons in Australia*. Trends and Issues in Crime and Criminal Justice No. 36. Canberra: Australian Institute of Criminology.

Harding, R. (1992b) 'Prison privatisation in Australia: a glimpse of the future', *Current Issues in Criminal Justice*, 4: 9–27.

Harding, R. (1994) 'Privatising prisons: principle and practice'. Unpublished paper.

Hatry, H., Brownstein, P. and Levinson, R. (1993) 'Comparison of privately and publicly operated corrections facilities in Kentucky and Massachusetts', in G.W. Bowman, S. Hakim and P. Seidenstat (eds), *Privatizing Correctional Institutions*. New Brunswick: Transaction Publishers. pp. 193–212.

HM Chief Inspector of Prisons (1993) *Report on Wolds Remand Prison*. London: Home Office.

HM Chief Inspector of Prisons (1994) *Report on HM Prison Woodhill*. London: Home Office.

HM Prison Service (1992a) *The First New Generation Prison: HMP Woodhill*. London: HM Prison Service.

HM Prison Service (1992b) *Model Regime for Local Prisons and Remand Centres*. London: HM Prison Service.

HM Prison Service (1994a) *Corporate Plan 1994–97*. London: HM Prison Service.

HM Prison Service (1994b) *Business Plan 1994–95*. London: HM Prison Service.

HM Prison Service (1995) 'Instruction to governors 74/95', *Incentives and Earned Privileges*. London: HM Prison Service.

HMP Woodhill (1994b) *An Evaluation of Woodhill Incentives Scheme*. Unpublished paper. Psychology Department, HMP Woodhill.

Home Office (1979) *Inquiry into the United Kingdom Prison Services*. London: HMSO.

Home Office (1983) *Prison Statistics, England and Wales, 1983*, Cmnd. 9363. London: HMSO.

Home Office (1988a) *Prison Statistics, England and Wales, 1988*, Cm. 825. London: HMSO.

Home Office (1988b) *Private Sector Involvement in the Remand System*, Cm. 434. London: HMSO.

Home Office (1988c) *Punishment, Custody and the Community*, Cm. 424. London: HMSO.

Home Office (1990) *Crime, Justice and Protecting the Public*, Cm. 965. London: HMSO.

Home Office (1991a) *Custody, Care and Justice: The Way Ahead for the Prison Service in England and Wales*, Cmnd. 1647. London: HMSO.

Home Office (1991b) *Tender Documents for the Operating Contract of Wolds Remand Prison*, London: HMSO

Home Office (1994) 'The prison population in 1993 and long-term projections to 2001', *Home Office Statistical Bulletin*, 16/94, Research and Statistics Directorate. London: Home Office.

Home Office (1995) 'Projections of long-term trends in the prison population to 2002', *Home Office Statistical Bulletin*, 4/95, Research and Statistics Directorate. London: Home Office

House of Commons (1981) *Fourth Report from the Home Affairs Committee, Session 1980–81: The Prison Service* (HC 412). London: HMSO.

House of Commons (1984) *First Report from the Home Affairs Committee, Session 1983–84: Remands in Custody* (HC 252). London: HMSO.

House of Commons (1986) *Twenty-fifth Report from the Committee of Public Accounts, Session 1985–86: Prison Building Programme* (HC 248). London: HMSO.

House of Commons (1987a) *Third Report from the Home Affairs Committee, Session 1986–87: State and Use of Prisons* (HC 35). London: HMSO.

House of Commons (1987b) *Fourth Report from the Home Affairs Committee, Session 1986–87: Contract Provision of Prisons* (HC 291). London: HMSO.

House of Commons (1995) *Committee of Public Accounts, Sixth Report, Session 1994–95: Wolds Remand Prison.* London: HMSO.

Howard League (1994) *Criminal Justice*, 12(2): 20.

Hudson, B. (1987) *Justice Through Punishment: A Critique of the Justice Model of Corrections.* Basingstoke: Macmillan.

Hughes, R. (1987) *The Fatal Shore: A History of Transportation of Convicts to Australia 1787–1868.* London: Collins Harvill.

Humphrey, C. (1991) 'Calling on the experts: the financial management initiative (FMI), private sector management consultants and the probation service', *Howard Journal of Criminal Justice*, 30: 1–18.

Jenkins, J. (1993) 'The hard cell', *New Statesman and Society*, 19 March: 18–19.

Jones, B. (1994) 'Crime and punishment', in B. Jones (ed.), *Political Issues in Britain Today* (4th edn). Manchester: Manchester University Press. pp. 355–76.

Kavanagh, D. (1990) *Thatcherism and British Politics: The End of Consensus?* Oxford: Oxford University Press.

Keating, J. (1990) 'Public over private: monitoring the performance of privately operated prisons and jails', in D. McDonald (ed.), *Private Prisons and the Public Interest.* New Brunswick: Rutgers University Press. pp. 130–54.

Kennedy, J. (1988) 'Final report of the Commission of Review into Corrective Services in Queensland'. Unpublished Government Report, Brisbane.

King, M. (1989) 'Social crime prevention à la Thatcher', *Howard Journal of Criminal Justice*, 28: 291–312.

King, R. and McDermott, K. (1989) 'British prisons, 1970–87: the ever-deepening crisis', *British Journal of Criminology*, 29: 107–28.

Kleinwort Benson Australia Ltd (1989) 'Investigation into private sector involvement in the New South Wales corrective services system'. Unpublished Government Report, Sydney.

Krisberg, B., Schwartz, I., Litsky, P. and Austin, J. (1986) 'The watershed of juvenile justice reform', *Crime and Delinquency*, 32: 5–38.

Lacey, N. (1988) *State Punishment: Political Principles and Community Values.* London: Routledge.

Learmont, J. (1995) *Review of Prison Service Security in England and Wales and the Escape from Parkhurst Prison on Tuesday 3rd January 1995*, Cm. 3020. London: HMSO.

Levinson, R. (1985) 'Okeechobee: an evaluation of privatization in corrections', *The Prison Journal*, 65 (2): 75–94.

Liebling, A. and Bosworth, M. (1995) 'Incentives in prison regimes: a review of the literature', *Prison Service Journal*, 98: 57–64.

Liebling, A., Muir G., Rose, G. and Bottoms, A. (1997) *An Evaluation of Incentives and Earned Privileges: Final Report to the Home Office.* London: Home Office.

Lilly, J. (1993) (Untitled) *New Statesman and Society*, 19 March.

Lilly, J. and Knepper, P. (1990) 'The corrections–commercial complex', *Prison Service Journal*, 87: 43–52.

Lilly, J. and Knepper, P. (1992) 'An international perspective on the privatisation of corrections', *Howard Journal of Criminal Justice*, 31: 174–91.

Logan, C. (1987) *Privatizing Prisons: The Moral Case*. London: Adam Smith Institute.

Logan, C. (1990) *Private Prisons: Cons and Pros*. New York: Oxford University Press.

Logan, C. (1992) 'Well kept: comparing quality of confinement in private and public prison', *Journal of Criminal Law and Criminology*, 83: 577–613.

Logan, C. and McGriff, B. (1989) *Comparing Costs of Public and Private Prisons: A Case Study*. Washington, DC: US Department of Justice, National Institute of Justice Research in Action.

Lomas, M. (1995) 'Experimenting with incentives at Woodhill', *Prison Service Journal*, 101: 37–40.

Lygo, R. (1991) *Management of the Prison Service*. London: Home Office.

Macionis, S. (1994) 'Contract management in corrections: the Queensland experience', in P.Moyle (ed.), *Private Prisons and Police: Recent Australian Trends*. Leichhardt, NSW: Pluto Press Australia. pp. 179–93.

McDonald, D. (1994) 'Public imprisonment by private means: the reemergence of private prisons and jails in the United States, the United Kingdom and Australia', *British Journal of Criminology*, 34 (Special issue): 29–48.

Melossi, D. and Pavarini, M. (1981) *The Prison and the Factory: Origins of the Penitentiary System*. London: Macmillan.

Morgan, R. (1992) 'Following Woolf: the prospects for prisons policy', *Journal of Law and Society*, 19: 231–50

Morgan, R. (1994) 'An awkward anomaly: remand prisoners', in E. Player and M. Jenkins (eds), *Prisons After Woolf: Reform Through Riot*. London: Routledge. pp. 143–160.

Moyle, P. (1993) 'Privatisation of prisons in New South Wales and Queensland: a review of some key developments', *Howard Journal of Criminal Justice*, 32: 231–50.

Moyle, P. (ed.) (1994) *Private Prisons and Police: Recent Australian Trends*. Leichhardt, NSW: Pluto Press Australia.

Nagle, J. (1978) *Report of an Inquiry into the New South Wales Department of Corrective Services*. Sydney: NSW Government Printer.

Nathan, S. (1994a) 'Privatisation: Factfile 7', *Prison Report*, No. 28, 11–18.

Nathan, S. (1994b) 'Privatisation: Factfile 8', *Prison Report*, No. 29, 13–20.

Nathan, S. (1995a) 'Privatisation: Factfile 9', *Prison Report*, No.30, 13–20.

Nathan, S. (1995b) 'Privatisation: Factfile 10', *Prison Report*, No. 31, 13–20.

Nathan, S. (1995c) 'Privatisation: Factfile 11', *Prison Report*, No. 32, 11–18.

Nathan, S. (1995d) 'Privatisation: Factfile 12', *Prison Report*, No. 33, 13–20.

National Association for the Care and Resettlement of Offenders (1992) *NACRO Briefing – Remands in Custody: Some Facts and Figures*. London: NACRO.

National Association for the Care and Resettlement of Offenders (1993) *NACRO Criminal Justice Digest*, October, No. 78.

National Association for the Care and Resettlement of Offenders (1994a) *NACRO Criminal Justice Digest*, July, No. 81.

National Association for the Care and Resettlement of Offenders (1994b) *NACRO Criminal Justice Digest*, October, No. 82.

National Association for the Care and Resettlement of Offenders (1995) *NACRO Criminal Justice Digest*, July, No. 85.

National Audit Office (1994a) *Report by the Comptroller and Auditor General: Control of Prison Building Projects* (HC 595). London: HMSO.

National Audit Office (1994b) *Report by the Comptroller and Auditor General: Wolds Remand Prison* (HC 309). London: HMSO.

Newburn, T. (1995) *Crime and Criminal Justice Policy*. London: Longman.

Player, E. and Jenkins, M. (eds) (1994) *Prisons After Woolf: Reform Through Riot*. London: Routledge.

Pollard, J. (1994) 'Jail officers cut overtime', *Sunday Times*, 15 May: 11.

Proband, S. (1994) 'Prison population exceeds one million', *Overcrowded Times*, 5/6: 4.

Roberts, A. and Powers, G. (1985) 'The privatization of corrections: methodological issues and dilemmas involved in evaluative research', *The Prison Journal*, 65 (2): 95–107.

Roper, C. (1989) *Prison Review: Te Ara Hou – The New Way*. Wellington, New Zealand: Ministerial Inquiry into the Prisons System.

Rutherford, A. (1990) 'British penal policy and the idea of prison privatization', in D. McDonald (ed.), *Private Prisons and the Public Interest*. New Brunswick: Rutgers University Press. pp. 42–65.

Ryan, M. (1994) 'Some liberal and radical responses to privatising the penal system in Britain', in D. Biles and J. Vernon (eds), *Private Sector and Community Involvement in the Criminal Justice System*. Canberra: Australian Institute of Criminology. pp. 9–18.

Ryan, M. and Ward, T. (1989) *Privatization and the Penal System: The American Experience and the Debate in Britain*. Milton Keynes: Open University Press.

Sellers, M. (1993) *The History and Politics of Private Prisons: A Comparative Analysis*. London: Associated University Presses.

Sellin, J. (1976) *Slavery and the Penal System*. New York: Elsevier.

Shaw, A. (1966) *Convicts and the Colonies*. London: Faber.

Shichor, D. (1995) *Punishment for Profit: Private Prisons/Public Concerns*. London: Sage.

Simon, J. (1988) 'The ideological effects of actuarial practices', *Law and Society Review*, 22: 771–99.

Sparks, R. (1994) 'Can prisons be legitimate?: penal politics, privatization, and the timeliness of an old idea', *British Journal of Criminology*, 34 (Special issue): 14–27.

Sparks, R. and Bottoms, A. (1995) 'Legitimacy and order in prisons', *British Journal of Sociology*, 46: 45–62.

Stacey, G. (1992) 'Progress report – operational review at the CW Campbell Remand Centre'. Unpublished Report, CW Campbell Remand Centre, Canning Vale, Western Australia.

Stern, V. (1993) *Bricks of Shame: Britain's Prisons*. Harmondsworth: Penguin.

Strategos Consulting Limited (1989) *Department of Justice Management Review*. Wellington, New Zealand: Strategos Consulting Limited.

Thomas, C. and Logan, C. (1993) 'The development, present status and future potential of correctional privatization in America', in G.W. Bowman, S. Hakim and P. Seidenstat (eds), *Privatizing Correctional Institutions*. New Brunswick: Transaction Publishers. pp. 213–40.

Twinn, S. (1992) 'Direct supervision with a British Accent'. Unpublished paper.

Vagg, J. (1994) *Prison Systems: A Comparative Study of Accountability in England, France, Germany and the Netherlands*. Oxford: Clarendon Press.

van Swaaningen, R. and de Jonge, G. (1995) 'The Dutch prison system and penal policy in the 1990s: from humanitarian paternalism to penal business management', in V. Ruggiero, M. Ryan and J. Sim (eds), *Western European Penal Systems: A Critical Anatomy*. London: Sage. pp. 24–45.

Weiss, R. (1989) 'Private prisons and the state', in R. Matthews (ed.), *Privatizing Criminal Justice*. London: Sage. pp. 26–51.

Windlesham, D. (1993) *Responses to Crime Volume 2: Penal Policy in the Making*. Oxford: Clarendon Press.

Woodcock, J. (1994) *Report of the Enquiry into the Escape of Six Prisoners from the Special Security Unit at Whitemoor Prison, Cambridgeshire, on Friday 9th September 1994*. Cm. 2741. London: HMSO.

Woodhead, P. (1995) *A Review of the Work of the Prisons Ombudsman: 24 October 1994–23 April 1995*. London: Prisons Ombudsman.

Woolf, Lord Justice (1991) *Prison Disturbances April 1990: Report of an Inquiry by the Right Hon. Lord Justice Woolf (Parts I and II) and His Honour Judge Stephen Tumim (Part II)*, Cm. 1456. London: HMSO.

Young, P. (1987) *The Prison Cell: The Start of a Better Approach to Prison Management*. London: Adam Smith Institute.

Zdenkowski, G. (1994) 'Foreword', in P. Moyle (ed.), *Private Prisons and Police: Recent Australian Trends*. Leichhardt, NSW: Pluto Press Australia. pp. 11–13.

Zimring, F. and Hawkins, G. (1994) 'The growth of imprisonment in California', *British Journal of Criminology*, 34 (Special issue): 83–96.

Index